Concerning Child Abuse

Papers presented by the Tunbridge Wells Study Group
on non-accidental injury to children

Edited by
Alfred White Franklin MB FRCP

Churchill Livingstone Edinburgh London and New York 1975

Churchill Livingstone

Medical Division of Longman Group Limited

Distributed in the United States of America by
Longman Inc., New York and by associated
companies, branches and representatives throughout
the world

First published 1975

ISBN 0 443 01224 5
Library of Congress Catalog Card Number 74–81992

Printed in Great Britain

Foreword

There has been growing interest over the last ten years in the problem of parents who 'batter' their children. There is of course a great deal we do not yet know about this subject, and there remains much work to be done on the diagnosis, care, prevention and organisation necessary for the management of cases involving non-accidental injury to children.

It is therefore of vital importance that, in the context of increased general concern over and discussion of the complex and delicate issues involved, we should aim at creating a public awareness that is at once informed and compassionate and an atmosphere in which more preventive work can be done. So the Department of Health and Social Security was glad to accept an invitation to participate in the study group which was set up in May 1973 by a number of people from varying walks of life, all of whom in one way or another encountered child abuse. This group provided an opportunity for the exchange of ideas and the sharing of experience between the people most directly concerned with the problem: doctors, nurses, social workers, the police and others. Because my Department believed that the four days of discussion and debate made an important contribution to the available knowledge of the management, care and treatment of families involved in a battering situation, they were glad to associate themselves with the report of the conference by circulating it to the relevant authorities.

I am sure that all the authorities, agencies and individuals who encounter this problem will find the full record of the four days' meetings and the resolutions which came out of them of immense value, and I hope that it will play a continuing part in the stimulating inter-disciplinary discussion and debate. I believe that in these papers there is also much that will be of interest to a wider public, who will, I am sure, join me in wishing success to all those who contributed in the important work which they perform on behalf of us all.

1974   BARBARA CASTLE

Introduction

Everyone is agreed that the present management of families in which children are abused is far from satisfactory. There are too many deaths and too many children suffer harm which damages them for the rest of their lives. To the extent that one factor is the mishandling of the parents during their own childhood, the condition is self-perpetuating and the management of the children of one generation must affect the children of the next. Rehabilitation of the family may therefore be more important to society than punishment.

Disquiet has been felt for a long time by paediatricians. The British Paediatric Association published a memorandum on 'the battered baby' in 1966, giving advice to doctors on the nature of injuries seen in babies and young children and on how to handle the resulting problem. The Department of Health and Social Security also circulated advisory documents about the benefits of collaboration between all the personnel involved in any area. Despite these encouragements, the situation of abused babies and children remained, and indeed still remains, serious. In 1971 Dr. Christine Cooper, who had been developing techniques of management in Newcastle since 1968, discussed with me what more could be done to achieve the desired improvement. We decided that, although much remained to be learned from both medical and surgical viewpoints, the time had come for the doctors' views to be presented cogently to those other non-medical professionals with whom the solution to the problem rested. In a 'Personal View' in the *British Medical Journal* (Franklin, 1971), I had suggested that two things were needed. The first was a free discussion between doctors and lawyers, the second was a change in public opinion about the nature of this condition.

After consultation with Sir Roger Ormrod, Mr. Brayshaw of the Magistrates Association, and Mrs. Hilary Halpin, JP, Dr. Cooper and I gathered together Mr. E. S. Higgins, Director of Social Services for Wandsworth, Mr. Leo Goodman, the Chief Clerk to the Bow Street Magistrates Court and Dr. Michael Power of the Medical Research Council's Sociology Research Unit, to form an *ad hoc* Working Party. We set ourselves two questions. First, under present law is it possible to improve the management of the families, perhaps with some change in court procedure? The second question was, if improvements cannot be made under present law, should the law be changed; if so, in what way, and by what means?

During our discussions it became clear that there are great differences in practice not only throughout the country, but between the different Metropolitan

Boroughs. In those areas where good solutions have been found and good methods of practice developed, too much depends on the chance that people of like mind and able to communicate well with each other form the teams. With a change in personnel owing to promotion and secondment, the working structure collapses. Reliance on this sort of chance is not good enough in the handling of so serious a matter.

A self-appointed *ad hoc* group such as ours might seem somewhat audacious in intervening in a problem which engages the attention of so many important bodies. We saw ourselves, not as pioneers, but as providing a link between the medical profession, the social services, the legal profession and the police. We wanted to share and to discuss with the other professionals the newer views which stem from Dr. Henry Kempe and his team in Denver and the ideas which inspire the casework of the NSPCC. The NSPCC uniquely combines the status of a voluntary society with statutory duties and through its Research Department has placed us all under a deep debt of gratitude.

Social service departments in many parts of the country are actively examining their methods of management. In Professor Trethowan's Department in the University of Birmingham, Dr. Selwyn Smith and his colleagues are conducting a research into the psychiatric aspects. Dr. Malcolm Hall in the Accident and Emergency Department in the Preston Hospital has forged a valuable and fruitful link with the police in the division. Dr. Christopher Ounsted and Dr. Janet Lindsay have a well-documented study of management at the Park Hospital, Oxford. In Newcastle Dr. Cooper and her colleagues, having formed a working party, produce a series of guidance memoranda. The NSPCC is establishing a National Advisory Council on the subject. And this is only some of the work in progress in England. Much attention is paid to the subject in the USA, Western European countries and Australia. The Department of Health and Social Security had early shown a deep and practical interest and, keeping a close eye on developments, circulates advisory papers from time to time. What seemed to be lacking was an opportunity for the exchange of ideas and the sharing of experiences.

The Working Party felt that benefit might follow a meeting between members of as many of the professional bodies as could be marshalled into a study group of manageable size. At this stage Dr. Ronald Mac Keith was invited to take an interest and he, with the support of Mr. James Loring, arranged for the Medical Education and Information Unit of the Spastics Society to sponsor the meeting. An added bonus was the administrative help provided by Mrs. Eve Kelly. A number of interested people, prepared to talk, were gathered in and, thus constituted, the Study Group met at the Spa Hotel, Tunbridge Wells, May 15–18, 1973. It is a pleasure to record the Study Group's gratitude to the Spastics Society for this timely help.

Encouraged by Sir Keith Joseph, at that time Secretary of State, the Department of Health and Social Security agreed to circulate copies of the report of the Tunbridge Wells Study Group and the resolutions which were later adopted. The members of the Study Group represented most of the professional bodies concerned with the problem. Each had prepared a paper for circulation before the meeting and it is these with the modifications which have resulted from further experience and further thinking since May 1973, that form the basis for this book. In the meantime the original Working Party continues to hold periodic meetings and is engaged in planning a residential meeting for 1975 when educational and preventive aspects of the subject will be discussed. The Tunbridge Wells Study Group itself also continues in being and plans to meet periodically to review progress. In order to preserve its status as a study group, the membership must remain selective and relatively small. Attempts to secure the attendance of a medical officer of health (new style 'community physician') have unfortunately failed owing to illness. Some surprise has been expressed at the absence of a general practitioner from the group. The membership, in the main, was recruited from those who were known to be actively engaged in work connected with non-accidental injury to children. No general practitioner answering to this description was known to the Working Party. It is hoped that a general practitioner will join the group for the next residential meeting.

Much thought has been given to the arrangement of the chapters in this book. On the whole the wisest plan seemed to be to divide the contributions into the appropriate sections, medical, social work, police, legal and educational. This has made for a lack of proportion between the sections and the medical part does greatly exceed the rest.

Since the May meeting some of the papers have been published and we acknowledge with gratitude permission to reprint the following: from the *British Medical Journal*, the two Birimingham Studies from Professor Trethowan's Department, Chapters 5 and 6; from *Social Work Service*, Miss Court's, Chapter 15; from *Justice of the Peace* and the Magistrates' Association Annual Report for 1972–1973, two chapters by Professor Cavenagh (chapters 21 and 23). Doctors Hall and Cooper have kindly contributed the illustrations from their unhappily large collections. The reader's attention is drawn to the appendices which describe proposals for the functions and composition of area review committees and of case conferences, with a note outlining the data necessary for the assessment of the effect which a plan of supervision or care is having on the child.

It hardly needs to be said that the British Paediatric Association continues to maintain a deep involvement in the whole problem, not only of child abuse but also of the effects on children of deprivation of all kinds. The Association has published in collaboration with the British Association of Paediatric Surgeons a statement which served as introductory comment to a guide on management prepared by a working party in the Department of Child Health, University of Newcastle upon Tyne (*British Medical Journal*, December 15, 1973, p. 656). This interest ensures the continuance of those clinical studies related both to diagnosis and to management, which are essential if progress is to continue. Despite the world wide interest in the whole subject, much research work is still needed. Such research, if hospital based, will include the expert contribution of psychiatrists. Epidemiologists and sociologists also have contributions to make. Until preventive measures can achieve a greater success, the actual disposition of children and their families will be in the hands of the social services departments and the courts, with the police more or less deeply involved.

The Tunbridge Wells Study Group attempted to expose and to explore the subject by the exchange of experiences and of ideas between professionals from the major disciplines concerned. Those taking part gained enlightenment in the process of giving it and hope that by publishing their papers, discussion and further study will be stimulated. Above all this book is intended to present the case for co-operation.

One of the Study Group's main functions will be to provide the opportunity for a free, frank and friendly interchange of knowledge, opinion and experience between these professionals. Without such interchange the problems of prevention and successful management will never be resolved.

1974   A. W. F.

Acknowledgements

The needs of the time prompted a few of the participants to publish their papers ahead of the publication of this full report of our Proceedings. Grateful acknowledgement for permission to reproduce articles is therefore due to the following:

The Editor of the *British Medical Journal* for the two articles by Dr. Selwyn Smith and his colleagues, and for the Newcastle guide to diagnosis included in Dr. Cooper's chapter

The Editor of *Social Work Service* and Her Majesty's Stationery Office for Miss Jean Court's chapter

The Editor of *Justice of the Peace* for Dr. Cavenagh's paper on battered baby cases in court and the Magistrates' Association for allowing us to reprint The Teaching of Legal Studies on Social Work Courses from their fifty-third Annual Report.

Thanks are due to Sir Keith Joseph for his encouragement while he was Secretary of State and to the Department of Health and Social Security for their continued interest and support

And to the Medical Education and Information Unit of the Spastic Society for so generously sponsoring the Tunbridge Wells Meeting.

Authors and participants

Sally E. Beer *Senior Medical Social Worker, representing the British Association of Social Workers*

Hugh Bevan *Professor of Law, University of Hull*

Raymond L. Castle, M.B.A.S.W. *Head of Battered Child Research, National Society for Prevention of Cruelty to Children*

Winifred Cavenagh, PhD., J.P. *Professor of Social Administration and Criminology, University of Birmingham*

Douglas R. Chambers, M.B., B.S., LL.B. *H.M. Coroner, Inner North London*

James Collie, LL.B. *Chief Superintendent, Young Offenders Section, New Scotland Yard*

Christine Cooper, M.D., F.R.C.P. *Paediatrician, Department of Child Health, University of Newcastle-upon-Tyne, British Paediatric Association*

Joan Court, S.R.N., S.C.M., H.V.Cert, M.S.W. *Department of Health and Social Security*

Jean M. Davies, S.R.N., S.C.M., H.V.Cert. *Vice-Chairman, Health Visitors Association*

Frances M. Drake, M.A. *Formerly Director of Social Services, Northamptonshire County Council*

Alfred White Franklin, M.B., F.R.C.P. *British Paediatric Association*

Leo Goodman, LL.B. *Chief Clerk to the Bow Street Magistrates Court*

Jean Graham-Hall, Her Honour Judge, LL.M. *One of Her Majesty's Circuit Judges*

Malcolm H. Hall, M.R.C.S., L.R.C.P. *Consultant in Charge of the Emergency and Accident Department, Royal Infirmary, Preston*

Ruth Hanson, B.A. *Senior Research Associate, Department of Psychiatry, University of Birmingham*

Edward S. Higgins *Director of Social Services, London Borough of Wandsworth*

Leo M. Honigsberger, M.B., M.R.C.Psych. *Consultant Electroencephalographer*

H. W. F. Ingram *Chief Superintendent, H.M. Inspectorate of Constabulary, Home Office*

Beti Jones, B.A. *Chief Adviser, Social Work Services Group (Scottish Office)*

Janet Lindsay, M.D., M.R.C.Psych., D.P.M. *Consultant Child Psychiatrist*

Ronald S. Mac Keith, D.M., F.R.C.P. *Director, Medical Education and Information Unit, The Spastics Society, British Paediatric Association*

Anita Loring *Research Associate Farmington Trust*

James A. Loring *Director Spastics Society*

Dorothy Morgan, M.R.C.S., L.R.C.P. *Director of Family Planning Services for Hampshire*

J. Mounsey, B.E.M., Q.P.M. *Detective Chief Superintendent, Lancashire Constabulary C.I.D.*

Sheila Noble, M.A. *Senior Research Associate, Department of Psychiatry, University of Birmingham*

Thomas E. Oppé, M.D., F.R.C.P. *Professor of Paediatrics, University of London, British Paediatric Association*

Rhoda Oppenheimer, B.Sc., M.B.A.S.W. *Social Worker, lately at the Park Hospital, Oxford*

Christopher Ounsted, D.M., F.R.C.P., F.R.C.Psych., D.P.M., D.C.H. *Consultant Psychiatrist, British Paediatric Association*

Michael J. Power, Dip S.S., J.P. *Member of Scientific Staff, Medical Research Council's Social Medicine Unit*

Eileen M. Ring, M.S., D.P.H. *P.M.O. Health Services for Children, Department of Health and Social Security*

Carol A. Smith, B.A. *Research Associate, Department of Psychiatry, University of Birmingham*

Selwyn M. Smith, M.B., B.S., D.P.M., M.R.C.Psych. *Lecturer in Psychiatry, Department of Psychiatry, University of Birmingham*

John Stroud, *Assistant Director (Field and Domiciliary Services), Social Services Department, Hertfordshire County Council*

Kenneth Till, M.B., F.R.C.S. *Neurological Surgeon, British Association of Paediatric Surgeons*

Contents

xiii

Part Three   Two Views from the Police

Part Four   Legal Aspects

Part Five   Education

Appendices

1. The nature of the task

Alfred White Franklin

'Child abuse', 'non-accidental injury to children', the 'battering of children' are some of the names that are given to one end product of family stress. So much effort is directed to providing an environment fit and safe for the nurture and education of children, of tomorrow's citizens, that society views with particular abhorrence those parents who turn against their children and do them harm. Positive harm reveals itself most clearly in physical injury, but the negative harm of deprivation, whether it be of love or food or any other necessity, shocks us too when we recognise it. These initial responses of abhorrence and shock are understandable but unhelpful. And because we feel this to be so, the last decade has seen serious attempts to look below the surface and to fathom how such things can be. The aim must be prevention. But successful prevention requires of us that we should recognise the many circumstances which in various combinations lead families into deprivation and abuse.

We have to begin somewhere. And because a critical period is reached with bodily damage, broken bones, bruises, brain haemorrhage, death itself, the obvious point of departure is medical. So it was John Caffey, a radiologist, and Henry Kempe, a paediatrician, who began to collect the information about these kinds of bodily damage, of end results which form a pattern that can be recognised. Clinical recognition is the prerequisite for medical study. When there is medical diagnosis there is always a differential diagnosis and this also requires the expertise of doctors.

But if diagnosis is to lead to treatment, it cannot be exclusively medical. To diagnose means to know through and through. What has to be known is not only that the clinical picture results from trauma rather than another pathological process in the child, but that these are parents who have traumatised their child within the family setting. The quality of the parents and the characteristics of the family setting must therefore be diagnosed, tasks which need both a psychiatric and a social approach.

To be parents to children requires rather more than the ability to reproduce. Perhaps good parenting can be taught, and if so, by example rather than by precept; perhaps it depends altogether on human character and instincts; in either case life experiences and the material environment play no small modifying part. Parents must have been seriously damaged by life before they can stub out their lighted cigarettes upon their baby's skin. The analysis of such deviant behaviour demands both epidemiology and insight. Common antecedents begin to emerge. Some of them point to a crisis from which recovery is possible, others to irreparable personality damage, with obvious implications for management. Unfortunately in some cases in present circumstances neither complete protection nor lasting rehabilitation is attainable.

Meanwhile epidemiological studies of accidents have begun to reveal patterns which suggest that recognisable aetiological factors are present in accidents of all kinds: poisoning, falls, traffic accidents, burns and scalds. Studies are also in progress about violence and intrafamilial aggression and about the results of deprivation and ineffective mothering upon the development of the child. Paediatricians have come to recognise increasingly the harm done by emotional deprivation to the child's emotional adjustment and behaviour and more recent studies have shown in addition stunting of physical growth (in height and weight) and slowing of intellectual development. Nurturing failure, especially in the early years of life, is now seen to be responsible for much damage to growing and developing children.

If our aim is the prevention of all such damage, the scope of studies and observations must be wide, linking the subject of child abuse to accidents in general on the one hand and to family pathology on the other. And this is concerned not only with the intrinsic psychopathology of the family and of the individuals who compose it, but also with the socioeconomic stresses playing upon the family from the environment in which the members live and work. The mother may have a below average intelligence, the father or stepfather may be an aggressive psychopath, but defective housing, unemployment, and the hostility of neighbours may also form part of the aetiology, though deprivation and abuse are not confined to families in the lower social groups. Today 'non-accidental injury to children' is seen to take its place in the wide context of social disorders in which defective care within the family leads to developmental failure, injury, or death.

When all the enquiries are set in train, medical, psychological, epidemiological, social, about the individual family, there remains a serious problem for the community, for society has to concern itself with crime and punishment. Non-accidental physical injury to a child is still a form of criminal assault, and criminal assault is confronted by the law, by the law's officers and the law's administrators. At the critical period of injury, behaviour emerges from the twilight of fantasy and imagination into a harsh world of accusing fingers, even of an accusing conscience. These two people are the parents who have battered their child. How can amends be made, how can life in the community be lived so labelled? The protection of the injured child, the punishment of guilty parents, how are these to be reconciled with the rehabilitation of the family?

The tasks of the police, the magistrates' courts and the judges may not be simplified by a better understanding of the nature of child abuse. Indeed for a time decisions may become more difficult. Better understanding of the parents could induce a lenience, a sympathy for them with the sacrifice of the safety of the child. At present the protection of the child, the siblings and of children yet unborn must be regarded as paramount, and the prevention of any repetition of injury to a child as a crisis demanding urgent decisions. The decision to remove the child or all the children may have the worst possible effect upon the eventual rehabilitation of the family. So may the imposition of prison sentences, and yet society must protect itself from the dangers of the aggressive psychopath. A place of safety order may be the only way of protecting the child from death or permanent disability. Safe solutions demand the most thorough medical and social study of the whole family or household.

Some practical measures are described in the following pages. Their success depends upon two prerequisites. Firstly, in every locality a working system must be devised to ensure protection for the children and all relevant help for the families. Secondly, all professional workers in the locality must use the system once their suspicions have been aroused. Mutual confidence must grow between the different services and each worker must respect the professional skill of his colleagues. The statutory responsibility for child protection by social services departments has to be reconciled with the clinical responsibility of the doctor and the legal obligations of the police. Consultation has everywhere to replace unilateral action. A system of area review committees and case conferences, proposed by the Department of Health and Social Security, has the whole-hearted support of the Study Group and is described in Appendices I and II.

Three main areas of difficulty exist: the doctor's problems with confidentiality; the policeman's reputed preoccupation with convictions; and the obstacles which the social worker's personal involvement with a family may place in the way of her objective assessment of a situation.

The general practitioner is less often consulted by these families because they tend to go directly to hospital. Nevertheless, he should be familiar with the type of family in which abuse may occur, and if his suspicions are roused he would be well advised to channel his patient into the system either through his attached health visitor or directly to his local paediatric department for immediate consultation and possible admission for protection and diagnosis. Sometimes with older children the school teacher or the educational welfare officer may be the first person to become concerned. The school medical service may then be the channel of entry directly through the general practitioner, or in the future through the paediatrician with community responsibility.

The complexities of this subject, commensurate with the complexities of human nature, are amply revealed in the chapters that follow.

Part One

Medical Aspects

2. A view from the emergency and accident department

M. H. Hall

INTRODUCTION

This paper, prepared for the Study Group, reflects the opinions developed over the last ten years by a physician who has been exclusively engaged in managing a busy emergency and accident department. A particular interest has been taken in non-accidental injuries in children and, with the co-operation of the hospital paediatric services, the services of the local authorities, the voluntary associations and the police forces, it has been possible to look at the problem from the point of view of the early recognition of physically abused children. It has also been possible to attempt an assessment of the incidence of physically abused children throughout the country and to contrast the nature of the injuries with those observed after major violence from other causes.

It is now becoming apparent that more attention must be paid to the study of the effect of violence on the skin; experience of the damage due to non-accidental injury has taught much that is of value in forensic practice in other cases of criminal assault by various means. There must also be a greater exchange of information between the pathologists and the clinicians if many of these cases are not to be missed.

During the past five years a considerable teaching programme has been carried out in north-west England. It is too soon to assess the value of this programme but there are indications that the incidence of the 'minor' cases is increasing and that the total number of cases is falling slightly. A final assessment of the work in progress will not be possible for many years but it does give some indication as to what is possible with maximal co-operation and minimal facilities.

DEFINITION

In 1962 the battered child syndrome was described by Kempe who deliberately chose an emotional name in order to produce an awareness of the condition in the medical and social service who, until that time, were unaware that children could be subjected to grave, and frequently fatal, injuries at the hands of their parents. As a result of research and a recognition of the condition by the medical profession there is no further need for this emotional term and it is now clear that the original name should cease to be used. The introduction of emotion hinders the management of the situation in which these children are placed and can only harm future developments in treating the condition.

Increasing experience in the recognition of these children enables many to be discovered at a stage where the injuries are minimal; on occasions these may amount to no more than a few bruises on the face. To label these children 'battered babies' is a complete misnomer. Previously the emphasis in these children has been placed upon their sustaining severe physical injuries, but now if a child sustains such injuries at the hands of a third person, it is clear that the preventive organisations have broken down.

Investigation of children with minor non-accidental injuries always reveals that the social circumstances are identical to those in which the full battering syndrome has occurred. The situation requires similar management and is of equal urgency, but full proof that these children with minor injuries are the 'precursors' of 'battered' children could only be obtained by allowing the children home into the unmodified surroundings in which they sustained their injuries. This is impossible and therefore it is the author's practice to identify these children as suffering from non-accidental injuries. Another name which has come into use is 'physically abused children'. Whichever name is preferred depends to some extent on where one works. In the Emergency and accident department 'non-accidental injury' seems more appropriate. Neither of these terms includes all aspects of child abuse.

Research has been initiated in the author's department to investigate the possibility that some so-called accidental poisonings in children and some cot deaths* may be deliberate. None of the above terms would be suitable for this latter group, but the term chosen should be one without emotional connotations. Isolated examples of poisoning in children do occur, but full investigation into the possibility of poisoning being a chosen method of injuring a child has not as yet been carried out. It is unlikely that it does not occur. The history of violence and other forms of personal abuse suggests that the persons responsible are always ahead of the detective agencies. Now that physical violence in children is becoming more easily recognisable those involved in treating the disorder must always keep the possibility of deliberate poisoning or other more esoteric occurrences very much in mind.

PREVALENCE

The prevalence of physically abused children is still very much a matter of informed guesswork. Kempe believes that it may, in Great Britain, amount to 3,000 cases per annum of which half could be significantly injured and the other half seriously deprived.

A study of non-accidental injuries in children has been in progress at Preston since 1963. The prevalence of the condition between that year and 1972 is shown in Table 1.

The large increase in 1970 is not the result of a major increase in the number of cases but follows the development of an efficient local organisation associated

* The term 'sudden infant death' should be reserved for the death of babies for which no explanation can be found after all possibilities have been explored and excluded.

with a very comprehensive teaching programme.

The Department of Health and Social Security published a memorandum in 1970 recommending that local co-ordination groups be established to manage the situation. As a result of work previously carried out in the area, a close liaison was built up between the hospital services, those of the local authorities and the general practitioners. The publication of the memorandum stimulated

TABLE 1. The prevalence of non-accidental injury in children in Preston between 1963 and 1972

Year	Definite*	Non-Proven†	Death	Total
1963	1	0	0	1
1964	0	0	0	0
1965	2	0	0	2
1966	1	1	1	3
1967	0	0	1	1
1968	5	1	0	6
1969	4	1	0	5
1970	9	10	1	20
1971	6	7	2	15
1972	9	4	2	15
Total	37	24	7	68

* A definite case is one in which action was taken for the protection of the child.
† The non-proven cases were those in which there was a strong suspicion of non-accidental injury but insufficient evidence to justify measures apart from supervision.

this process and resulted in the establishment of local services to deal with the problem. It was also decided that all cases occurring in the locality should be referred to the author for initial assessment. This method can only be carried out in an area where one hospital serves the surrounding community and where co-operation between the emergency services and the other hospital units is at a high level. Liaison must also be maintained with the voluntary organisations and the police authorities in order that all cases in the locality may be directed through the same channels. Because of this approach it is reasonably certain that the prevalence of the condition in the Preston area in the last three years is accurate. It is depressing to realise how many cases may have been missed during the previous period.

The majority of the cases are minor in nature. Only one example of the full-blown battering syndrome has been seen during this period but it is disturbing to find that the number of deaths is remaining constant at between one and two per annum.

The cases are divided into groups:

1 Those which require definite steps to be taken for the protection of the child; this is usually admission to hospital or other place of safety.
2 Those which are highly suspicious yet which the degree of uncertainty is such as to make it justifiable to manage them by social measures. These are a particularly difficult group for, even if the situation is recognised as being

uncertain, the grounds for a place of safety order are insufficient to support either the initial order or any subsequent legal proceedings.

In 1970, 1971 and 1972 a total of 29 definite cases, including five deaths, were seen. The average number per annum is 9·6 and the mortality rate is 17·2 per cent. Fifteen million patients are treated annually in the emergency departments of the country. In Preston 34,000 patients were treated in 1972. The incidence of these cases is 1 in 3,400 of the attendances at the Preston Emergency Department. If this is related to a national figure of fifteen million attenders per annum, then it might be expected that 4,400 such children would be seen throughout the country every year. A mortality rate of 17·2 per cent would give 757 as the annual number of deaths to be expected in the whole population.

No claim is made that these figures are accurate and it is unlikely that all cases are recognised in every area. For example, the study in Preston of bruising patterns, particularly of the face, has led to the early recognition of many children who would not previously have been included.

The relation of the numbers to emergency department attenders rather than to the total local population enables variations caused by the parents using different hospitals for different injuries to be excluded. It may also exclude regional and local variations caused by geographical and industrial factors, e.g. an industrial area where housing and social conditions are poor might well be expected to have a higher prevalence but an area such as this would also have a larger total attendance at the emergency and accident departments. A rural area, where the prevalence of the condition might be lower, would also have a lower number of attendances at the emergency department. The use of the emergency department figures also serves to reduce inaccuracies caused by relating a hospital prevalence to the population of the area which the hospital serves, because in many instances there is a considerable overlap of hospital boundaries and accurate population figures cannot be obtained.

Two of the five deaths since 1970 might have been avoided. In one there was a history of previous bruising of the child. Unfortunately the mother did not take any action before the child was killed. In the other, the child was admitted three months before its death with a dummy stuck in its throat. This was considered to be an accident but subsequent events showed that it was a wrong assessment. In future any peculiar incident happening to a child will be subjected to a full social investigation. The others, as far as can be ascertained, gave no premonitory signs of instability in the family. The mortality is unlikely ever to be reduced much below 10 per cent unless the social circumstances giving rise to the syndrome are recognised at a much earlier stage than at present.

The prevalence of the condition can be assessed from figures supplied by the Lancashire Constabulary, which serves approximately three million people. In 1972 throughout the county area 26 children under three were killed. In a population of fifty million persons, 450 deaths would be expected per annum. If the fatality rate is assumed to be 10 per cent, the national total would be estimated to be 4,500 a figure closely related to that based on the casualty attendances. The fatality rate based on the hospital figures is very much higher and it is difficult to know why this should be.

The North-West area may have a high population of physically abused children, but this results from improved recognition rather than from a higher than average local prevalence. Many of the children included are by no means badly injured, but, sadly, they all show the typical parental or home disturbances associated with the full-blown syndrome.

Both the hospital and police figures suggest that between 4,000 and 5,000 children every year in this country will require legal action to be taken by the hospital or social services to ensure their future well-being and survival. An equal number will also require close supervision for their protection as the evidence will be insufficient to support an application for a care order.

A reliable figure for mortality is not available. This may well be of the order of 10 per cent since head injuries feature largely in the medical records and sub-dural haematoma is a common cause of death in the group. These cases are usually referred for treatment to neurosurgical departments where the relevant social investigation is unlikely to be carried out. Finding evidence of non-accidental causation at a later stage is particularly difficult when the specialist unit is not part of the hospital which originally receives the case. When the child is seriously ill, the medical profession has to concentrate on the clinical state to save life. Little time can be devoted to social background investigation. Yet this information is so important that the possibility of a non-accidental origin for the condition should be investigated by an experienced department which is not involved in the immediate care of the child.

None of the Preston cases which have been investigated or in which action has been taken for the protection of the child have sustained further injury. The majority are back with one or both of their parents. One child has died in a local authority home and a 'cot death' was diagnosed by the pathologist. A parent of one of the children died with severe head injuries after walking into a lorry whilst crossing a road. Her husband on that day was due to appear in court for theft and it was considered that preoccupation with this event made her careless.

CLASSIFICATION

Although classification may be premature, a tentative division into five groups is suggested.

A classification must be based both on the circumstances of the child, i.e. whether it be mentally or physically injured, and on the state of the parents at the time when the child was harmed.

The injury to the child may be produced by active or passive means. In the active injury groups the child is harmed by physical intervention on the part of the parents. In the passive groups harm arises from a process of neglect. The violence in the active group may be further divided according to whether the injury is of a normal or of bizarre or sadistic type.

The situation can be expressed diagrammatically in the form of a tentative classification proposed for discussion (Fig. 1).

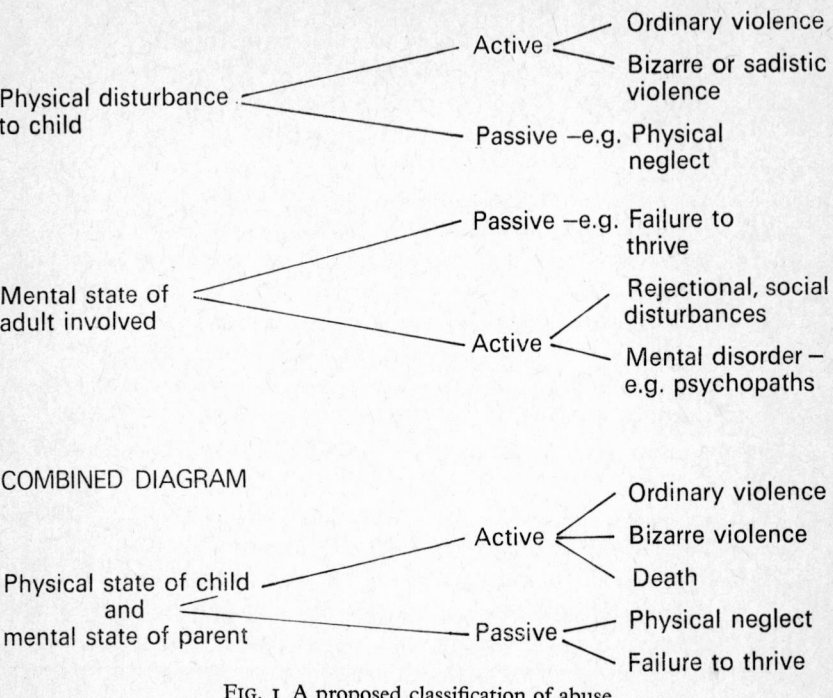

FIG. 1 A proposed classification of abuse

One person cannot possess a full enough specialist knowledge in all the disciplines involved in treating the situation. A satisfactory classification of child abuse would simplify management and enable necessarily limited facilities to be directed into the areas where help would be most productive. The present blanket approach to treatment fails in approximately 20 per cent, which means that much of the treatment effort is wasted. Suggested methods of classification are crude, nevertheless rather ill-defined groups can be discerned even at this early stage and this aspect is worth further investigation.

DIAGNOSIS

The final diagnosis in a case of non-accidental injury depends on a correlation between the physical signs obtained on examination, the alleged history as to the cause of the injuries and the results of investigation into the social background of the family.

Alerting signs

The recognition of the major case is straightforward and few are likely to be missed. The doctor who first sees the child often fails to appreciate the significance of the minor and less spectacular injuries because he lacks experience. Those working in an emergency department need to pay extra attention to the history in all cases of injury to children under three years. A precise statement must always be obtained from the adult who accompanies the child as to how the injuries are alleged to have happened. This may take only a few seconds. It is usually easy to relate the injuries to this history but from time to time slight incongruities appear and then expert advice must be sought immediately.

Most cases are missed because the possibility of a non-accidental injury is not considered. Certain features are well recognised, such as delay in attending the hospital after injury. This delay may vary from a few hours to several days and frequently the child is brought to hospital by one or other parent at the suggestion of a third party. From time to time the child is brought for attention by a member of the local health authority services or an officer of the NSPCC who has observed bruises on the child's body. In these cases the parents frequently allege that they were going to take the child to the doctor that day or that the appointment was going to be made for this purpose. Many phrases are well recognised as having a non-accidental injury connotation. The child is alleged to bruise easily or he fell out of someone's arms when they were carrying him downstairs. The child may on other occasions be alleged to fall over easily or to have fallen off a table, off a cot and so on. One very important phrase is that the parents do not know what has happened but 'the child was alright when he was put to bed last night and when I got him up this morning he could not use his arm or his leg'.

These alerting signs are useful and should be known to all members of emergency departments. It is of equal importance to recognise that the vast majority of children attend the emergency departments after injuries that are truly accidental. Non-accidental injury is much less common.

The author has not found, as Kempe has, that in his own department 25 per cent of all fractures seen in the first few years of life are due to child battering, nor that 10 to 15 per cent of trauma in children under three years of age is attributed to the syndrome.

In a daily review of the X-rays taken in the department in 1971, only four suspicious cases were observed; when these were investigated they were found to be true accidents. Similarly in 1972, when only three slightly suspicious incidents were investigated following review of the X-rays, all were due to normal accidents. The X-ray films are always considered in conjunction with the clinical record and particular attention is paid to the children with fractures who reported back on a second occasion with another fracture, but in spite of this close attention no case was found. This experience does bring into question the value of attempting to recognise these children retrospectively using X-ray findings and clinical records without knowledge of the family's social background.

In the final analysis the recognition that there is an incongruity between the injury found and the history given must depend on the clinical acumen of the doctor concerned. Unfortunately in many hospitals at the present time the quality of the medical staff in the department is not as good as one would wish. Much greater assistance can usually be obtained from the skill of experienced casualty nurses, particularly those who have raised families of their own. In the author's experience the nursing staff have recognised many more cases than the medical staff. Strangely enough the medical staff tend to suspect the syndrome in conditions which are clearly of accidental origin and when non-accidental origin is postulated they find it difficult to accept the reasoning.

The significance of bruises

The most valuable clinical finding in the minor case is the presence of bruises (see Plate 1). These are of frequent occurrence. A child who has been subjected to manual pressure on the face can be recognised from several yards away. Too little attention has been paid to bruising patterns and to the characteristics of bruises caused by various external agencies. It is of great significance that in a large number of major road accidents which involved young children, the author has never yet seen a pattern of bruises presented which is similar to that caused by manual pressure.

The classical finger-tip bruises on the face are round or oval and the diameter varies between 0·5 cm and 2·0 cm. They occur in crops on the face and are frequently of different ages. On some patients it is possible to recognise that they have occurred on three different occasions, fresh ones being bluish in nature and the older ones going through a greeny blue and finally into a yellowish colour. The bruises are usually all of a slightly different size and they all appear within the skin. The overlying skin is never swollen or shiny and the overlying cuticle is always damaged.

On the forehead and cheek areas the bruises tend to remain distinct but on the sides of the chin and the neck they tend to cohere into a single area. When crops of bruises are seen the first requisite is to see if they will fit the pattern of the hand. Bruises of the same age should conform without difficulty to the pattern of the thumb and fingers with usually the thumb imprint, which is larger, on the left hand side of the face and the larger number of smaller bruises fitting the pattern of the fingers very clearly. It is possible to recognise three distinct patterns of facial bruising.

1 The forehead pattern consists of a large thumb bruise over the right eye with a crop of two or three or four small finger-tip bruises on the left side of the forehead.
2 The cheek pattern is similar with the large bruise on the right zygoma area and a smaller crop on the left zygoma area.
3 The chin pattern consists either of a small number of larger bruises along the right side of the jaw with a crop of smaller bruises along the left side of the jaw or alternatively the bruises may coalesce and produce a bruise which runs along the whole of the ramus of the mandible.

The above patterns are those which are caused when the bruises are inflicted by a right-handed person from the front of the child; the pattern inflicted by a left-handed person will be reversed and it has, in one instance, been possible to identify the battering parent because of a left-handed bruising pattern on the child's face. The mother was right-handed and the father was left-handed and this distinction was clearly evident on the child's face. Indeed facial bruising with this type of distribution is not seen after road traffic accidents and the single bruise over the right eye is almost pathognomonic of the condition.

On the neck bruises are not so well defined; they tend to run into bruises on the chin and if excessive pressure has been applied there are usually petechial haemorrhages in the skin and the conjunctivae indicative of asphyxiation rather than simple pressure.

The parents often claim that the cause of the bruise is a fall. Apart from the difficulty of falling in a way which would give several bruises on each side of the face at the same time and then possibly repeating the incident later to cause a crop of different ages, certain injuries to the face do have characteristics which tend either to support or to disprove the alleged cause of the injury.

Blows to the face with a hard object almost invariably cause oedema of the skin. The finger-tip bruise is always flat and never swollen, but the blow against a table, a piece of wood, a wall or the floor is always associated with swelling and a shiny appearance of the skin. If the fall is against a table or other irregular object, then a pattern of the object may even be apparent.

If the fall is as alleged on a rough ground surface such as a concrete path there will be a disturbance, however small it may be, of the overlying cuticle. This is never seen in finger-tip bruising and it is thus possible, to some extent, to support or disprove the history given by the parents.

Frequently black eyes (see Plate 2) are alleged to be caused in falls. These are seen infrequently after road accidents and only rarely in games, when there is usually a witness. To cause a black eye, a round object must fit into the orbit. A black eye cannot be produced by a fall against a flat surface. This would result in a bruise around the orbit whereas these children, when seen soon after injury, exhibit bruising of the eyelids due to an object of corresponding shape striking the eye. It is impossible for a child to sustain two black eyes in one fall and therefore any child who exhibits two black eyes as the result of a home incident must, unless proved otherwise, have been injured by a third person.

These characteristic facial bruises do not in general apply to bruises in other areas. Most children exhibit bruises of the legs, varying in size, shape and situation, but from time to time it is possible to recognise, either on the one limb or on both legs looked at together, the pattern of finger-tips. This should always be looked for, but swelling and disturbance of the cuticle is less reliable on the limbs than on the face.

Head injuries can sometimes be shown to have a non-accidental causation. The back and front of the trunk should always be examined in children who exhibit subdural haematoma. The back (see Plate 5) may exhibit finger-tip bruises about one to two centimetres in diameter, in the skin and lying opposite the 12th dorsal or 1st lumbar vertebrae about 5·0 cm from the midline on each side. On one or the other side a third bruise will be present at a higher level than the previous two. Many of these subdural haematomas are caused by violent shaking of the child. If a child is picked up as if to shake him it is found that in order to obtain an adequate purchase the thumbs fall accurately into the above-mentioned positions. One hand is usually at a higher level initially, and to obtain balance it has to be slid down thus causing the three bruises. Cooper in a personal communication states that she has observed a bruise over the centre of each clavicle associated with manually produced subdural haematoma.

The author has also observed bruises opposite the centre of the medial border of each scapula in a child who was forcibly pulled from the mother's arms by the co-habitor.

When a child is struck on the back, trunk or limbs with a hand or an object such as a belt or a piece of wood characteristic marks are produced. The pressure of the object in contact with the skin drives the blood out of the capillaries under increased pressure to an area of reduced pressure. The inflow of blood into this latter area is sufficiently great to rupture the capillaries and this causes a linear type of cutaneous marking due to ruptured capillaries. This intradermal haemorrhage around the outside of the contact area of the object produces a negative image of the object on the skin.

The shape of the contact area will vary depending on the curvature of the body tissues at the point of impact, thus a rectangular piece of wood applied to a curved surface such as the buttocks may give a 'D'-shaped mark. The flat of the hand applied to the skin will give an outline of the fingers with an increased area of bruising around bony prominences such as the base of the little finger, and the impression produced on the side of the face from a child being slapped with the flat of the hand is completely characteristic in that there are four or five parallel intradermal haemorrhages usually running forwards from the front of the ear. Such a mark may appear on the cheek of the buttock and the thumb imprint can lie along the natal cleft.

When the body is hit, the shape of the object can only be seen when the limb or trunk is examined in the position that it was in when the injury was inflicted. Thus a mark with a straight object over a flexed joint will only appear straight when the joint is examined in the flexed position; scratch marks on the back will only assume a recognisable pattern when it is inspected in the position in which it was when the injuries were caused. A belt will give rise to an outline caused by an intradermal haemorrhage around the tongue or buckle parts. The holes in the tongue, may be marked by small circumferential haemorrhagic areas. When a child is gripped firmly through the clothing, the pattern of the clothing may appear; the areas where the clothing is in firm contact with the skin will not be marked but in the areas where the pressure is less, as for example in a patterned vest, the negative imprint of the clothing may be clearly visible.

All these points should be appreciated so that the type of object that has been used to damage the child may be investigated. They assist in assessing the dangers inherent in the situation and may allow the alleged accidental cause to be absolutely excluded.

The marks of cigarette burns (see Plate 6) are characteristic and may occur anywhere on the body. Scars of old cigarette burns may be present and from time to time tooth marks are seen in areas which are, to a normal person, completely inconceivable. The impressions of a fresh bite mark (see Plate 6) are unmistakable and, if forensic dental tests were applied, the identity of the person responsible might well be established. This technique, which involves matching the bite marks to an impression of the suspect's teeth, has been introduced into criminal practice in recent years but it has not yet been introduced into forensic paediatric medicine in non-fatal cases.

PROBLEMS AND DIFFICULTIES

Emotional, intellectual, professional and, from time to time, physical demands will be placed upon a person who is handling these cases. A doctor who is involved in the initial or early stages of the management of such a case is in particular difficulty because he is in the unfortunate position of being unable to fulfil all his various obligations. To injure a child is still a legal offence and therefore if this information is withheld from the police he is breaking the law, particularly as the child is his patient. The child is in the care of the parents and if he examines this child without their consent he could, theoretically, be held to commit an assault. Much information may be given him by the parents. What is his ethical position in relation to making this information, which is frequently highly confidential, available to other authorities?

When he goes to court he may appear to be acting against the parents who gave him this confidential information, yet it is largely on the strength of the doctor's evidence that the success or otherwise of the legal proceedings will depend. The doctor is thus in a commanding position, and it is therefore essential that he act in a fully professional manner if he is to avoid being involved in major ethical disputes with his colleagues.

In earlier times, it was not appreciated that children could be severely injured or killed by their parents. More recently, the Children and Young Persons Act of 1969 has failed to recognise the high incidence and importance of this condition so that the legal basis of management is inadequate. A successful conclusion is only possible with close adherence to the ethical tenets of the profession, coupled with a recognition that the child is the person at risk. The child is the patient and all other considerations must be subservient to this paramount requirement, that the child must be protected.

The ultimate aim of the exercise must always be kept clearly in view. That aim is restoration of a fit child to a rehabilitated family in which there is no further risk of physical or mental violence being offered to the child or to any other children in the family.

No one body of persons can achieve this end result. A successful conclusion demands the whole-hearted co-operation of the medical profession, the social services, the voluntary societies and the police forces. Co-operation between these bodies must be absolute. There must be no concealment, no unilateral action on the part of any section and communications throughout must be full and comprehensive. It is essential at the commencement of the proceedings for the medical and social services to work closely in harmony, and it is equally important later when a child is to be returned to its parents that co-operation should be as great. No one person has the right to make a decision which may have a serious or fatal result for a child by returning it to its home before the fullest discussion has taken place between the various bodies concerned.

The role of the police force is, in many areas, extremely unclear. There is no place for the view that under no circumstances whatsoever should the police be involved in these cases. The injury of a child is a crime and the police have a legal right to be aware of it. If they are excluded from these situations they will take unilateral action whenever such a situation comes to their notice. If the case could be managed without a prosecution for causing injury to the child, the surest way to stimulate legal action is to exclude the police. The only satisfactory way to avoid unilateral police action is to involve them in the management of the situation at the earliest possible moment. In general the services managing these cases will obtain from the police the degree of co-operation which they themselves show towards the police and, whilst the prosecution of the parents would be a tragedy in the majority of cases, it must be remembered that the police are responsible for both the prevention of crime and its detection. The police have the safety of the child as their paramount interest. The management of the parents, whilst of importance, is in their view of less importance than ensuring that the child will not sustain any further harm. It is both helpful and stimulating for the services managing these cases to have to satisfy an authority, such as the police force, that they are taking adequate steps for the protection of the child.

A depressingly large number of children in recent years have been killed after they have been returned to their parents by the courts on the advice of a social services department. This kind of unilateral action should be discouraged, and there should be a moral if not a legal obligation on social services departments to consult fully with the medical profession and with the police before applying to the magistrates to allow the return of a child to the parents. If either of these two other bodies should hold the opinion that the child should not be returned home, the application should not be allowed to proceed.

When the social services department was part of the medical officer of health's domain, medical influence could be exerted, but now that they are independent they may take such action as they think fit without reference to any other person. Whilst in the majority of cases they do consult with other authorities, the absence of a legal requirement to do so does, unfortunately from time to time, lead to serious and fatal errors of judgement. These may arise from a lack of knowledge about the condition but they may also result from a failure to recognise that man is not necessarily always like an angel. There are evil people loose in the community and the assessment of human nature is a very skilled and difficult task. If the person involved in supporting a family has relatively little experience, the recommendations made may fail to safeguard the child.

The social services departments are now large organisations with many teams working in various areas. All communication about cases of non-accidental injury should be made through one nominated senior officer or his deputy. This one person can then disseminate the available information to the members

PLATE 4

David, who proved to have been scalded at 13 months and assaulted at 17 months by his mother's consort, illustrates the discrepant history and the value of the skeletal X-ray survey.

1. The fresh bruises: 'he must have bumped himself on his cot this morning'.
2. The 4-month-old scald: 'he pulled a kettle over himself', but his chest and abdomen in front are uninjured, all the scalds being on the back.
3. Skeletal X-rays revealed an unsuspected spiral fracture of the left tibia and when repeated after an interval a healing fracture of the head of the left fifth metatarsal bone, possibly sustained on the day of admission.

PLATE 8

Michael was brought to hospital at 7 months by a frustrated mother because he was irritable, vomiting and not feeding well. He was found to be thin and underweight, and had the characteristic appearance which Ounsted has labelled 'frozen watchfulness'. The right cheek showed fresh bruises.

The skeletal X-ray survey revealed periosteal bruising on all four limbs (see plate 10) and multiple rib fractures of three different dates.

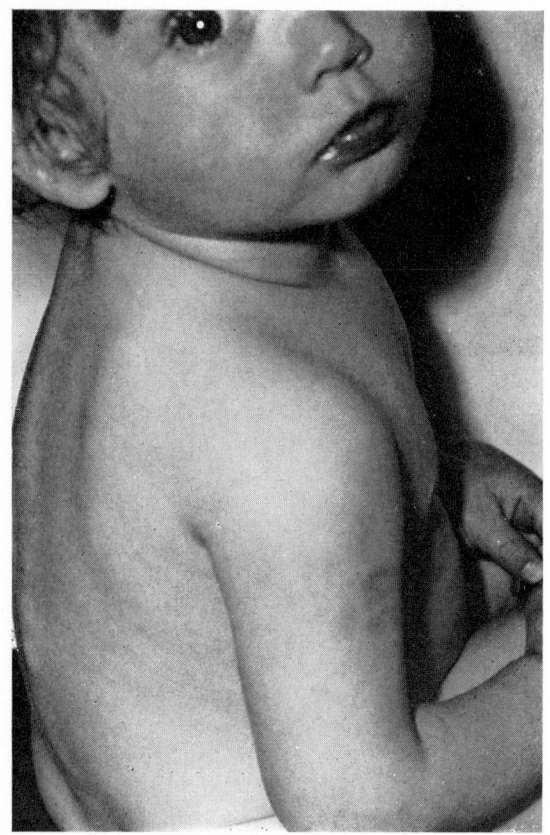

PLATE 9a. Photograph on day of admission showing swelling of the right shoulder joint and bruises with cigarette burns on the right upper arm.

PLATES 9a, 9b, 9c, AND 9d

Cathy, aged 20 mths. Brought to hospital with the complaint that the right shoulder had looked a little swollen for 24 hours and that she would not use her right arm (Plate 9a). The mother had brought her to casualty 3 months before for a similar swelling of the right elbow. An X-ray of the elbow had shown no abnormality (Plate 9b) and a sprain was diagnosed.

The shoulder X-rays (Plate 9c) showed a normal shoulder joint but there was now gross distortion from a healing 3-month-old fracture at the elbow joint. X-ray of the shoulder 2 weeks later revealed gross calcification in a large haematoma (Plate 9d).

This story illustrates that fractures will be missed unless X-rays are repeated 2 or 3 weeks after the injury. Normal X-rays at the time of the 'accident' do *not* exclude fracture.

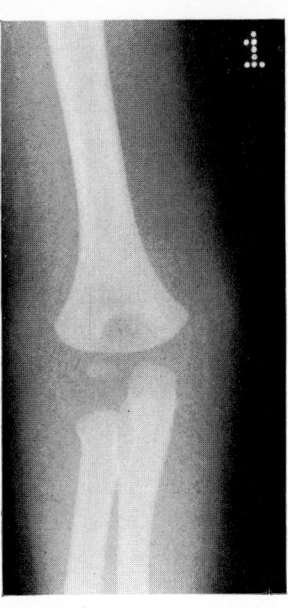

PLATE 9b. Normal radiograph of elbow joint 3 months before admission.

PLATE 9c. On day of admission—healing lesion at lower end of humerus and double contour line. There is swelling of the shoulder joint but no bone changes.

PLATE 9d. 2 weeks after admission, the damage to the upper end of the humerus is apparent. Calcification is seen in the periosteal bruise.

9b

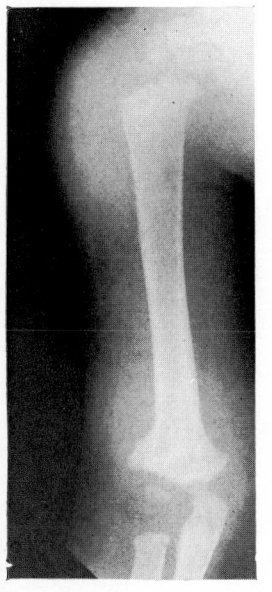

9c

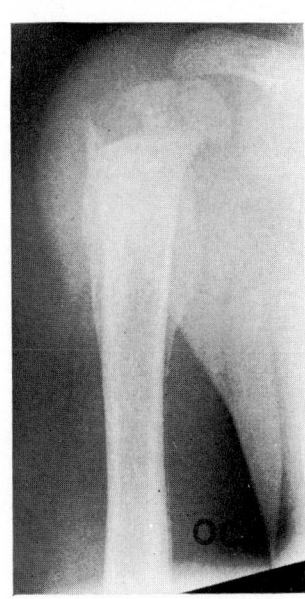

9d

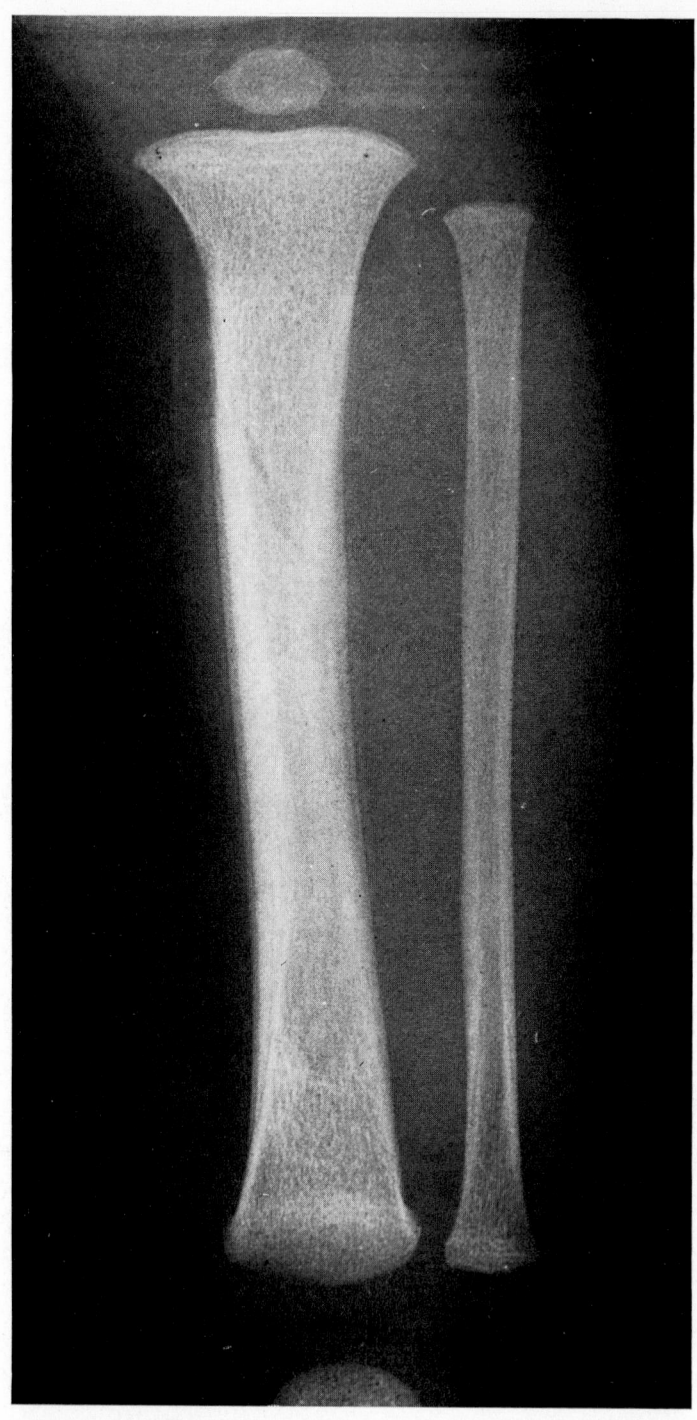

PLATE 10. Radiograph of the leg showing double contour lines indicative of periosteal bruising.

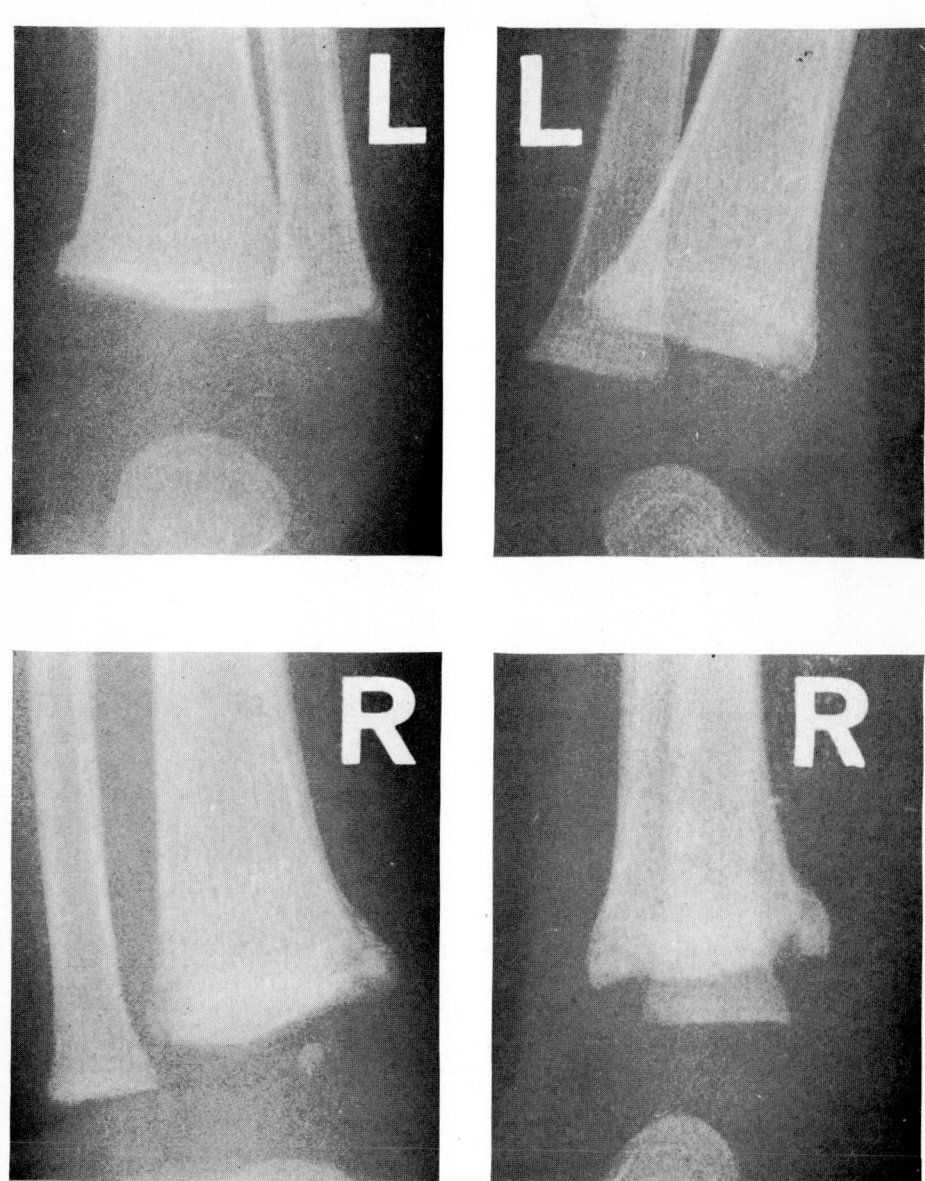

1   2

PLATE 11. Typical chip fracture of metaphysis. 1. Anteroposterior. 2. Lateral

of the appropriate team. Medical information must be restricted to the smallest number of people possible, as it is highly confidential and any leakage could give rise to gossip with serious consequences for the families involved.

Communications with the police force offer no difficulty if the information is made available to senior officers who have a large amount of discretion. At lower levels in the police force action has to be taken as there is no room for discretion. The attitude of the police in the author's experience has always been most helpful and it is interesting to note that in the last five years, during which time regular lectures have been given to the new recruits in the Women's Police section of Lancashire Constabulary, the response is now much more sympathetic due to the recognition that the battering adults are, in the main, sick people who are needing help rather than prosecution. Where a police force is not co-operative and co-operation cannot be achieved, information should not be made available. No doctor, except in a case of major injury, would report these cases knowing that it would inevitably result in a prosecution for injury. This dilemma is one which the individual doctor has to resolve for himself.

At present the medical profession holds two widely polarised views about involving the police in these situations. This springs from the dichotomy of views between doctors and police about the management of these cases. The establishment of a uniform national policy will require these bodies to accept views which may be diametrically opposed to those which they now hold. The present uncertainty can only cause harm, since concealment of the cases with lack of communication to the other bodies is known to be responsible for the deaths of many children.

The current interpretation of the law actually interferes with protection of the children by giving excessive and dangerous attention to the 'rights' of the battering parent. The legalistic approach by court officials and the legal profession, many of whom appear to regard these cases as exercises in forensic skill, completely disregards the fact that the reward for this expertise may be the death of a child. Perhaps one day these cases may be removed from the court room atmosphere into the quiet of a committee room where the whole situation may be weighed up and decided on the basis of what is best for the well-being of the child and the family.

The management of a complex medical social problem should not be subjected to the limitations imposed by the arbitrary requirements of a court of law designed only to produce a Guilty or Not Guilty verdict. It is of little consequence, in most cases, who was or was not the 'guilty' party, but what cannot be in dispute is that rewards for a successful end result are high and that the penalties for failure are equally great.

DISCUSSION

In discussing this paper, which covers the subject widely, the Study Group concentrated on three main questions: the variety both in the family situations and in the nature of the injuries, the need to disseminate knowledge and the problem of identification of cases. It was wrong and dangerous to look on non-accidental injury as a homogeneous syndrome. Undoubtedly there were local variations in the kind of injury as well as in the effects of injury. Variations depended on the availability of the means of injury. For example an increased availability of prescribed drugs could raise the proportion of poisonings. Cultural differences were probably active too. Was the injury the result of crisis or was it premeditated? Cigarette burns and poisoning are more likely to be premeditated than physical attack which accompanies a family crisis. Premeditation characterises schizophrenia.

At present ignorance of the powerful forces that underlie non-accidental injury causes society to reject these families, and this is clearly demonstrated by the aggressive attitude displayed towards them even by hospital personnel when the victim is being admitted. The antagonism of neighbours can be a precipitating factor in causing injury or re-injury and the noise of crying in the household increases neighbourly hostility. The fact of injury itself produces a crisis and at such a time the parents become inaccessible, so that the first aim, to arrive at truth in order to secure the proper protection of the child, is unattainable. An aggressive or an accusatory attitude towards the parents isolates them still more completely. A better understanding by society is essential. But so too is an understanding by the parents if this can be achieved.

The families are identified by a variety of agencies, and information should come from the family doctor as well as from the paediatrician and the obstetrician. The success of referral of injured babies and children to hospital depends on what arrangements have been made for the recognition there of the dangers inherent in the situation. Casualty departments are being used increasingly for primary care but staffing is unsatisfactory. Mainly surgical training is conducted in them, whereas the physician's approach is essential. For babies and children, the attention of the paediatric staff, possibly by providing a paediatric casualty officer, is to be desired although some prefer a specially trained casualty staff. With employment of overseas doctors changing every six months and not altogether conversant with the English language, the responsibility for the management of injured babies and young children should be strictly limited and decisions never taken without reference to experienced medical or nursing staff. Casualty consultants should be appointed for all major emergency and accident departments. The proportion of cases of non-accidental injury to all the other patients in these departments will always be small. This decreases awareness and increases the importance of consultation with senior staff.

3. The doctor's dilemma—a paediatrician's view

Christine Cooper

All those who have to deal with child abuse are aware of the need to improve their general understanding of all the problems as well as to develop their own expertise. Many professions and disciplines are concerned and adequate opportunities to share knowledge, experience, opinions, and doubts and difficulties are few. Free communication between all involved should enhance confidence between the disciplines and this is nowhere more necessary than in this difficult, controversial and time-consuming problem of non-accidental injury to children.

In Newcastle in 1966 to 1967 four deaths occurred in young children already diagnosed as 'battered babies' and reported as such to the medical officer of health, the children's officer, the family doctors and the health visitors concerned. Therefore it seemed that further thought needed to be given to the protection of battered children, and so a working party of six was set up in the University Department of Child Health to study the problem. The working party consisted of three paediatricians, a child psychiatrist, the Medical Officer of Health and the Children's Officer. A *Guide to Management* by doctors and social workers was drawn up for use in casualty departments, in wards where children were admitted with injuries, in child health clinics, family practice and social work departments. The *Guide* was modified at intervals, and *Guidance Notes on Diagnosis of Non-accidental Injury* were issued with it and similarly modified from time to time. The latest version of *A Guide to Management* was published in the *British Medical Journal* on December 15, 1973, pages 657 to 660. *The Guide to the Diagnosis* is printed below.

A study was made of the children seen in Newcastle with non-accidental injuries from 1965 to 1971, representing 148 episodes of injury to 136 children from 124 families. The histogram, Figure 2, shows the age and sex distribution and the deaths. It should be noted that the majority of the children were under 1 year of age, and that a high proportion were under 6 months. All those who died were under 3 years old. It was worth emphasising that there were 9 children over 4 years of age and this probably represents an under-estimate of cases in the older age group owing to the greater problems of diagnosis.

Table 2 shows the outcome in these children, with a death rate of 10·3 per cent which is similar to that found in other series. The male to female ratio was eight to six. Permanent brain damage was present in 30 per cent of the 60 who were followed up, and a later study of all the children will reveal the

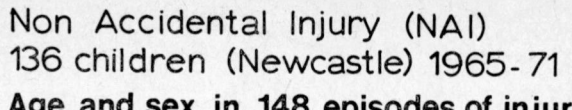

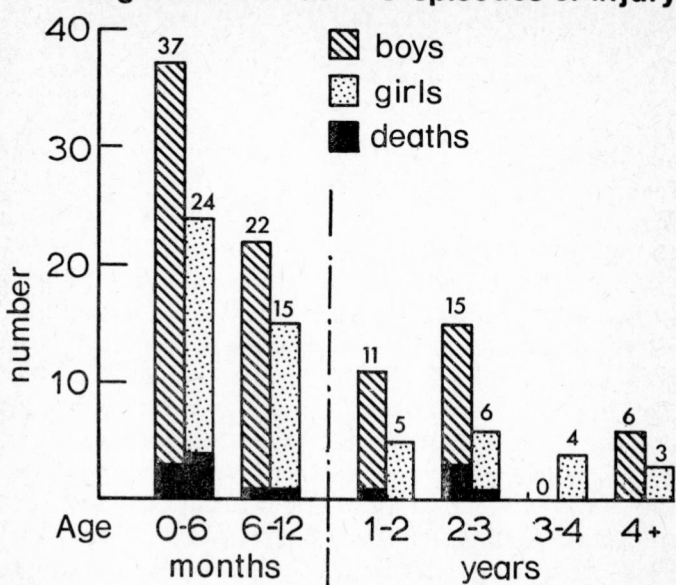

FIG. 2   Histogram showing distribution of death and sex in age groups

number of damaged personalities. It is expected that this will be high. One mother was murdered by her aggressive psychopathic consort 10 days after her child died from head injuries (probably also inflicted by the consort). Two other mothers were considered to be seriously at risk of severe injury, and many others were 'battered wives', appearing from time to time with black eyes, multiple bruises and other injuries.

Table 3 shows the frequency of the various injuries to the children. Bruises and other skin manifestations were present in 93 per cent, and expertise is increasing in recognising the various skin lesions, especially the adult human bites, cigarette burns, bizarre skin markings and petechial haemorrhages. The high rate of fractures (46 per cent) indicates the severity of the injuries which occurred, and the large proportion (28 per cent) with subdural haematoma

TABLE 2. NAI 136 children (Newcastle) 1965–1971

Outcome		
Deaths	14	10·3%
Boys	8	
Girls	6	
Permanent brain damage	c. 30% of 60 followed up	
Damaged personalities = Many		
One mother murdered 10 days later		

further underlines this point. The subdurals were usually bilateral, from shaking the child, and generally associated with retinal haemorrhages, an important clinical sign. Swollen joints, abdominal injuries, burns and scalds and poisoning were other noteworthy features in these children.

TABLE 3. NAI 136 children (Newcastle) 1965–1971

Frequency of injuries (148 episodes)

Bruises, including lacerations, small burns etc.	127	93·4%
Fractures	63	46·3%
S.D.H.	39	28·7%
Other (abdomen, eyes, synovitis, bites)	21	15·6%

Doctors in various branches of medicine face a number of dilemmas in handling families where child abuse (non-accidental injury or NAI) is occurring. The following *Guide to the Diagnosis of Injuries to Children* is used in Newcastle at the present time.

GUIDE TO THE DIAGNOSIS OF INJURIES TO CHILDREN (Newcastle 1974)

The question always is:

'IS IT ACCIDENT, CARELESSNESS, NEGLECT OR INFLICTED INJURY?'
(NB Most 'accidents' to young children follow environmental and family stress.)

Injured children often tax the doctor's diagnostic skills to the utmost and may require a multidisciplinary approach for full elucidation of the child's injuries (physical and mental) and the family psychopathology.

REMEMBER THE HIGH MORTALITY AND MORBIDITY OF INFLICTED INJURY.
Where inflicted injury is suspected (and it should at least be considered in the differential diagnosis of all injuries to young children) four studies are needed to make a complete diagnosis:

1 *The physical signs in the child*, including radiological signs which may take 2 weeks to manifest themselves completely.
2 *The full history of the injury*, how it occurred and details of the environment before and actions taken immediately after the injury.
3 *The personality of the parents* (or caretakers), together with their attitudes and behaviour with the child and his injury.
4 *The social circumstances* of the family, including previous injury to this child or injuries to siblings.

When inflicted injury is suspected in a casualty department or in family practice or elsewhere in the community (health clinic, school, social work department) it is recommended that the paediatric registrar at the nearest hospital paediatric unit be contacted by telephone and *admission for investigation* arranged. Rarely an immediate outpatient consultation or a domiciliary visit will be more appropriate. Sometimes the injury itself, but sometimes other problems, such as failure to thrive or the possibility of coagulation defects or bone disease, will be given to parents as the reason for admission.
The following are some of the more important clinical signs which should be carefully looked for and evaluated in injured children. Sometimes the skin and bones tell a

tale which the child is too young or too frightened to reveal: *Look for signs of the discrepant history.*

1 BRUISES

(a) Any bruises on a baby in the first year, especially when on the cheek or head
(b) Bruises from adult human bites (Plate 6)
(c) Two black eyes without gross bruising of the forehead (Plate 2)
(d) The 'purple ear' (Plate 3) from bruising, or fading bruises of the ear and surround-ing scalp
(e) Petechial haemorrhages (from rough handling of a young baby) or bizarre marks and bruises on the skin
(f) 'Finger-and-thumb-mark' bruises on the face, trunk or limbs, especially on the trunk of a young baby who has been firmly held and shaken (Plate 1 and 5)

2 FRACTURES

(a) Any fracture in the first year which does not have a clearly accidental history. Repeat X-rays in 2 weeks will reveal the full extent of the injuries. A vague history of: '. . . must have hit his arm on the side of the cot . . .' will be suspect.
(b) Unsuspected fractures of the clavicle, ribs and long bones may be present even in a healthy looking child. Epiphyseal and metaphyseal injury and periosteal bruising are typical of inflicted injury but only detectable on X-rays.
(c) Spiral fractures in the first 3 years need careful study of the history and family factors.

3 JOINTS

A tender swollen joint with a normal X-ray at first needs further X-rays in 2 weeks when any periosteal haemorrhage will be revealed as it calcifies.

4 BURNS AND SCALDS

(a) Circular blebs, sores or scars from cigarette burns are often found in clusters and may be of different ages. (Plate 6)
(b) Other burns and scalds in young children need detailed studies of the history and findings in child and family, to screen for inflicted injury. (Plate 4)

5 MOUTH

(a) If there is a small blood-clot on the gum or tongue, examine for a minute tear of the frenulum (Plate 7) or elsewhere in the buccal mucosa. (This is usually caused by ramming the bottle or a fist on the mouth of a crying baby.)
(b) Sundry cuts, scratches, excoriations or sores around the mouth, often of different ages.

6 EYES AND BRAIN

(a) Retinal haemorrhages from chest compression or shaking
(b) Subdural haematomata, easy to suspect when large and acute, but when small and chronic present as a puzzling picture of vomiting, irritability and failure to thrive.

7 VISCERA

Injuries to a solid or hollow viscus may present with puzzling signs in the abdomen (or chest) without any external bruising of the abdominal (or chest) wall.

8 POISONING

Ingestions of tablets, medicines or other 'fluids' may not always be accidental careless-ness, although very hard to prove otherwise.

9 OTHER SUGGESTIVE SIGNS

(a) Repeated injuries to a small child or to siblings
(b) Delay in reporting the injuries
(c) Failure to thrive, short stature, excoriated skin and other signs of neglect

(d) Repeated consultations for trivial symptoms in an apparently healthy baby but with a worried mother may be the prodromal stage of inflicted injury

(e) Some cases of apparent 'cot death' are non-accidental.

CLINICAL DIFFERENTIAL DIAGNOSIS OF INFLICTED INJURY

Birth injury	Leukaemia
Osteitis	Congenital syphilis
Arthritis	Neurogenic sensory defect
Rickets	Congenital indifference to pain
Scurvy	Ehlers-Danlos syndrome
Haemophilia and allied	Acute abdomen
coagulation defects	'True' accident

RADIOLOGICAL SIGNS

Multiple bony lesions (There is sometimes only one, especially in an infant)
Various stages of healing
Epiphyseal displacement
Metaphyseal fractures and 'chips'
Avulsion of part of provisional zone of calcification ⎫
Double contour lines of periosteum   ⎬ 2 weeks later
Massive calcification in periosteal bruise ⎭
Cortical thickening is a late sign
(See Plates 9, 10 and 11)

RADIOLOGICAL DIFFERENTIAL DIAGNOSIS, additional to CLINICAL

Infantile cortical hyperostosis	Metastases
Osteopetrosis	Fragilitas ossium
Osteoid osteoma	Fatigue fracture

FURTHER DIAGNOSTIC STEPS

All injuries to young children should be carefully screened for child abuse.

Poisoning, burns and scalds, and sudden unexplained deaths may not always be accidental, a fact not fully realised by all the specialists into whose wards such children may be admitted, so that the appropriate enquiries and investigations are not made. The Department of Health and Social Services recommends that the paediatrician should collaborate in the care of all children in hospital. In these cases it is especially important in surgical wards where doctors tend not to accept that a non-accidental cause is relatively common.

The consultant should be involved from the start, despite the problem of finding time.

The paediatrician should not leave these difficult cases in the hands of his juniors. Telephone consultations for guidance, often helpful when emergencies arise in much serious physical illness, are not sufficient. The juniors will be involved as part of their training and time must be found for all the discussions with parents and for case conferences when child abuse is suspected or diagnosed. Because this taxes all concerned, some doctors are tempted not to become deeply involved in 'minor injuries'. Yet the next injury may kill the child.

To assist and expedite diagnosis, a central register is needed for all proved or suspected cases and their families or, possibly, of all young children with injuries. This register should be kept in each locality or perhaps computerised for a region. The families are notorious for changing addresses and moving the homes of their children, as well as for attending different hospitals in the same city, or for moving off to some new area. Whatever the anxieties of lawyers about registers and human rights, all doctors experienced in handling such families are agreed on the need for them. Registers are already in experimental operation in some cities where they prove useful in speeding up diagnosis or raising the index of suspicion in busy casualty departments. How the register should be kept and by whom are still open questions (see p. 133).

The problem is a medical one initially. Many of the children who die from inflicted injury have previously been taken to a doctor for major or minor injuries or problems of behaviour or failure to thrive. All doctors who treat children should understand these early warning signs or 'cries for help'. Such children should always be referred to hospital at least for paediatric consultation and the majority will be admitted:

1 Some for urgent medical or surgical treatment.

2 All for confirmation of the physical diagnosis, which will involve X-rays (to be repeated in 2 weeks), blood tests and photographs. Rare forms of bleeding diseases and bone disease must be excluded. The child's behaviour and growth can be studied as well as parental attitudes and behaviour.

3 Meanwhile the hospital provides a safe place for the child. The family and siblings can come freely to visit and to be studied during this time. Cherishing the anxious parents is an important task for doctor, nurse and social worker.

4 The parents have to gain confidence in the treatment and in the concern and understanding of medical and nursing staff before they relax enough to discuss the difficulties which they are having with the child and with their social problems. At first they are frightened, guilt laden and full of fantasies concerning the child, as well as about 'authority'. Medical and nursing staff need special understanding and skills to handle the situation appropriately.

5 With time and delicate handling, parents whose difficult behaviour during this stage is often taxing, can be brought to unfold the problems, whereas a 'confrontation' at the outset results in antagonism and removal of the child from hospital, and a failure to reveal crucial facts.

6 A family diagnosis will be arrived at within 2 or 3 weeks with help from a psychiatrist and from all who know the family, including the community services, GP's, health visitors, social services, police, voluntary services such as NSPCC, FSU etc., and also from other hospitals which the family may have attended. Immediate and long-term management can then be planned, although modification from time to time may become necessary.

7 When mothercraft is adequate, the subtle signs of disturbed mothering and parenting are often missed, and doctors and others unaware of the emotional tensions just beneath the surface may be misled by 'obsessionally good' household care.

MANAGEMENT

Management begins at the first contact of any worker, medical or social, with the family and if the diagnosis is confirmed continues for several years at least. A doctor or health visitor is usually the first to be consulted or to suspect the problem but, as our predicting skills improve, midwives and those in touch with ante-natal and recently confined women or young families at home will be alerted to early signs. Nursery matrons, school teachers or playgroup leaders, social workers or neighbours may be the first to recognise the problems and referral for full assessment should be the next step, a step unfortunately not always taken. Liaison by doctors with colleagues in the community demands that the various disciplines concerned need to know much more about each other's work and about the skills and the limits of expertise of any one professional group. Case conferences and full communication will help to develop mutual trust and increase the value of the contribution made to the family.

Reorganisation has imposed a heavy burden on the understaffed social services. In many areas child care suffers especially from lack of specialisation and the employment of inexperienced, junior and often untrained members. Long delays and inadequate reporting are common. Senior trained workers are essential for this work.

The attitude that 'Case work can cure everything' for these unfortunate clients is still too prevalent. Only experienced workers understand that clients with seriously damaged personalities are unable to respond.

The mistaken notion that separating a child from his family is always a last resort and harmful is widely believed by social workers. In fact the contrary is true. Whatever the age of the child, removal from traumatic physical and emotional battering is always beneficial if the substitute care provides adequately for the child's needs. There is no one answer, and assessment and reassessment of the family diagnosis must accompany the medical treatment and the measurement of growth and development.

INVOLVEMENT OF THE POLICE

Ideally senior members of the police, specially trained, should be involved and take part once the multidisciplinary consultations have resulted in strong suspicion or certainty. These discussions should begin as soon as possible, but at any rate within three or four days of the child's admission. At this stage it is desirable, except in very occasional or very severe cases, that the police share their previous information on the family and then keep a watching brief, having satisfied themselves that the child is safe. Police interrogation or investigation at an early stage generally disturbs the developing confidence of the parents and delays the unfolding of the true picture, besides interfering with therapeutic relationships. As trust develops between police and doctors relationships will become easier, and both disciplines will learn much from each other. If the first studies of the family reveal dangerous attitudes, clearly the police will need to start early investigation. In the majority of cases, however, the full family diagnosis takes two or three weeks to establish and at the outset NAI may not be certain. Information from the police about previous violent behaviour is a helpful contribution to the discussions where the injuries are slight and diagnosis is being attempted at an early stage.

Problems of confidentiality arise on both sides, which mutual trust and the employment of senior staff will lessen. A senior police officer has, unlike a junior, the power to use discretion about immediate investigation provided he is satisfied that the family is safe.

Written reports from doctors to police are frequently requested and given. The police seldom give written reports to doctors. Reciprocity is desirable.

LEGAL DILEMMAS

These are many and ill understood, as practice among police, lawyers and courts and medical attitudes varies so much.

Place of safety orders. The threatened removal of the child by the parents from hospital can usually be prevented by explanation and persuasion from a senior member of the staff, provided that the atmosphere of the ward is cherishing and friendly and not punitive and angry. If necessary the department of social services (or police or NSPCC) may be approached for an emergency order. There are two difficulties here:

1 Social workers, especially the junior ones, are more and more reluctant to obtain such an order.
2 In at least one area the Clerk to the Justices advises the magistrates to grant the order for seven days only. As the juvenile court meets only once a week, this may leave only one or two days for the investigations and consultations, and this time is far too short. The Act allows for 28 days which should give adequate time and is much more desirable.

Care orders. These are of invaluable assistance in the rehabilitation of the child to his family in suitable cases. Only a short separation from home may be necessary when a care order is in force. When rehabilitation is not expected the order is needed for removal of the child. The police are often content not to prosecute the parents when a care order is to be made and this is advantageous when the long-term welfare of a particular family is taken into consideration. When the family is prosecuted, a probation order can be more helpful than a short term of imprisonment. The care order may be discharged by the court after several years when the family problems have been resolved.

Supervision orders. These do not give enough room for manœuvre to be of much value and have little strength.

Evidence in court. In the juvenile court it is not necessary to prove 'who did what' but only that the child is suffering and needs care which he is not likely to receive from his family without help. A senior member of the medical staff must see it as his duty to give evidence, as the medical evidence is often the major or the only evidence of any value. When the parents have admitted to injuring the child or to being unable to cope with him without help and will agree to the care order, a shorter and simpler hearing takes place. The parents should be encouraged always to be legally represented, and so should the local authority or the NSPCC who bring the case.

With regard to the doctor, the parents and evidence: if the juvenile court can be understood by the parents to be a 'helping' and not a prosecuting court, with all its deliberations in private, it can be a therapeutic agent. Nevertheless doctors do find it hard to reveal in court confidential material obtained during doctor–patient consultations, even when it is in the interest of the young patient. If the parents agree to the care order, this material will not need to be produced.

Lawyers, especially those who act for the parents in care proceedings, ought to understand the serious nature of the problem and the dangers of subsequent injury. They would see the matter less as a 'game of advocacy' which they hope to 'win' if they realised that 'winning the case' could result in the child's death. The writer has experienced increasing understanding and help from the parents' lawyers, particularly in changing the emphasis of the cross-examination in contested cases.

CONCLUSION

The paediatrician sees this as one kind of 'psychosomatic' disorder. He is accustomed to seeing many children whose 'illness' is due to parental attitudes, neglect or rejection which is not of a degree to reach the court. This initial handling of the NAI families will not differ much from that of the other disturbed families that he sees, unless premature police interrogation upsets the delicate interaction which the multidisciplinary team tries to develop, Yet doctors can appreciate the police point of view and sincerely hope to learn better ways of working with them.

4. The psychopathology and psychotherapy of the families: aspects of bonding failure

Christopher Ounsted, Rhoda Oppenheimer and Janet Lindsay

INTRODUCTION

The battered child syndrome is a common one. Kempe and Helfer (1972) give a rate of 300 per million population per year. This is probably a low estimate. If this rate applies to England and Wales then we would have 15,000 new cases a year. All workers agree that the syndrome has been diagnosed more frequently in recent years. Whether or not there has been a true secular increase is not known. Our impression is that the syndrome is truly increasing. In our service at the Park Hospital there has been a notable increase in the demand for treatment of the syndrome in the last few years. Our current rate is now about 20 per thousand referrals. In the past it has been of the order of 2 or 3 per thousand. Kempe and Helfer (1972) have given details of the sociology and the psychopathology of the syndrome.

In this paper we consider systems of treatment and of prevention that are evolving in our service. We shall deal with two series: one of approximately 86 families referred to the Park Hospital for Children, and the other of 24 selected mothers who were treated as outpatients because of fears that they might injure their babies, but who in fact had not done so when they were taken on for treatment.

DIAGNOSIS, THE FIRST STEP IN THERAPY

Diagnosis, as Kempe has pointed out, is the first step in psychotherapy. It is an integral part of the classic syndrome that the babies will have been brought by their parents to doctors on a number of occasions before the diagnosis is made. When the parents present their injured child at casualty or to the paediatrician they give a story in which both have colluded. The story is often accepted by the doctors and social workers. In spite of recent intensive propaganda more than half of all our cases are known to have been injured on a number of occasions before they are finally diagnosed.

The first step in therapy is that the diagnosis should be made and maintained with equanimity. The parents are told at our first interview that the injuries are such that they must have been inflicted by an adult. We find that the parents often accept this with relief, though this relief may not be explicit until therapy has advanced.

The assessment of the family prognosis

About one-third of the families referred to us are found to be untreatable in the sense that permanent removal of the proband under a care order is required. A single example will suffice.

Case 1   A female child aged 20 months was admitted to hospital with the classic syndrome. There were numerous bruises of different ages on all parts of the body. The child was dwarfed being below the 3rd percentile in length and weight. Her skull circumference was just below the mean. She had a severe iron deficiency anaemia. Radiological survey showed two recent fractures of the skull probably of different dates. There were two fractured ribs, probably three weeks from fracture at the time of the radiograph.

On admission the child showed notable 'frozen watchfulness' (which syndrome we describe below). She did not raise her head. She did not move her hands in any useful way. She was entirely silent, neither crying nor cooing. The only exception to this behaviour was when she was approached by a male adult. If any such approached her she would gaze-fixate him and, as he picked her up, she would utter a brief piercing scream. Apart from this behaviour she gave out no active signals.

Two and a half months after admission, during which time she had been given intensive care, she showed approximately ten months of developmental advance. She was attempting to walk with assistance. She was feeding well. Her weight was rising. Her anaemia was cured. She had formed selective affectional bonds with some members of the staff.

Investigation of the family background revealed that the mother, who was 21, had been reared hard in another country. She had conceived the proband out of wedlock. She had been deserted by her fiance when this occurred. After the child's admission she was found to be suffering from pulmonary tuberculosis and to be pregnant by her second spouse. She was an inadequate weak woman who refused to come into the Mother's Unit to be with her. These refusals were in response to the demands of her husband. The stepfather was the eldest of 11 children and came from a harsh background. Since he was 12 years of age, he had been repeatedly in trouble with the police. He had served sentences in detention centres, approved schools, borstals and, just before marrying the proband's mother, had completed a sentence of 3 years for infliction of grievous bodily harm. The parents on one occasion expressed a weak wish to have the child returned to them for two days, but in practice made no steps to obtain care of her. In a follow-up of five years they have made no further contact.

In such cases there is an urgent need for the infant to be found fresh and safe surroundings where he can develop social bonds with healthy adults. Too often this decision is delayed, the maturational stage for bonding passes by, and the child is left with a chronic deprivation syndrome likely to perpetuate itself in the next generation.

Both for separation and for therapy, early action is essential. In its absence we see that paragenetic perpetuation which Sir Keith Joseph (1972) named the 'cycle of deprivation'.

Diagnosis of other disease in the proband

We have found that many children who are battered have unrecognised physical and/or behavioural abnormalities or are thought to have them by their mothers. This obtained in about a half of all the Park Hospital group of treated families. The abnormalities were very varied. For example, one child had had seven hospital admissions before it was found that he was blind and hence could not gaze-fixate his mother. The parents had maintained a totally defensive attitude, until they were told that their child was blind, and had been from birth, then their defences fell. 'He cried and cried and he never looked at me,' said the mother. The father said 'It's my fault. I knew what was happening really. I should have stopped it.' They asked the physician, 'Could you have done it?' He answered 'Yes.' This empathic answer led to an open relationship. This second stage in diagnosis is also therapeutic. One shares with the mother and father those features of the child's development and behaviour that could be provocative of abuse in anyone.

Diagnosis of the parents

A thorough, delicate and psychiatrically sophisticated diagnosis of both parents is essential. It must be a progressive process.

Serious mental illness, psychopathy and inadequate personalities were found. Precise statistics cannot be had and we think that statistical treatment of data is likely to mislead more than to clarify.

Diagnosis of the family

The family diagnosis extending back into the pedigree should be made in detail. It is well recognised and our own data confirm that parents who abuse their children often come from families where violence has ruled down the generations. This must be made conscious to both parents. Then they can see their task as one of breaking what often seems to them like a family curse extending down the generations. The parents are themselves unloved children, specifically children to whom very little was given but from whom much was demanded. Many of the mothers have a dependent, yet angry and hating relationship, with their own mothers. Since in therapy we give to these mothers the mothering of which they have been deprived, it is essential to elicit a clear and precise diagnosis of their own developmental experiences.

Diagnosis of family relationships

All these families are by definition disturbed, but it is desirable as treatment proceeds to try to define the nature of these different disturbances. For example, jealousy is relatively common. By this we mean that one of the parents is morbidly jealous of the other's feelings towards the baby. A father can often feel that the baby has replaced him in his wife's affections. In one case a social class I father came into the maternity ward and saw his wife breast-feeding their new born infant. He physically tore the infant from the breast and flung it violently across the ward, shouting out, 'Those breasts are mine!'

THE IN-PATIENT SERVICE

Both the architecture and the setting of the in-patient service are essential aspects of the treatment we give. The mothers' house consists of a domestic dwelling, closely annexed to a children's hospital. The house contains three comfortable bedsitting-rooms, a communal sitting-room, a dining area, a kitchen, a laundry, and the usual offices. It is set in a garden with peaceful views on every side. The hospital where the children and their brothers and sisters are treated has a great diversity of rooms and territories in it. There is an active school. There is a large occupational therapy department with a number of environments. The play rooms are equipped and furnished for children of all ages. There is a separate day nursery, staffed with experienced nurses and removed from the rest of the day space. The night nursery is physically removed from the day space and from the Mothers' Unit.

ADMISSION TO THE UNIT

When the diagnosis is first made the parents are defensive, thus a crisis arises that must often be resolved by law. This can be a therapeutic action. The doctor and the parents know that the child has been injured. The child must be put where this will not recur. This is done by obtaining a place of safety order, through either the appropriate department of social services or the police. This order names the hospital and gives 28 days in which the plan of treatment can be put in action.

When the order is obtained we explain what this means and we offer to admit the mother together with any brothers and sisters. In the great majority of cases this offer is accepted.

THE FIRST FEW DAYS OF THERAPY

The first few days of therapy are crucial. The mothers and children have been living a life of extreme tension, punctuated often by outbursts of rage. Communications have been shouts and blows. The families usually have been existing in social isolation.

Almost universally the mothers have felt trapped, unwanted, unloved and unequal to their roles as children, as spouses and as parents. These feelings must be reversed.

In the first few days the mothers and children experience for the first time total care. Without having to ask, they are provided with food, warmth, with privacy, with tranquillity, with an undemanding routine and with the attentive care of large varieties of mature adults.

The standard reaction of the mothers to this experience is one of astonishment. It is a situation quite new to them. We see at first the phenomenon which we have named 'second day packing'. On the second day after admission the mothers often panic and wish to leave. It is a situation analogous to the sudden cessation of chronic pain. Calm intervention by the staff soon overcomes this and the mothers settle down into a regular routine.

Frozen watchfulness

The abused child must also receive his initial treatment. Once the injuries have received attention there remains a behavioural syndrome to treat. Repeatedly abused children show a characteristic behaviour which we have named 'frozen watchfulness' (Ounsted, 1972). Children with frozen watchfulness make no sounds. If they are toddlers, they do not chatter in the presence of adults.

If they are approached, they stand quite still. They will gaze fixate but they do not smile. They are often silent even when their wounds are dressed.

Frozen watchfulness we see as an adaptation to unpredictable behaviour by the loving and loved parent who without provocation becomes transformed into an aggressor and then immediately reverts to good parental behaviour. Treatment aims primarily to provide care that is predictable. Characteristically the child with frozen watchfulness has been unable to establish basic trust in the regularity of his life. This must now be given him. The routine is designedly regular. Bed times, meal times, bath times and play times are all on a fixed schedule and the behaviour of the nurses is equally predictable.

An extreme example of frozen watchfulness (see Plate 8) and its change under treatment is exemplified by this case history.

Case 2   The patient was admitted to hospital with his mother at the age of 9 months. The mother had a chronic schizophrenic illness which had been manifest for at least 8 years. The father was unknown. The mother and infant had lived in isolation. The mother had not allowed any interactions with the infant by any person other than herself. On admission the child's physical measurements were on the 25th centile for his age. Examination revealed no stigmata. He was well washed. On inspection he was found lying completely immobile. When picked up he made no response. His body was held in tonic extension. He showed no interest in toys. If a plaything was placed in his hands he would drop it without a glance. When food was placed in his hand he did not move it to his mouth. He did not react to sounds. There was no stepping response. If sat up, he lay down at once. He did not smile. He did not vocalize or babble.

He was gently separated from his psychotic mother and given intensive mothering by the staff. His development was dramatic. Within a month he had made at least 4 months advance. At 25 months his skills were measured on the Griffiths Scale and he performed as follows:

Locomotor Scale	22 months
Personal Social Scale	21 months
Hearing and Speech Scale	21 months
Eye/Hand Co-ordination	22 months
Performance	20 months

Observation of the child in the presence of his foster mother showed what appeared to be a natural and warm bonding between the two and no significant abnormalities in their interactions. The child showed disturbed behaviour at and after visits to his mother in a mental hospital. These were stopped when he was 2 years 6 months. At the age of 3 years 6 months the foster parents abruptly rejected him and ended the fostering. They gave no reason.

THE OPEN RELATIONSHIP

Earlier we have mentioned the 'open relationship'. The parents of battered babies have developed an overgrowth of fantasy not only in respect of battering, but also in respect of other matters in their lives. The fantasies protect the parents from a reality which they see as unbearable. This perception is often distorted. In the setting outlined above these fantasies are not needed. The situation moves forward and during the second week of treatment it is common for clarifications to occur in which, with relief, the parents will admit to the assaults and will abreact the emotions they have denied.

The timing of this crisis is critical. Behind the treatment is the consultant who does not interfere in the day to day therapy. He has to judge when the moment has arrived to see the parents. Both parents are seen together and in privacy. It is usual for them to condense what happened into a few emotive sentences. 'His crying,' said the mother of one battered baby, 'seemed to follow me round the house. I could not stop it. I could not escape.' They then go on to tell how alien to themselves the assaultive behaviour seemed to be. 'It did not seem to be me that did it.' They express the feeling that they could not incorporate into their egos the alien behaviour which they had shown.

During the interview weeping, sobbing and mutual comforting behaviours are prominent. Towards the end of the interview they begin to express their feelings of alienation. 'I did not think that I could be part of the human race.' At this point it is essential for the physician to make clear to them, with empathic communications, that cataclysmic breakdown in parental behaviour is an integral part of the human ethogram. One has to convey that all of us could, given adequate provocation, batter babies. Later it is useful to go over each violent act and elicit in detail what really happened so that the fantasies can be eliminated.

By the end of the second week of in-patient treatment we aim to have established with the families an 'open relationship'. By this we mean that:

1 We have released the proband from his frozen watchfulness. We have let him find a safe and predictable world in which he can begin to explore, to learn and to mature, both as an individual and as a social being.
2 We have helped the mother to feel free. She no longer feels trapped in a vicious circle. She begins to mature. She learns by precept and example how to care for her young.
3 We have helped the parental relationships and the intrafamilial dynamics to lose their quality of fantasy.
4 We have let the future be seen afresh, as hopeful for growth and change.

We must here make a theoretical digression to explain our terminology: we use the term 'closed relationship' and 'open relationship' as analogous to Bertalanffy's (1968) division of general systems into closed systems and open systems. In the former the laws of classical thermodynamics apply—a closed system over time proceeds inevitably towards complete disorder, just because it is closed in on itself. These families seem similarly to have been closed in for generations. By removing, both physically and emotionally, all the constraints which have held the family closed, we allow an open relationship to develop. Open systems are those which show increasingly expressed orderliness as they develop over time. The classical example is the realisation of the zygote's potential as it evolves into the adult organism through a series of metamorphoses.

We place the families in a highly regressed state. They are fed, housed, and cared for as though they were infants. It might seem a paradox that, in this situation, they can change and mature. But consider how a caterpillar changes into a butterfly—the regression of pupation is essential. Thus we see the simultaneous occurrence of psychodynamic dissolution and psychodynamic developmental advance, not as a paradox but rather as the 'coincidentia oppositorum' in Nicholas of Cusa's sense: a resolution by the coming together of opposites.

The therapeutic court

Court hearings need not damage the open relationship between the hospital and these families. Properly handled the small drama of the juvenile court can itself be a useful catharsis. These parents have been dogged by guilt, denial and fear of exposure. Their upbringing has often been unjust. They have fantasied another world of 'them', of police, of magistrates, of parental figures that they must dread but obey.

They expiate their guilts in reality and this enables them to feel themselves to be responsible persons for the first time (Ounsted, 1968). After the court hearing the parents usually express relief. The court usually makes an order placing the child in the care of the local authority but in treatable cases this does not mean separation from the parents. It does mean that the parents have an organisation which protects both them and the child.

The liberating bond

The notion that firm bonds to mature adults are preconditional for the capacity freely and responsibly to choose is another apparent paradox. Yet analogous concepts are basic to the physiology of stability and change. Claude Bernard's 'La fixité du milieu intérieur est la condition essentielle de la vie libre' expresses the matter precisely.

When part of a system is employed in choice, in idiosyncratic development or in movement, then another part of that same system must be stable. The stable bond for the battering parents is with the hospital and its staff. It is important that this trusting bond should not be seen as a kind of 'transference neurosis'. Specifically we make no attempt to end the families' relationship to us, nor do we interpret it to them. In an open relationship mutual courtesy between all parties is the goal. Verbal discussion has limited utility, and interpretations of private feelings are apt to destroy the self-respect which we aim to create.

The outcome

No statistics of outcome would be meaningful, since both our ideas and our practice are in a state of evolution. In most cases there has been a notable improvement in the intrafamilial dynamics. Many cases still cannot be treated, and in others only palliation is possible. We now turn to the more hopeful area of prevention.

THE PREVENTIVE STUDY

Kempe and Helfer (1972) showed that prevention is practicable and effective. We now describe a study of families treated on an out-patient basis.

The referral

Certain children were referred by their general practitioners because of a grossly abnormal mother-child relationship and also because the doctors thought that the children were at risk for battering. From our referrals we selected for detailed study and treatment 24 families where the mother and child were of normal intelligence and where the child was not older than 4 years.

Two-thirds of the mothers had complained to their family doctors that the child was driving them crazy. One-third had admitted to hitting the child too often and too hard. At the time of referral over 90 per cent of the mothers were on tranquillisers or antidepressants and 66 per cent of the children were receiving sedatives. Fifty-four separate factors were examined for each of the 24 families and then arrayed in order of increasing frequency within the sample as a whole.

Parental characteristics

The early lives of both parents were often disturbed. Over 60 per cent of the mothers had had unhappy, emotionally deprived childhoods. The most striking aspect of their personalities was their extremely low tolerance to any form of pain or to any form of frustration. Two-thirds of the mothers were labile in mood. Migrainous attacks of sufficient severity to require withdrawal to bed had occured in 66·7 per cent of the mothers. Of all the parents 37·5 per cent had suffered from Besnier's syndrome (asthma, eczema). The fathers showed immature and dependent personalities in 41·7 per cent and the mothers in nearly 80 per cent.

In general the families were isolated and lonely. They had made few friends in their neighbourhood. Many had removed themselves from their own part of the country and were new settlers in the area. Not one of the 24 mothers went out to work.

The mothers were on average 24 years old at the time of the birth which is 2 years younger than the median age of maternity in our region at the present time.

Parental relationships

Parental relationships were in general bad. 16·7 per cent of the mothers had an illegitimate child by a different father, which had been kept in the family by the mother. The mothers had conceived six further children before marriage to their present spouse. In about one-quarter of the sample, housing and work difficulties were prominent. In 41·7 per cent one or other parent had been sterilised by the time of referral. Nearly two-thirds of the mothers complained that the fathers lacked understanding of their difficulties and were impatient and unhelpful. Sexual difficulties were an outstanding complaint of the mothers in 80 per cent of the sample.

Proband pregnancy

From the beginning, most of these families had an unhappy and disturbed mother-infant interaction. Nearly two-thirds of the mothers complained of and were treated for puerperal depression. The colicky child syndrome (Barrett, 1971) was a prominent feature of most of the probands in infancy. A third of the children were described as vomiting frequently in the neonatal period.

Complaints of tics and other displacement activities figured in 41·7 per cent. Asthma and/or eczema afflicted 45·8 per cent of the probands. Sleeping difficulties, crossness, excessive crying and irritability were present in two-thirds. This had led to the same proportion of children being treated with some form of sedation or tranquilliser before they were referred to the clinic.

Referral state

At the time of referral the mothers had a multiplicity of complaints. They saw the child as too clinging, too aggressive, too timid, too defiant, disobedient.

They made quite unrealistic demands on the children for obedience and for love. Two-thirds of the mothers complained that the child could not be cuddled.

As part of the general failure in communication which was in evidence in every case, it was striking that selective speech retardation was present in half of the children.

Thus we were faced in these families with a situation where the interaction between all members had become distorted and fixed in a pattern of a closed system. This was made explicit by the mothers often in terms that they felt trapped, in prison, unable to break out except in outbursts of rage. The vicious circle of mal-communication was present in every case.

Treatment

On referral the parents and the child were seen by the physician. Individual therapy was first instituted for the parents and the child by the social worker in their own home as this made it more easy to involve the father.

When judged ready, the mothers were introduced into a group situation. At the same time the child was also introduced into a toddler's group. The two groups were run simultaneously in adjoining rooms with free access between the two. The goal of therapy was simultaneously to help the mothers with their own problems and at the same time to teach them to cope in a more constructive way with all their children.

The mothers were encouraged to telephone to the social worker whenever a crisis arose. As the mothers learned to cope, many of them reported that simply thinking of using the telephone was enough to enable them to regain control.

The mothers were helped to keep a daily diary of the situations in which their child drove them to explosive anger. This was brought along to the sessions with the therapist for detailed discussion.

The groups were found to be therapeutic. The mothers were able to receive mutual support from each other. The group size was held between five to eight on empirical grounds.

The children soon learnt to play and explore naturally and associated this with their mother's presence. The mothers came to be regarded by the children as bringing them to a place where they were safe and free. Babies who were too small to join in play activities actively themselves were involved by being cuddled and loved by any staff member available. The mothers saw their children handled cheerfully when they showed any signs of the colicky child syndrome or when they soiled, vomited or were angry.

During the course of the study we began to be able to make assessments at earlier and earlier stages so that by the end of the study we were ascertaining mothers ante-natally and instituting treatment before the birth of the child.

Outcome

The 24 mothers who attended regularly over one to two years all showed some improvement. In no case did battering occur.

It must be emphasised that this group was a selected one. We deliberately chose those likely to respond for treatment, and a good outcome should not be generalised to the whole of the battered child syndrome.

Summary

1 There is an increased demand for the prevention and treatment of child abuse.
2 In cases where child abuse has occurred, about one-third are regarded as untreatable except by removal of the child from the family at the present time.
3 Diagnosis and therapy proceeds in the following sequence:
   (a) the firm diagnosis that battering has occurred
   (b) the diagnosis of other diseases in the proband
   (c) the diagnosis of the parents
   (d) the diagnosis of the pedigree
   (e) the diagnosis of family relationships.
4 The admission crisis is described. The family must be got to a place where all of them are safe.
5 The novel therapeutic environment is organised to provide what has been lacking in the family histories.
6 The syndrome of frozen watchfulness is described and its treatment outlined.
7 The method of establishing what is called an 'open relationship' with the family replaces the closed system of fantasies which had formerly existed.
8 Court hearings are sometimes needed. The therapeutic nature of these dramas is explained.
9 The concept of the liberating bond is discussed.
10 A system of preventive treatment is described.
   Twenty-four families were treated intensively on an individual and group basis. The family characteristics are described. The colicky child syndrome and the frequent occurrence of irritating illness in the child are noted. The parental characteristics are those described by Kempe and Helfer. The outcome in these cases was generally good but a warning is given against generalising from selected groups.
   The goal in preventive treatment should be the early ascertainment of families at risk during the ante-natal period.
11 Knowledge of this syndrome is advancing fast. We think both theory and practice should remain tentative and flexible.

DISCUSSION

To break through this problem and, in the individual case, to prevent re-battering, not only assessment and short term management of battering parents and their children has to be considered but also the more long term treatment. The psychopathology of these families has been sufficiently well worked out to allow identification of potential battering in parents.

A psychosocial history could easily be included when a pregnant woman presents at an ante-natal clinic, and a specially trained psychiatric social worker could work in liaison with maternity departments to help select suitable cases. Although the diagnosis of disturbed parents is not difficult, considerable psychiatric sophistication is required for their prolonged treatment. A psychiatrist should therefore be involved at an early stage when battering has occurred. It is unfair to put the whole burden of treatment on to the social services department, where not enough cases are seen to build up the necessary experience.

Importance is attached to the careful evaluation of the results of schemes at present under trial. Basic to success is the establishment of the full diagnosis and the recognition of serious family psychopathology. There is a place for both individual and group therapy. In the Park Hospital series, two-thirds of the patients have been amenable to some form of treatment and battering has not recurred.

Should the fathers be treated? The clinical data presented and the results of this Oxford Study differed from those in Birmingham where psychopathic fathers and mothers of low IQ seemed commoner. No adequate explanation was forthcoming for these differences. The behaviour of the newborn baby, its sleeping, feeding and crying habits appeared to be important factors and the question was raised of a possible chemical basis for this behaviour.

5. Parents of battered children: a controlled study

Selwyn M. Smith, Ruth Hanson, Sheila Noble

Though generalisations describing the characteristic features of parents who batter children have recently become prominent, there is a scarcity of controlled studies. Recent observations have suggested that battering parents are not confined to any particular personality type, intelligence level, or social class (Steele and Pollock, 1968) and that 'child abuse is psychodynamically related and has nothing to do with race, colour, creed, sex, income, education, or anything else' (Kempe, 1969). By way of contrast other authors have noted that battering parents are young (Gil, 1968) and from the lower social classes (Young, 1964; Skinner and Castle, 1969). Mental illness, psychopathy and subnormality have been observed by several authors (Woolley and Evans, 1955; Birrell and Birrell, 1968; Lukianowicz, 1971). In addition Gibbens and Walker (1956) mention that criminality and alcoholism are often found.

Because we believe that a knowledge of the parental characteristics of child batterers is of prime importance in the management of the battered child syndrome and because previous studies have led to conflicting conclusions it was decided to undertake a controlled investigation of battered children and their parents. This paper compares age, class, psychiatric state, criminality, and intelligence in 214 parents of battered children and 76 control parents.

SUBJECTS AND METHODS

Index cases

Over a two-year period 134 battered infants and children aged under 5 years and their parents were studied in detail. Most children had been admitted to hospitals. All the parents who had either confessed to inflicting trauma or had inadequately explained their child's injuries were referred by the consultant paediatrician who first saw the child.

Control group

The controls comprised 53 children admitted to hospital as emergencies. Accidents and trauma cases were excluded. Parents of these children were matched with the index group on the basis of mother's age and age of infant. The following variables were held constant: consultants referring cases; area of origin; research team; and the particular circumstances in which the parents of children who were suddenly and unexpectedly taken ill became involved in the research.

In both groups parents were seen as soon as possible after their child's admission to hospital and their co-operation was requested in a research study into the background of children with injuries or conditions similar to that of their own child. All parents underwent standardised psychiatric, psychological and social interviews.

Classification

Personality diagnosis was classified on the basis of the American Psychiatric Association classification (1952) into normal and abnormal. Abnormality of personality was further subdivided into mild, moderate and severe.

Mild (character disorder). Personality is disordered to the extent that the person is dissatisfied with the quality of his relationship with other people. Such persons may think they cannot make satisfying contacts with others owing to emotional inhibition, dependence on others, or because of their own overbearing behaviour.

Moderate (personality disorder). Impaired personal relationships are sufficiently noticeable to be evident to others. Such persons are perceived as unusual, odd or eccentric.

Severe (psychopathic). Personality disorder is so gross that the subject harms others either through commission of aggressive acts or through omission of ordinary obligations. Thus psychopaths may be classified as *aggressive* or *inadequate*. Their work record is often poor (Walton and Presly, 1973).

Other factors

Neurosis was diagnosed at psychiatric interview and classified according to the International Classification of Disease (WHO, 1968). Non-psychotic disturbance was measured by the General Health Questionnaire (Goldberg, 1972). Subjects scoring 12 or over on this scale have a high probability of being diagnosed as abnormal. Neuroticism (instability) was measured by the Eysenck Personality Inventory (Eysenck and Eysenck, 1964).

Four subtests of the Wechsler Adult Intelligence Scale (Wechsler, 1955) were given (vocabulary, block design, comprehension, and picture arrangement).

The Criminal Records Office was searched for the names of parents interviewed.

RESULTS

Age: The mean age of index mothers was 23·5 years, a high proportion of whom were age 21 at the time of the child's injury (Fig. 3). The mean age of index fathers was 27·0 years, and their age distribution was similar to the mothers.

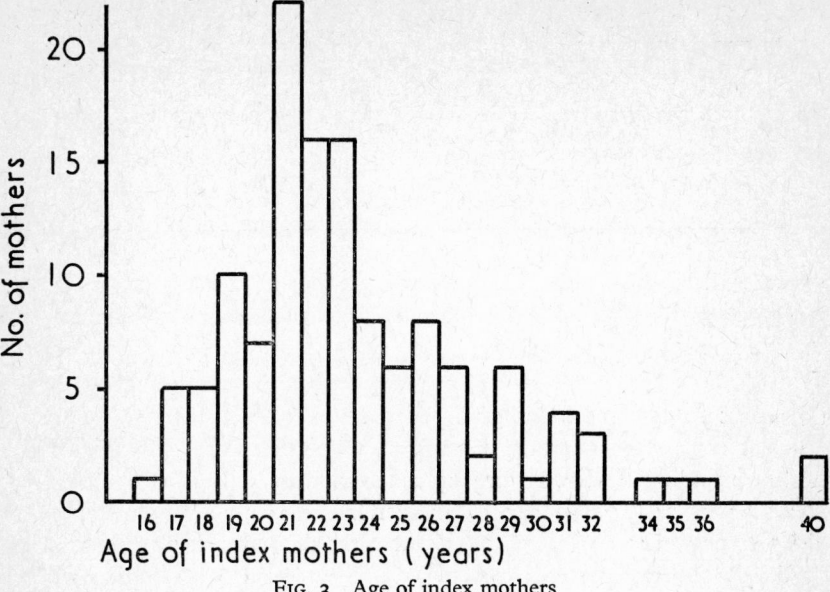

FIG. 3   Age of index mothers

Social class: It was found that index group cases were of significantly lower social class than the controls (*P* 0·001). Among the index parent none came from social class I and only three were from social class II (Table 4).

TABLE 4. Social class distribution among index and control groups

	I	II (Non-Manual)	III	IV (Manual)	V
Index group (%)	0 (0)	3 (2·5)	26 (22)	56 (47·5)	33 (28·0)
Control group (%)	5 (9·6)	4 (7·7)	26 (50·0)	14 (26·9)	3 (5·8)

χ^2 with 1DF = 26·29, P<0·001

Personality: 95 of the 125 mothers (76 per cent) and 57 of the 89 fathers (64 per cent) in the index group had an abnormal personality. Compared with the controls this amount of abnormality is highly significant ($P < 0·001$) (Table 5).

Severity of personality disorder: 78 (62·4 per cent) of mothers had personality disorders of mild or moderate severity compared with the controls. This is a significant finding (for 1 DF and $\chi^2 = 45·32$, $P < 0·001$). 24 (27 per cent) of fathers had mild or moderately severe personality disorders and this also was significantly different from the controls (for 1 DF and $\chi^2 = 5·63$, $P < 0·05$). 17 mothers (13·6 per cent) and 33 fathers (37·1 per cent) in the index group had severe personality or psychopathic disorders. None of the controls were psychopathic. Nine mothers (7·2 per cent) and 29 fathers (32·6 per cent) were aggressive

TABLE 5. Comparison of personality findings in parents in both groups

	Normal No.	%	Abnormal No.	%	Significance
Index mothers	30	24·0	95	76·0	} $\chi^2 = 55·12$, DF = 1
Control mothers	44	86·3	7	13·7	} P < 0·001
Index fathers	32	36·0	57	64·0	} $\chi^2 = 18·15$, DF = 1
Control fathers	21	87·5	3	12·5	} P < 0·001

psychopaths. Eight mothers (6·4 per cent) and four fathers (4·5 per cent) were inadequate psychopaths. Alcoholism and drug dependence were not features among the index cases or controls.

Neurosis: Among the index group 60 mothers (48 per cent) and 9 fathers (10·1 per cent) were neurotic. Compared with the controls neurosis was a significant finding ($P < 0·001$) among index mothers only (Table 6). Of the index mothers 34 (27·2 per cent) showed mixed neurotic symptomatology, 21 (16·8 per cent) were depressed, 2 (1·6 per cent) showed anxiety reactions, and 2 (1·6 per cent) had hysterical reactions. One subject (0·8 per cent) showed a mixed neurotic picture. One index mother had anorexia nervosa. She starved one child to death and battered another who was older. Her case has been described in detail elsewhere (Smith and Hanson, 1972).

TABLE 6. Comparison of neurosis findings in index mothers and controls

	Non-neurotic No.	%	Neurotic No.	%
Index group	65	52·0	60	48·0
Control group	46	90·2	5	9·8

$\chi^2 = 12·08$, DF = 1·, P < 0001

General health questionnaire: Index mothers had a mean score of 19·2. They scored 12 plus significantly more often (1DF and χ^2 8·37, $P < 0·01$) than the controls. For other groups the mean scores were normal (index fathers, 11·0; control mothers, 7·2; control fathers, 6·1). This finding supports the validity of clinical diagnosis of neurosis found among the index mothers (mentioned above).

Eysenck personality inventory: High scoring (20 plus) on the neuroticism (N) scale of the inventory is significantly more characteristic of index than control mothers (for 1 DF and χ^2 4·69, $P < 0·05$).

Psychosis: Psychotic reactions were observed in four mothers (3·2 per cent and one father (1·1 per cent). None of the controls were psychotic. Two mothers were paranoid schizophrenics; one of them killed her two children under the influence of hallucinations. She was found unfit to plead and committed to a special hospital. Two mothers and one father were psychotically depressed. The injuries inflicted on the children by psychotic parents were bizarre.

Criminal records: Excluding juvenile court appearances among the index group 29·2 per cent of the fathers and 11·2 per cent of the mothers had a criminal record (Table 7). Of the control group none of the mothers and only two of the

TABLE 7. Number of parents with criminal records in index group

	Number of criminal records investigated	Number with criminal records after child abuse incident	Total number with criminal records
Fathers	89	6 (6·7%)	26 (29·2%)
Mothers	125	5 (4·0%)	14 (11·2%)

fathers had a criminal record. After the child abuse incident subsequent criminal convictions for offences other than child abuse occurred in 6·7 per cent of fathers and 4 per cent of mothers. 23 fathers (25·8 per cent) and 13 mothers (10·4 per cent) in the index group had been convicted for theft or larceny (Table 8). Convictions for violent crimes were recorded in 8 fathers (9·0 per cent) and one mother (0·8 per cent). Four of the fathers (4·5 per cent) had convictions for sexual offences including rape. Cruelty and neglect to children were recorded for only one mother and one father.

TABLE 8. Types of criminal offences in index group

Criminal offences	Fathers (n= 89)	Mothers (n= 125)
Theft, larceny etc.	23	13
Crimes of violence	8	1
Serious sexual offences	4	0
Cruelty and neglect to children	1	1
Motoring and traffic offences	2	0
Drunk and disorderly	1	1
Breach of probation order	0	1

Intelligence: The mean IQ's (based on the combined subtests) were 80 for index mothers, 95 for controls, 92 for index fathers, and 102 for controls. The difference in distribution of IQ's between index and control mothers is highly significant (for 2 DF $\chi^2 = 28\cdot61$, $P < 0\cdot001$). Index and control fathers were also different in ability, but the difference was not as statistically significant. The distribution of mothers' IQ's are shown in Figure 4. Nearly half the sample of index mothers were of borderline subnormality or below.

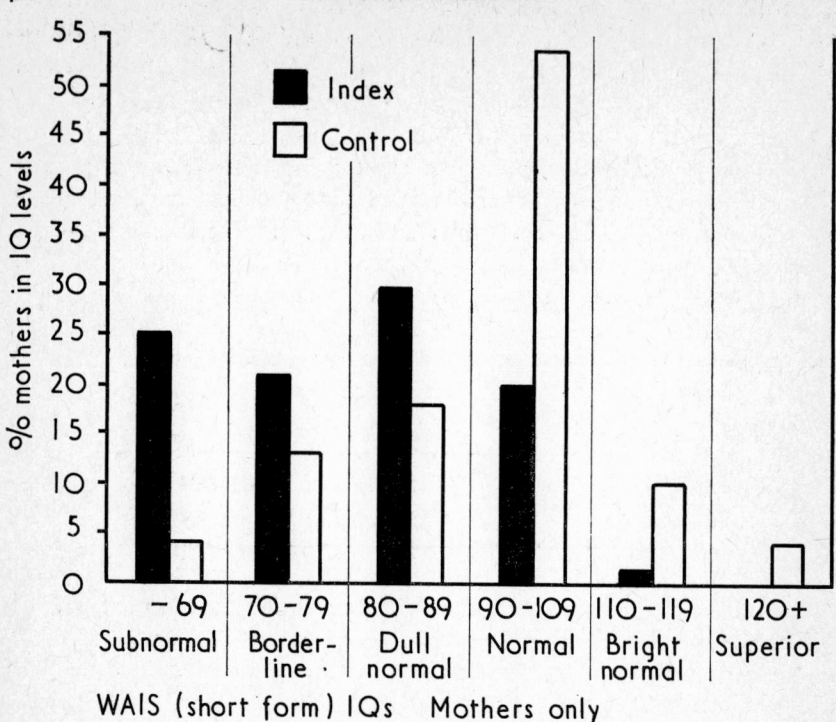

FIG. 4   Distribution of IQ in index and control mothers
(Wechsler Adult Intelligence Scale)

DISCUSSION

The young age of mothers closely compares with the age distribution described by other authors (Gil, 1968; Skinner and Castle, 1969). On average index mothers were aged 19·7 years at the birth of their first child. This compares strikingly with the national average age of 23·3 years (Registrar General, 1972). Even in the lowest social class the average was 22·6 years (Newson and Newson, 1965). Index mothers were thus nearly four years younger than the national average when they gave birth to their first infant. Taking into consideration our other observations that most battered babies were first or second born and that half were under 18 months old when battered it may be concluded that battering is associated with youthful parenthood. This argument is further exemplified by the infrequent occurrence of battering in older parents with large families observed in this and other series (Bennie and Sclare, 1969; Lukianowicz, 1971) and suggests that the risk of battering diminishes with parental age.

The parents in the present series were predominantly from the lower social classes. The association of low social class with battering parents has been commented on by several other workers (Young, 1964; Skinner and Castle,

1969). We found no support for the statement that all social classes were represented (Kempe, 1969). Of the index group 76 per cent were from social class IV and V compared with only 32 per cent in the Birmingham population (City of Birmingham, 1972). It may be argued that such a large discrepancy is due to the youthfulness of the parents and type of admission (emergency) of the children. Nevertheless, despite allowing for these important factors we found that the control group also contained 33 per cent of social class IV and V. This strongly suggests that battering is mainly a lower social class phenomenon. Furthermore, as the criteria for referral of cases were medical we are reasonably confident that if more children from high social class families had been admitted with unexpected injuries then consultant paediatricians would have referred them.

Abnormality of personality was a significant finding among the parents of battered children. The less severe types of personality disturbance were more commonly found among the mothers, who in general had features of emotional immaturity and dependence. Many of these mothers had in addition little concept of appropriate child-rearing practices. Battering may at best be regarded as an ineffectual method of controlling their child's behaviour. Techniques of teaching child-rearing skills based realistically on their low intelligence should perhaps be explored further as a possible means of correcting such ineffectual parental care.

Among the fathers studied one-third were psychopaths. The association of battering with psychopathy has been commented on before (Birrell and Birrell, 1968; Lukianowicz, 1971; Smith et al., 1973) but contrasts with Kempe's (1969) finding that psychopathy is a feature in only 2 or 3 per cent of battering parents. Though most of these fathers had not killed their children it is disconcerting to observe that they share similar personality characteristics with a group of fathers who did kill their children (Oliver, personal communication, 1973; Scott, 1973).

29 per cent of the fathers had a criminal record. Though the follow-up period was brief, nevertheless 6·7 per cent went on to commit subsequent crimes. Furthermore, though 19 per cent of the children's siblings had been previously battered, only 1 per cent of parents had been charged with cruelty or neglect, highlighting the capriciousness of the legal system towards parents who batter children. Criminality and recidivism, particularly if associated with a psychopathic personality, should caution against an optimistic outcome, and in our view invoking a care order is essential if further battering incidents are to be prevented. No association was found with alcoholism or drug addiction, which agrees with Steele and Pollock's (1968) findings but differs from those of Young (1964) and Gil (1968), who maintained that battering is precipitated by alcoholism.

We found that mothers were neurotic by three different measures. 58 per cent were non-psychotically disturbed on the general health questionnaire, and 48 per cent were diagnosed as neurotic at interview—the usual symptomatology being depression, anxiety, or a mixture of both. The diagnosis of neuroticism on the Eysenck Personality Inventory lends some support to the clinical findings of neurosis and the questionnaire results. One-third (34 per cent) reported having had an unhappy childhood. In general neurotic mothers (in contrast to psychopathic fathers) confessed to harming their children and expressed willingness to discuss their difficulties further. For this particular group of mothers the combination of symptomatic relief with a programme of social relearning conducted by skilled therapists seems to us to be far more beneficial than relying solely on programmes of 'mothering' and other methods (Kempe and Helfer, 1972) that tend to reinforce their dependent behaviour.

Our findings confirm the view that only a minority of battering parents are psychotic (Steele and Pollock, 1968). The bizarre nature of the injuries inflicted by psychotic parents suggests that they form a separate subgroup among child batterers whose management must differ accordingly.

CONCLUSION

Oliver and Cox (1973) showed that the tendency to perpetuate child abuse in successive generation is not diminished by supplying extensive medical and social help to battering parents. Furthermore, 60 per cent of children who are returned home are rebattered (Skinner and Castle, 1969). While every effort must be made to rehabilitate battering parents this should not be at the expense of the safety of the child. In the light of our findings we believe that strong consideration should be given to permanent removal of children from parental care in those cases where after an overall psychiatric assessment the likelihood of parents responding to treatment is thought to be remote.

SUMMARY

A controlled investigation of 214 parents of battered children shows that they were young and predominantly of lower social class. Premature parenthood is an associated feature. Among the mothers 76 per cent had an abnormal personality and 48 per cent were neurotic. Nearly half were of borderline or subnormal intelligence; 11 per cent had a criminal record. Of the fathers 64 per cent had an abnormal personality, more than half being psychopaths. 29 per cent had a criminal record. Recidivism is an associated feature.

The risk of battering possibly diminishes with time. The teaching of appropriate child-rearing skills, symptomatic relief, and social relearning are suggested as realistically based treatment methods and should be combined with a care order. When response to treatment appears unlikely, permanent removal from parental care should be considered.

We are grateful to Mrs. Carol Smith, who helped with the psychological testing, and Mrs. J. Harold and Mrs. Irene Brown, of the Department of Medical Statistics, United Birmingham Hospitals, who helped with the statistical analysis. Professor W. H. Trethowan provided valuable criticism. We are also most grateful to Detective Chief Superintendent Harry Robinson for his ready help. The department of medical illustration of the Birmingham Children's Hospital provided the figures. We are especially grateful to the paediatricians who referred patients to us. Mrs. Sue Knight typed the manuscript. The study was supported by a grant from the Barrow and Geraldine Cadbury Trust.

6. EEG and personality factors in child batterers

Selwyn M. Smith, Leo Honigsberger and Carol A. Smith

Growing interest in the subject of 'battered children' has led to a belief that those who injure their children are not aggressive criminals but relatively normal persons who are exposed to unusual and excessive stress (Helfer and Kempe, 1968). The view has also been put forward that psychopathy is not a significant finding (Steele and Pollock, 1968). Despite this it has been shown that a high proportion of child batterers have a history of blackouts or fits (Gibbens and Walker, 1956). Because of this and because we believe that insufficient emphasis has been placed on the possible organic background of this type of antisocial behaviour we decided to undertake an investigation of EEG findings among child batterers and any attendant abnormal personality correlates.

It is known that between 5 and 10 per cent of the general population exhibit EEG abnormalities (Hill and Watterson, 1942; Cobb, 1963). In selected groups such as university students and flying personnel EEG abnormalities occur in fewer than 5 per cent (Williams, 1941; Harding, 1973). In contrast, among those who are known to have committed acts of violence, for example motiveless murder, abnormalities may be found in 20 per cent or more (Hill, 1943; Stafford-Clark and Taylor, 1949).

SUBJECTS AND METHODS

As part of a comprehensive study in child battering which will be reported elsewhere and which involved 134 battered children in all, EEG's were recorded from 35 subjects who either confessed to inflicting injuries on their children or in whom the index of suspicion was high enough to make it virtually certain that they had done so. In addition to these, 16 of their husbands and wives were also subjected to EEG examination. In 13 other instances there was either no spouse or he or she was not available. Five subjects failed to co-operate while one other who attended fainted, leading to abandonment of the procedure.

The EEG's were divided into two groups. Those graded as *normal* either consisted of alpha activity with negligible amounts of theta activity or contained alpha activity together with small amounts of theta activity (Fig. 5) or showed only low voltage beta activity or harmonically related frequencies and prominent mu activity. Those graded as *abnormal* contained noticeable theta activity in the absence of drowsiness, though with some alpha activity (Fig. 6) or showed a

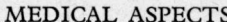

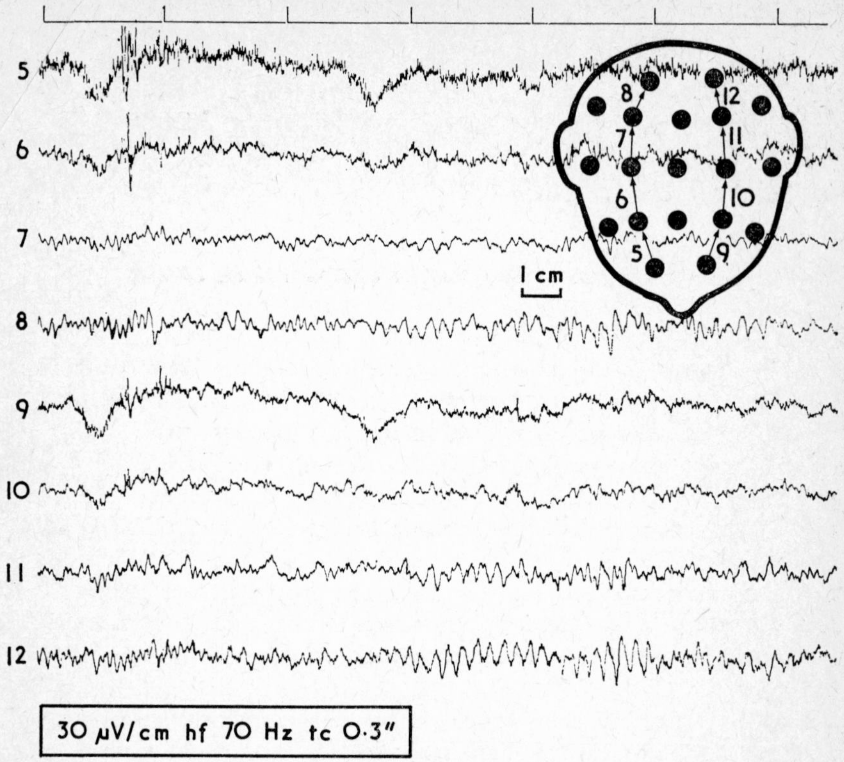

30 μV/cm   hf 70 Hz   tc 0·3″

FIG. 5   Normal EEG showing alpha activity and small amounts of theta activity

dominant activity of low frequency or the presence of marked asymmetry (Figs. 7 and 8) or transient or complex activity of the type associated with epilepsy. No abnormal response to three minutes of hyperventilation occurred in any of the subjects.

In addition to the EEG recordings the subjects underwent a standardised psychiatric interview and were given a shortened form of the Wechsler Adult Intelligence Scale (WAIS) (Wechsler, 1955).

In all cases assessment of the EEG findings and psychiatric interviews were done 'blind'. Each assessment was made without knowledge of the results of the other, and the electroencephalographer did not know whether the patient undergoing EEG was a batterer or a spouse.

RESULTS

Of the 35 parents who battered their children 8 (23 per cent) had demonstrably abnormal EEG's. In the case of the other 27 batterers and 15 of their spouses no EEG abnormality was shown. The one remaining spouse who was known to have epilepsy but was not responsible for the battering had a characteristically abnormal EEG.

On further investigation the eight batterers with abnormal EEG's were

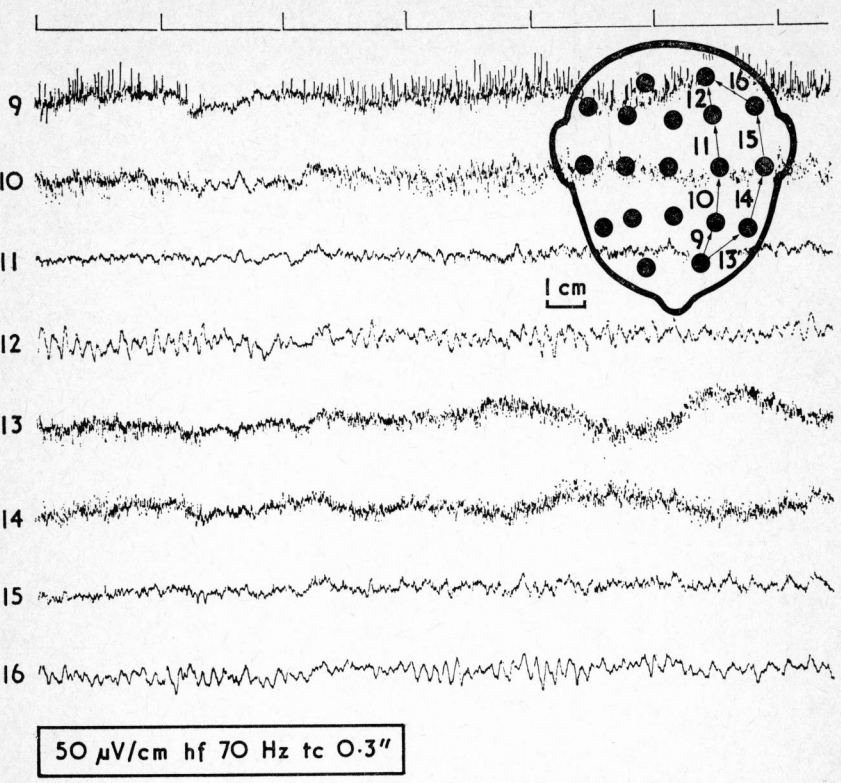

50 μV/cm hf 70 Hz tc 0·3"

FIG. 6   Abnormal EEG showing noticeable theta activity

TABLE 9. Performance IQ and EEG findings

Performance IQ (WAIS)	EEG Normal	EEG Abnormal
Subnormal to borderline	8	1
Dull normal to average	4	5

Males are not included in this table since there was only one with an abnormal EEG.

generally found to be of low intelligence though no lower on average than were those subjects in whom no EEG abnormality could be shown. Of the women tested those with an abnormal EEG tended to score higher on performance subtests than did those with a normal EEG (see Table 9). All eight subjects with abnormal EEG's could be defined according to the American Psychiatric Association (1952) classification as having a personality disorder (Table 10) without reference to the act of battering. They were also found to be persistent batterers, having battered one child more than once and sometimes more than one of their children.

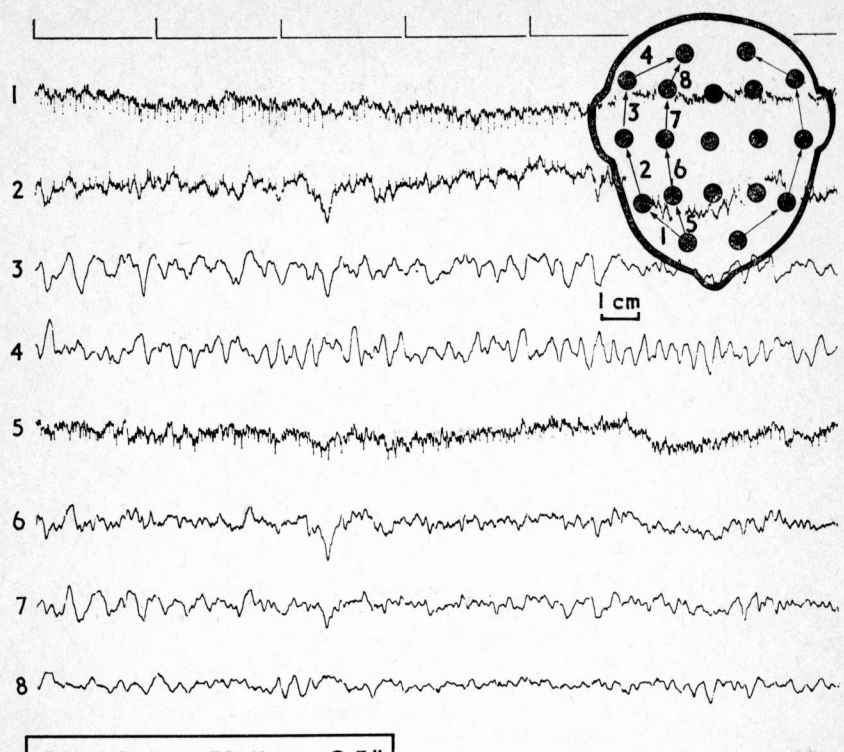

50 μV/cm hf 70 Hz tc 0·3″

FIG. 7   Abnormal EEG showing dominant activity of low frequency

TABLE 10. Personality diagnosis and EEG findings

Personality diagnosis	EEG Normal		EEG Abnormal	
	Male	Female	Male	Female
Personality disorder (mild and moderate severity)	3	9	—	2
Aggressive psychopathy	6	3	1	5

DISCUSSION

Because the numbers are on the small side only tentative conclusions can be drawn. Nevertheless, the prevalence of abnormal EEG findings strongly suggests that some child batterers at least are much more closely related to other groups committing acts of violence than they are to the general population. This is borne out also by the results of psychological testing, particularly of the group with abnormal EEG's, which also showed a consistent variation from the normal population. It therefore seems clear that child batterers are not a homogeneous group about whom it is safe to generalise. Whereas in some instances

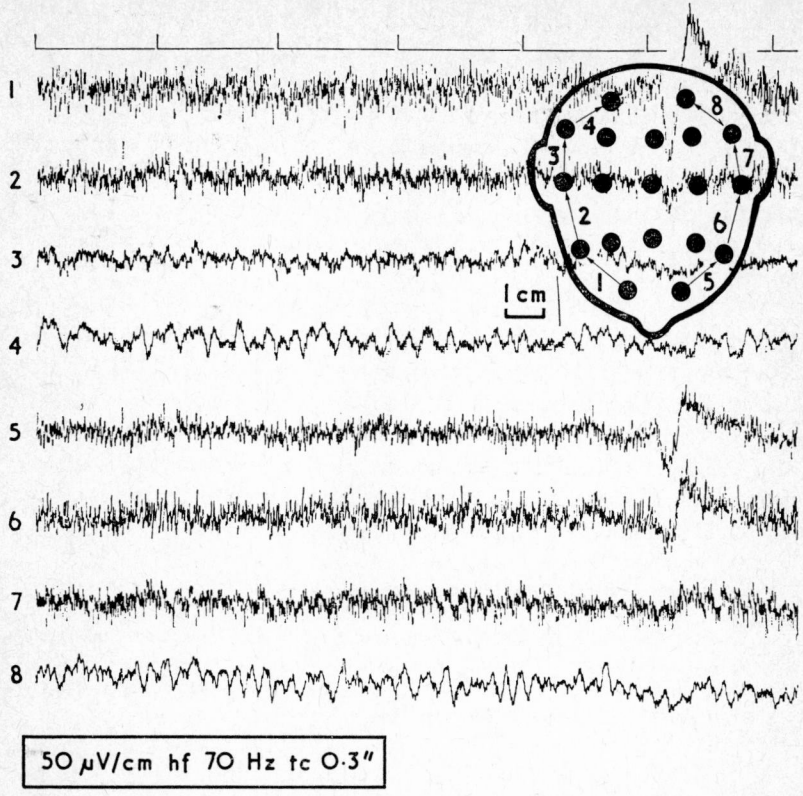

50 μV/cm hf 70 Hz tc 0·3"

FIG. 8   Abnormal EEG showing marked asymmetry

battering may be a response to unusual and excessive stress situations, though this needs further investigation, the presence of a definitely abnormal EEG in almost one-quarter of the cases points to what may well be a separate subgroup to which special attention should be paid. This is further borne out by a demonstrable relation between personality diagnosis and abnormal EEG's. Indeed five female batterers and one male batterer all with abnormal EEG's could undoubtedly be classed not only as having a personality disorder but as aggressive psychopaths (Walton and Presly, 1973). The male subject also had a criminal record. The two other female patients exhibited a personality disorder though this was not primarily of an aggressive type.

CONCLUSION

The findings reported here suggest that it may be wrong, even dangerous so far as the children are concerned, to rely too heavily on seemingly facile explanations of why parents batter their children. There is an over-ready tendency to assume that battering parents have experienced inadequate mothering in their own childhood and are therefore recreating in their own child-rearing practices the same maltreatment that they themselves had experienced as children (Steele and Pollock, 1968). This tendency should be resisted. Retrospective assumptions of this kind are attractive in that they are difficult to disprove. They are also equally difficult to prove. To assume that all such parents or even the great majority can be adequately treated by 'a transfusion of mothering', as has been suggested (Court and Kerr, 1971) may not be altogether justified and in the light of our own findings may even be dangerous to the children concerned.

SUMMARY

Out of 35 parents who battered their children 8 had an abnormal EEG. All of these were found to be psychopathic, of low intelligence, and to be persistent batterers. The presence of an abnormal EEG strongly suggests that some child batterers are more closely related than is usually accepted to those who commit acts of violence and that they are not therefore a homogeneous group about whom it is safe to generalise. The possibility that they form a separate subgroup among child batterers needs close attention.

We wish to thank Mrs. Ruth Hanson who gave valuable advice in the selection of material for this study and carried out the psychological testing. Dr. P. Jeavons, Dr. G. Fenton, Dr. W. Cobb and Dr. D. Williams kindly made available their EEG tracings. Professor W. H. Trethowan gave helpful advice, encouragement, and criticism throughout the study. Mrs. Sue Knight typed the manuscript. The study was supported by a generous donation from the Barrow and Geraldine Cadbury Trust.

DISCUSSION

Ruth Hanson and Selwyn Smith described the results of a study of families where there was an inadequately explained or unexplained accident. Seven major hospitals took part. The parents were seen separately. Convicted parents were interviewed in prison. Assessments were made on the parents from the psychiatric, psychological and social sides and on the children from the medical, psychological and other sides. Attention was paid to special relationships to grandparents. Criminal records were noted. The child's investigation included haematology, skeletal survey, photograph, an EEG (20 cases), a Griffiths development score and any previous hospital records. Controls were children under 5 years old admitted as emergencies to a Birmingham Children's Hospital other than for injuries and accidents. Of the 134 index children, 15 per cent died (33) and of the CNS injuries, 24 per cent had intracranial haemorrhages, subarachnoid, subdural or intracerebral, and 11 per cent had ophthalmic problems. Some became epileptic, spastic, blind and one had myoclonic jerks. There were recent burns in 9 per cent and old burns in 11 per cent.

There was initial denial of deliberate injury by mother in 80 per cent, reducing later to 69 per cent, but 71 per cent constantly for fathers. The precipitating cause was crying in 20 per cent and there was premeditation in 10 per cent.

Camps described four groups of cases: true infanticide, wasted and neglected, deliberate cruelty, and battering. Congenital defects were present in 13 per cent, reduced to 8 per cent when birth marks are excluded. The premature rate was 10·7 per cent. The lower social classes, with more prematures, had a higher incidence. 40 per cent were primips (young parents): in 19 per cent there was a second case. No case was seen in Social Class I. There was no correlation between the date of confinement and the lesion. 46 per cent of pregnancies were premarital. Few wanted the baby (control figure 19 per cent). 34 per cent were illegitimate as compared with 4 per cent in the controls. Some confess to having been maltreated in childhood: emotionally (males 26 per cent, females 10 per cent) and physcially (males 12 per cent, females 6 per cent). The criminal record was checked with the consent of the parents.

In the discussion the differences were brought to light between this Birmingham group and those within the experience of others working elsewhere. The incidence of paternal aggressive psychopathy seemed unexpectedly high in Birmingham, the 'frozen watchfulness' described by Ounsted was not seen and the families were all in the lower social classes. There was no confirmation either of the reputedly high incidence of childhood maltreatment in the parents or of the frequency of cries for help in the form of attendance at the general practitioners' surgery for a variety of trivial ailments.

Concern was expressed at the length of the psychiatric interview, stated to last for 5 hours, and the question was raised whether this could be harmful and unethical for controls. Concern was also voiced over the timing of the interviews with index parents who were seen within 24 hours of the child's admission by the psychiatrist and within one week by the social worker. A more gradual approach was favoured by other workers. The EEG report and its interpretation might be helpful to magistrates, but an abnormal EEG could not be treated.

It was suggested that at first knowledge of the family a social flying squad akin to a coronary care unit should visit them to work out what was happening, to care for the family and to decide on the nature of help needed. The first decision even if erroneous was difficult to reverse. How are you to know, asked the cynic after all this psychology, that the parents were not drunk and will not be doing it again?

Finally came two questions: were the criteria for assessing recent treatment valid? and to what extent could group psychotherapy help?

7. A neurosurgeon's viewpoint

Kenneth Till

Few workers in the medical and social fields will dispute these two propositions. First, each of us feels that his or her management of the problems arising following child abuse could be improved. And second, the more one knows about all the aspects of this complex subject, the more effective will one's management be—whether one's personal concern with child abuse will be therapeutic (medical, surgical, psychiatric), supportive (social services), investigatory and legal, or legislative.

In presenting my own factual experiences accompanied by my personal impressions, I hope to further a little the better understanding of the parents' situation. Child abuse is generally regarded in most instances as a long-standing disorder affecting one or more members of the family. The only occasion when it is regarded differently is when the police are investigating an occurrence which they think may constitute an indictable offence.

One of the earliest clues to the existence of child abuse is that the two parents' explanations are not compatible one with the other. Both explanations are usually intended to show how 'accidental' were the injuries. Enquiry at this stage, therefore, by police or doctor is unlikely to elicit the truth and will certainly make it more difficult to do so later.

HOSPITAL ADMISSION

The admission to hospital of an injured child is an acute episode adding for a time several new dimensions to an already complex situation. It is precisely during this time that we are required to gain the parents' confidence, make assessments, judge degrees of risk and make plans for the future. It is because the impact upon the parents of the condition of the injured baby, his admission to hospital and the treatment needed, is added to the effects of the previous situation, that all concerned with the problems, whether within the Health Service or not, should be acquainted with the physical situation, the better to order their own attitudes and management.

There are many forms of child abuse and the child victim may be admitted to one of several hospital departments. My own experience has limitations and in some ways is atypical. While to generalise from this experience would be unwise something may be learnt from it. All children referred to my small department within a general children's hospital come from other hospitals, already selected as probably having an intracranial lesion requiring neurosurgical care. The infant may arrive hours, days or even weeks after the initial incident which led to hospital admission. This varying interval together with the wide variety of referring hospitals and geographical areas from which the children come have produced over the years an impression that early management frequently leaves much to be desired, illustrating that all have much to learn. Whereas in some instances the paediatrician and his co-workers have established a satisfactory and profitable relationship with the parents, in most cases the doctors (and possibly the nurses) have so managed the early care that it is difficult to get the parents to attend, let alone to talk in any relaxed manner.

Diagnosis

My hospital, largely a referral hospital not serving a defined geographical area and receiving patients from other centres, admits 30 to 35 babies per annum who are suffering from some form of child abuse. About half of these are admitted to the neurosurgical department because they appear to have sustained some form of head injury. If admitted early, the baby is characteristically pale and inactive with a tendency to stare motionless into space and without any of the familiar posturing of a baby when asleep. The importance of appreciating what this very unnatural behaviour is like lies in its almost certainly closely resembling the condition of the child after he has sustained injury at home, possibly following a period of irritating and perhaps maddening crying which has led to the physical abuse. It does not require much imagination to enable one to understand that the rapid change from noisy vigour to quiet inactivity as a result of inflicted injury fills the parent with fear. It is probable from the parents' descriptions that, at some time before calling a doctor or before admission to hospital, not only has the child become silent and inactive but breathing may appear to have stopped. It is significant that of all the many babies admitted, often seriously ill from a wide variety of conditions some of which have been equally dramatic (e.g. after severe seizures), only in this abused group is there a story from the parents that mouth-to-mouth respiration was used. It has always surprised me that this attempt at resuscitation is related by the parents so frequently. It is extremely difficult to do properly with a baby and probably represents a panic reaction on the part of the parents. Vigorous resuscitation of this sort is sometimes the reason given by parents for bruising on forehead and cheek and for the fracturing of the ribs which is later reported to them. This may indeed occasionally be a correct explanation.

My thesis is then that, whatever social or psychological circumstances have led to the abuse, the dramatic effect upon the baby where head injury has been sustained is such that the parents' emotions are likely to be very intense and disturbing. It may or may not be profitable at this early stage to go into details of the circumstances with the parents, but it is far more useful for the medical, nursing and social service staffs to concentrate upon keeping the parents closely in touch with their child's condition, its significance and the treatment, if any is needed, while awaiting the gradual emergence of the parents' confidence in the staff and the more frank revelations which follow.

The most important effect of physical abuse is likely to be injury to the brain. In the first few hours and days this is apparent from the baby's apathy or even loss of consciousness. Vomiting, fits, weakness of limbs and shallow slow breathing may be other manifestations of brain contusion. Not infrequently the cerebral damage is diffuse and partly irreversible, so that the pattern of the child's future development may be determined at this time, when we have very little scope for improving matters. X-rays of the skull taken later at hospital reveal fractures in only approximately 10 per cent of these babies. Even medical people frequently forget that the skull of a baby under 6 months of age is thin and elastic so that considerable injury may be sustained without leading to any fracture of the bone. Hence the absence of fractures should not lead one to suppose that the brain has not been damaged. Conversely the presence of a fracture does not provide a clue as to the extent of brain damage, since fractures are well known to occur in quite mild accidents without leading to brain damage.

The neurosurgeon's role

The reason for transferring such babies to the care of the neurosurgeon is not because he has some special means of treating brain contusion with or without fractured skull. It is because a complication of a head injury arises in the form of blood clot and later watery fluid collection over the surface of the brain. This collection of fluid, commonly referred to as subdural haematoma or subdural effusion, does not subside spontaneously except after a very long delay and thus exerts a harmful pressure upon the brain both at the time of the acute injury and later, so that permanent damage may result. It is for the relatively simple diagnosis of this complication and its surgical treatment that the child is transferred to a special centre, a form of selection of patients which restricts the neurosurgeon's experience.

The long bones of the limbs of a baby may be fractured but more commonly rough handling causes not breakage but haemorrhage under the periosteum which shows on later X-rays as a thickening of the bone. The first suspicion of such an injury is the observation that an otherwise moving baby keeps one limb motionless. This may be due to weakness from brain injury but equally may be 'pseudoparalysis', the limb being kept motionless to avoid pain. The handling of such an injured limb will often be seen to cause distress to the baby.

The way in which a parent injures his or her infant tends to be the same over a period of time. There is evidence to support the belief that certain forms of abuse are more characteristic of one part of the country than of another. Probably all victims of abuse, however, are likely to sustain chest injury resulting from a vigorous grasping and shaking of the child. The revelation of fractured ribs on chest X-rays is not uncommon, present in about 15 per cent of the babies admitted to the neurosurgical department. Within broad limits it is possible to deduce from the chest X-ray films the date of such fractures and it is sometimes only too apparent that a succession of injuries have been sustained pre-dating the head injury by a substantial period of time.

Half the babies who have subdural effusions as a complication of head injury also have retinal haemorrhage, that is the formation of very small blood clots in or in front of the retina. This type of bleeding is known to occur as the result of rapid rise of pressure within the head. Retinal haemorrhage has therefore often been taken to indicate that there has been a fairly severe blow to the head. More recently it has been realised, however, that a more likely explanation in many cases is that thoracic pressure had been suddenly increased through grasping of the chest and compressing or shaking it. The rise of pressure within the veins of the head which result from this handling may lead to haemorrhage within the eye.

The numerous other forms of abuse, such as burning with cigarettes and biting I omit from this brief outline through lack of personal experience of such children. Instead I follow with a description of the treatment of the physical ailments and the later sequelae.

The treatment of injury

The duration of hospital stay may vary from many days to many weeks and during this time a decision has to be made concerning the future care of the child. Those who have sustained brain injury must be observed with particular care during the first few days but later it is usual to see a steady improvement in the baby's activity. Those parents, few in proportion, who visit the hospital regularly are soon encouraged by the improvement, and self-confidence may be seen to return. The baby may need blood transfusion through severe anaemia, and those who are referred to me usually require removal of the subdural fluid either by frequent aspiration through a needle or by an operation to carry the fluid away from the head and allow the brain to be relieved of its compression. In more severe cases the baby must be left in his cot, that is not lifted for feeding or other attentions, but I have often had the impression that parents do not find this an irksome situation, since they show little or no inclination to touch the baby. If operative treatment for the subdural effusion is required, the baby needs to stay in the neurosurgical unit for at least a further week.

The fractures of skull or ribs and even of the long bones of the limbs only very rarely require any direct treatment. Awareness of their presence is essential if the baby is to be handled without causing further harm. Satisfactory healing of the fractures, however, almost always occur.

The retinal haemorrhages are not susceptible to treatment and must be allowed to resolve slowly and spontaneously. When these haemorrhages are large they cause loss of vision and indeed a frequent question from parents and others is 'Can the baby see?' The apathy and staring referred to earlier may continue for days and the lack of apparent awareness of surroundings and the failure to be attracted by bright objects is more often due not to visual loss but to the diminished activity of the whole brain. It is therefore very difficult to judge at first whether there has been a true loss of vision or not. It is wise to suspend judgement unless the degrees of retinal haemorrhage is so great as to make it probable that the baby is partially blind. Only a very small percentage of those who have survived and have been followed up for several years have been shown to have lost useful vision.

The physical treatment of the baby is not complex but to the parents appears dramatic, involving, as it may, blood transfusion, an operation upon the head, the baby remaining throughout the early days very obviously ill. If the baby were equally ill but from a different type of disorder, I would normally have the opportunity to fulfil the parents' need for explanations and would be able to 'carry' them through the anxieties of the illness through frank explanations of what is happening. But the parents of abused babies tend to be infrequent visitors. This is partly due to the distance of my hospital from the home of the parents, but clearly there are other factors at work. This is one reason why the baby should be returned to the referring hospital in the neighbourhood of his home as soon as possible.

Some sequelae

The physical sequelae of the type of abuse that I have described are indeed serious in many instances. The overridingly important aspect is the brain injury. This leads to ineducability in between 5 and 10 per cent of this sub-group (those with head injuries). Over 10 per cent prove later to be educationally sub-normal, leaving about 80 per cent with normal intelligence. Data does not exist to show what if any harm has been done to those who remain 'normally intelligent', but it is highly probable that some loss of intelligence has been sustained. Less important and affecting probably fewer than 5 per cent of all the children is the development of epilepsy later. This probably reflects localised brain damage. Epilepsy appears to develop in between 1 and 5 per cent of those children who have sustained head injury and subdural effusions.

The third important sequel is loss of vision which is fortunately rare.

All assessment of the results of treatment are necessarily of doubtful value because permanent harm may have been done by abuse preceding the incident leading to hospital admission and by abuse which undoubtedly occurs following discharge from hospital.

SOME GENERAL RECOMMENDATIONS

It was suggested to me that I might take the opportunity to express my views about possible improvements in the management of these problems although my experience is limited to one small facet of this complex problem. For I deal with only one type of injury, and that in a hospital geographically far removed from that to which the child has been admitted initially. Prompt recognition that a child has sustained a non-accidental injury is of paramount importance. Understanding this we should face the problems of the abused child as objectively as we would face any other disease process and towards this end there should be far better communication among us. A small handbook should be prepared, possibly by the Department of Health, so that the medical and nursing, together with the social and legal aspects, could all be expounded. To improve communication there should be a central registry in every area recording the admission of children with certain forms of disorder. This should be confidential and should not contain any judgement as to the origin of real or suspected injury. This would help to ensure that admissions to different hospitals with a succession of injuries would be known. The medical officer of health should keep a record (if he were properly informed of cases) which would enable him to alert hospital clinicians or family doctors to the probability that child abuse is occurring.

The police authorities should be involved in the problem as soon as there are reasonable grounds for suspecting that there has been inflicted injury, although I realise that this is a very difficult and controversial area. We all share these objectives, namely the protection of the child at the present time and in the future, and the protection of the siblings. Essential to this achievement is the true assessment of the situation. The truth is unlikely to emerge in the initial stages from direct questioning of the parents; it will come from the gradual gaining of parents' confidence. If police authorities could see their way to having confidence in the medical staff's approach there would, I believe, be a great improvement in our management. Such confidence in the medical staff would sometimes have been misplaced when children have been discharged from hospital to meet their death later. Mutual confidence, however, will come from free communication and better understanding. The real difficulty is associated with the policeman's legal duty to investigate what he has reason to believe to be a criminal offence. To seek to interfere with this duty of a policeman is not only an offence but, more importantly for society, would be very ill-advised. A far better working relationship will arise if we concentrate upon the main purpose of law enforcement in the context of child abuse, that is prevention and cure. To this end we wish to elicit the true facts and these will come not from confrontation of the parents but only from patient enquiry and consultation. This takes time during which the child must be retained in some form of care until all are convinced that the child may safely return home. I would like to see, therefore, very specially selected members of the police force, chosen for a number of reasons and provided with a special insight into these problems who could be consulted and informed by hospital staff and family doctors following an incident of child abuse and who, while retaining that right which we cannot remove in any case (the right to bring a charge against the parents), acts always in close collaboration with the medical staff and the social services.

DISCUSSION

This informative paper raised the question of whether the inaccessibility of parents to discussion was part of their crisis of anxiety over what they had done, or was due to faulty previous handling. In either case the injuries described in infancy were so rarely due to birth injury or infection (perhaps 5 per cent) that the doctor's duty was to pursue closely the possibility of non-accidental injury. The dangers of bleeding within the skull from severe shaking of the baby with its unsupported head should be more widely known. This knowledge was fairly recent for doctors and the mother, who so dangerously shook her baby, did so in ignorance of the severity of the damage that might follow.

8. Speculations on some possible long-term effects

Ronald Mac Keith

In all countries, children sustain non-accidental injury (NAI). Among the various injuries, head injury is not infrequent. Sometimes it is severe enough to cause death. It is probable that less severe cerebral injuries also occur which are survived. Many of these will recover fully. But it seems likely that between the NAI head injuries which kill and those followed by complete recovery, there are others which lead to lasting brain injury sufficient to produce deficits of cerebral function. It is therefore possible that sometimes cerebral palsy and mental deficiency are late sequelae of cerebral injury by NAI, although there is as yet no adequate long-term follow up to prove it. The justification for exploring this possibility by examining the available data is that no sufficient explanation can be found in half the children with cerebral palsy.

THE HEAD INJURIES SUSTAINED FROM NON-ACCIDENTAL INJURY

Writing of the necropsy findings in children dead of child abuse with no previous history, Weston (1968) says that 'The most commonly encountered pathological finding was that of subdural haemorrhage. This was acute . . . and in most instances was associated with . . . underlying contusion of the cerebral cortex identified by light pink-purple discoloration, slight softening, and sharply outlined dark red-purple/petechial haemorrhages. In the children thrown or hurled against the wall or to the floor, there was evidence, not only of a primary contusion adjacent to the scalp lesions but also of a contrecoup injury, reflected by contralateral subarachnoid haemorrhage and cerebral contusions . . . Among the 23 children who expired as a result of injuries superimposed on previous injuries, the internal injuries were essentially the same . . . but of considerably greater magnitude'.

Among 42 children admitted to hospital for NAI, Birrell and Birrell (1968) found intracranial haemorrhage in 9 (21 per cent) and skull fracture in 12.

THE POSSIBLE LATE EFFECT OF SHAKING A BABY

Caffey (1972) has suggested that shaking a baby may damage its brain. The greatest risk is said to be in the first six months, when shaking gives a whip-lash effect that bumps the brain against the side of the skull and causes pinpoint haemorrhages and damage to blood vessels. Follow-up studies of two small groups of 'shaken' children uncovered a surprisingly high prevalence of mental retardation. He suggested that cumulative damage occurs and that some, perhaps many, of the cerebrovascular injuries attributed to pre-natal infections, congenital malformation, birth injuries and genetic metabolic diseases are really caused by undetected whip-lash shakings during the first weeks or months of life.

THE SEQUELAE OF SUBDURAL HAEMATOMA

I have not located the two follow-up studies of 'shaken' babies. There is, however, an oblique way of approaching the main problem. Cerebral contusion is potentially much more likely to give fatal or lasting cerebral deficit than is subdural haematoma. While it may be difficult to confirm the existence of a cerebral contusion it is easier to establish the presence of a subdural haematoma which, as Weston's work showed, usually implies the presence of a cerebral contusion. By studying the sequelae of subdural haematoma in fact we shall be discovering the effects of the common combination of cerebral contusion plus subdural haematoma. This view finds confirmation from the conviction of neurosurgeons that NAI is a major, though not the only, cause of subdural haematoma (9 of 21 cases, Köttgen, 1967).

In a follow up of 76 children with subdural haematoma, Till (1968) found that 5 per cent were dead, 8 per cent were ineducable and 12 per cent were educationally subnormal.

In a follow up of 65 children with subdural haematoma, Aicardi *et al.* (1971, 1973) found that 6 per cent were lost, 10 per cent were dead, 25 per cent were severely incapacitated and 25 per cent were moderately incapacitated.

Of 14 who had status epilepticus at the onset, 12 were severely incapacitated. Of 16 whose coma continued for more than 12 hours after the haematoma was tapped, 11 were severely or moderately incapacitated. The duration of the effusion did not affect the prognosis.

These two series taken together suggest that for every child dead with a subdural haematoma, there may be two or three who survive to be severely incapacitated and another two or three who survive to be moderately incapacitated, notably in intelligence. A tentative conclusion is that for every death from NAI, there may be four children with incapacitating chronic neurological sequelae.

DEATHS FROM NON-ACCIDENTAL INJURY

In 1962 Kempe reported on a sample of 749 cases and said that 10·4 per cent of the children had died. The UK department of Health pamphlet (1970) calculated that 2 per cent of deaths of infants between 4 weeks and 1 year are due to wilful violence. In 1967 there were 679 such deaths in the UK. On this estimate about 13 infants under 1 year of age die every year as the result of wilful violence. This suggests that there are at least 50 new cases a year of chronic neurological handicap resulting from NAI. In West Germany, Trube-Becker (1971), reporting on 1,385 necropsies, found that 6·4 per cent of children under 6 years of age died of neglect or maltreatment.

INCIDENCE OF NON-ACCIDENTAL INJURY IN CHILDHOOD

The incidence of NAI is believed by Kempe (1971) to be 6 per 1,000 live births. For the USA with a population of 225,000,000, he calculated that there are 40,000 cases a year. We should remember that the number of reported cases in the USA in 1967 was 6,000 (Gil, 1969).

For the UK with a quarter of the population of the USA the *Lancet* (1971) gave 3,000 cases each year of NAI. Kempe (1971) also suggested 3,000 cases a year in the UK, a figure derived from the assumption of only 500,000 births a year, instead of 800,000, so that Kempe's estimate should be revised to at least 4,500.

MORTALITY RATE OF NAI IN CHILDREN

The mortality rate for battered children has been varyingly reported at:

4 per cent	(Kempe *et al.*, 1962)
1·4 per cent	(California Pilot Survey; Gil, 1968)
1·3 per cent	(Skinner and Castle, 1969)
3 per cent	(Gregg and Elmer, 1969)
1·3 per cent	(Skinner and Castle, 1969)
6 to 14 per cent	(Moszer and Bach, 1969)
13 per cent	(Barnmishandel, 1969)
10 per cent	(Cooper, 1972)

Two comments may be made on these figures. One is that they suggest that over the last ten years doctors are revising their ideas on the mortality rate of NAI in an upward direction. The other is that these mortality figures are largely based on children who have been seen in hospital and hence on children who have suffered more severe injuries.

At a guess for the UK the case mortality is at least 3 per cent, though it may be several times that figure. The lower estimate of 3,000 cases in the UK each year suggests 90 deaths a year, a figure three times the amount the *Lancet* estimated (1971) and seven times the 13 based on necropsy studies.

Bierman (1969) states that in the German Federal Republic with a population of 50 million, about 1,000 children die every year of NAI and that the number is increasing.

If for every child dead of NAI, four children have a lasting incapacity, and if the estimate of 90 deaths a year in the UK is correct there should be 400 new cases a year of lasting incapacity due to NAI.

INCIDENCE OF LASTING NEUROLOGICAL DISORDER AFTER NAI

Another estimate could be based on the reports published of the proportion of children suffering NAI who are left with permanent neurological disorder. From a sample of 749 cases Kempe (1962) estimated that 15 per cent were left with 'permanent brain damage'; motor disorder was not differentiated from the mental handicap which might result from accompanying deprivation. Gil (1969) reported 'permanent damage' in 5 per cent of NAI not specifically of the brain.

Kempe (1971) stated that 'half' of the NAI children will be significantly injured, but not necessarily in the CNS nor permanently.

Martin (1972) reported that when 42 abused children were re-examined three years after the abuse, 43 per cent were impaired neurologically and 33 per cent were mentally retarded. 'They were a pathetic lot and had little capacity for enjoyment and spent time mothering adults around them and a minority had given up relating normally to other people.' Martin, Beazley and Conway (1973) tried to follow up 159 children but only 58 could be persuaded to co-operate. The injuries they had had were relatively mild. 53 per cent had a poorly functioning nervous system, including 31 per cent with serious neurological deficits.

Aicardi et al. (1971, 1973) reported that of children who had had subdural haematoma, 25 per cent were severely incapacitated and 25 per cent were moderately incapacitated. Of 40 children admitted for NAI at the Park Hospital, Oxford, 17·5 per cent had subdural haematoma. If from 8 to 25 per cent of children with subdural haematoma are liable to be left with severe neurological handicap, the Park Hospital figures suggest that 1·5 to 4 per cent of NAI children have lasting neurological handicap.

These papers provide data from which firm conclusions cannot be drawn. Yet if 3 per cent of NAI children develop cerebral palsy, visual defect and so on, then on the lower assumption of 3,000 cases of NAI annually in the UK, NAI will be responsible for 90 new cases of neurological deficit every year. This compares with the estimated 1,600 new cases a year of cerebral palsy in half of which no cause is found. So perhaps NAI may be responsible for 6 per cent of the current new cases of cerebral palsy in the UK.

INCIDENCE OF MENTAL HANDICAP AFTER NAI

There are rather more definite data about the later educational difficulties of some of the children who have had NAI.

According to Gil (1969) 3 per cent of children of school age had never attended school and 13 per cent were in grades below those expected of their age. The figures given by Morse et al. (1970) are 2 of 25 children severely retarded and 6 of the 25 were retarded, 5 were disturbed, 8 normal, and 4 were lost.

Gregg and Elmer (1969) studied a group of 30 who had had NAI and found that 24 per cent more children were retarded in development than in a control group of non-abused children.

Martin's re-examination (1972) of 42 children three years after being abused revealed that 33 per cent were mentally retarded.

These reports may be compared with those of children who had had subdural haematoma; of these 8 per cent were ineducable (Till, 1968), 25 per cent were severely incapacitated (Aicardi et al., 1971, 1973), 12 per cent were educationally subnormal (Till, 1968) and 25 per cent were moderately incapacitated (Aicardi et al., 1971, 1973).

If, as seems possible, after NAI only 5 per cent of survivors are severely subnormal and given 3,000 of NAI a year in the UK, this means 150 new children with mental deficiency a year. This is 25 per cent of the known 600 new mentally deficient children each year. It also seems possible that some 20 per cent of those who have suffered NAI in their early years are likely to be mentally handicapped in later life. This would be some 600 new cases a year of moderate mental handicap. The educational handicap of children who have had NAI could originate in actual cerebral injury but it could also result from the emotional and intellectual deprivation which are very much parts of the syndrome as Birrell and Birrell (1968) have emphasised.

When a child is first assessed several years after infancy, deprivation and NAI as possible causes may be less likely to be considered because the parents may have grown and developed into a more reasonable competence.

MALADJUSTMENT

Another late effect of the maltreatment syndrome is emotional maladjustment. Depression and pseudo mental retardation were shown by 6 of 106 survivors (Ebbin et al., 1969). 'Only a few of the (20) battered children gave promise of becoming self sufficient adults' (Elmer and Gregg, 1967).

Even if battering parents are amenable to treatment—and probably most of them are—they are sick people who treat their children in a sick way. 90 per cent have serious problems in mothering or fathering their children and this would be expected to affect the child's personality development. It is generally thought that many battering parents were, as little children, themselves mal- treated. Hence one late sequel of NAI is that the child who has had NAI is at high risk for injuring his or her own children. This risk is largely the consequence of the deprivation or maltreatment, but any person with brain injury is probably more vulnerable to untoward environmental experiences and hence is liable to break down under stresses with which ordinary individuals can cope. Nau (1968) stated that from large-scale studies in Germany, he was able to note that a large proportion of criminals, killers and murderers come from the group of people who had been maltreated in childhood.

Fortunately, attention is now being directed to prevention. One way is to attempt to recognise at pre-natal clinics the mothers-to-be who are at risk for inflicting NAI and to follow them up, treat them and support them when the baby is born. Another is to step up the measures in lying-in wards which promote good bonding between mothers and their infants.

CONCLUSION

In one-half of the children with cerebral palsy and half of the mentally deficient children, no adequate cause of their disability can be identified. Speculation on incomplete data suggests that NAI and the associated deprivation may account for 90 new cases of cerebral palsy each year, that is about 6 per cent, for about 150 or about one-quarter of new cases of severe mental handicap each year, and also for a considerable number, perhaps 3,000 a year, of new cases of children with disturbed personality at risk for developing anti-social behaviour and for injuring their own children. An alternative method of calculation yields a figure of 400 new children each year with chronic neurological deficits.

9. A coroner's view

D. R. Chambers

The coroner's involvement and his jurisdiction over cases begin when it is brought to his attention that in the area for which he holds the office there lies the body of one whose death he may reasonably consider to have been sudden and of unknown cause, violent, or unnatural. Clearly the death of a child which has been criminally brought about could fall into any of these categories which are not mutually exclusive. Deaths of all persons in such circumstances are reported to the coroner through one of his officers usually by the police, although a direct reference by hospital staff or even the public does happen. Unexpected death in childhood is uncommon and medical awareness of the existence of child abuse is now so widespread that the police are commonly called only to find themselves involved in deaths of children which, though sudden and of unknown cause, are found after post-mortem examination to be natural. A large number are cases of the so-called sudden infant death syndrome. I have not known any example in my jurisdiction of the finding at post-mortem of a violent or unnatural cause for a sudden death in a child when it was not suspected beforehand, whereas it is fairly frequent for a 'battered baby' to be found to have died a natural death.

STATISTICS

The registrar-general's statistical review of England and Wales, 1971, gives figures for deaths caused by accident and by homicide in the age groups 0–4 and 5–14. When deaths from road traffic accident and poisonings are excluded the ratio of homicide to accident was 1:2 for 0–4 and 1:9 for 5–14. These figures compare with 2:10 and 0:5 in the respective age groups in the author's own small series.

COURT PROCEDURE

When a young person has died an apparently accidental death, the presence of the CID at the post-mortem is almost routine. When the violent and unnatural nature of a child's death is confirmed at post-mortem the circumstances of the death are reviewed by the CID officers concerned, for it is now a legal requisite that an inquest be formally opened. If either parent is likely to be charged with murder or manslaughter (or, in the case of the mother, infanticide), such a person is not called at the inquest to give evidence of the deceased child's identity. Where no such charge is envisaged, either parent may be so called.

The coroner's next decision is whether to hear the inquest with a jury. This he is required to do by law if he thinks that there is ground for suspecting that the death came about as a result of one of the crimes noted above. If the jury takes this view too after hearing the evidence, it may return a verdict to this effect with the result that the person or persons named by the jury are committed for trial at the next Crown Court sitting. This situation can arise where the police, often on the advice of the DPP, do not think that there is sufficient admissible evidence to charge a person with the unlawful killing of the child. When they consider that there is, this charge is brought and the coroner can adjourn his inquest to await the outcome of criminal proceedings. When the coroner considers that the facts do not merit the hearing of the inquest before a jury, he sits alone. The verdict which he returns cannot impute crime, but often neglect is clear on the part of those having the lawful custody of the child. Such a verdict appears not to affect the possibility of bringing proceedings under other statutes such as the Children and Young Persons Act.

Deaths of children under 5 years of age, particularly of girls, have to be investigated quickly and thoroughly, where there is a possibility that they have been caused by intentional harm. Procedurally it is better that a charge be brought in the magistrates' court than as a result of a coroner's jury finding. When the cause of the child's death clearly cannot result in a charge of murder, manslaughter or infanticide, the coroner can sit alone and bring in a verdict which seems not to leave the matter in doubt.

10. *The place of family planning*

Dorothy Morgan

Whatever the aetiology of the 'battering families' may be, it is likely that at least one of the partners in the union has had, in the process of growing up, some contact with officialdom. This may be through the education service, social services, housing or police. Because of their own immaturity, their failure to communicate, or aggression on the part of the officers concerned the couple may be anti-establishment, so that they in turn are aggressive in their attitudes to anyone whom they consider to be in a position of authority. Whenever possible, therefore, the first family planning approach to the family 'at risk' is ideally made through a neighbour, a friend, or a medical or social worker with an already established relationship.

One should bear in mind the confused 'morality', for the want of a better term, of these families. It is my belief that frequently these parents have known child abuse in their own upbringing so it is to some extent their 'norm' in the rearing of their own children; and yet the delay that so often occurs before seeking help for the injured child and their preference for the impartial casualty department of a hospital rather than their general practitioner suggest that they feel guilty about their actions.

In giving family planning advice one has to be very sensitive to the attitudes of these families. They rarely seek advice on their own initiative, nor are they willing to attend the clinic, hence the need for the home visit, permission having first been obtained from the family doctor. The first visit must be casual, merely to identify oneself and one's services, and to let the couple know that such advice is available to them. A return visit to meet both partners of the union at a later date is offered. It is immaterial whether this first visit takes place on the doorstep or whether one is invited into the home.

The joint interview is of the greatest value. Firstly, it creates some rapport with the couple and secondly it enables family planning information to be given. In the home setting the husband is far more at ease, and there is adequate time to discuss the fears and the fantasies that are so often associated with methods of birth control. The role of the doctor should be merely to give information on the various methods of birth control and to leave to the couples themselves the choice of the method to be used. It may often happen that the method chosen is not the safest, but if it is the one that is acceptable, there is greater motivation to use it. For example, where the husband is obviously inadequate and his insecurity is shown in the way he dominates the joint interview, it is important that he should be the one to use the method of birth control. It is unusual for some method of birth control not to be accepted. In my own limited experience of child abuse it is evident that the second or third child is the one who becomes battered. We know that the stress of inadequate housing, too many children in cramped conditions, and marital disharmony contribute to produce the battering situation, although we do not yet know to how great an extent.

Subsequent visits should be made at regular intervals, both to give support and to form a greater rapport and a deepening relationship with the couple. This may eventually lead not only to help with their methods of birth control but to the couple's beginning to talk less about themselves and more about their children. When they produce meaningful statements such as 'Why is it that my baby is always crying or why is this particular baby . . . ?', some analytical work with these families becomes possible.

In conclusion, the doctor must be a person known to the family. The visits must have the consent of both partners of the union. It must be a continuing relationship, for work in depth can begin only when a true rapport has been established. Thus one hopes that further tragedies may be averted.

DISCUSSION

The Family Planning doctor was accepted as someone with an important function in battering families. Her experience of handling parents and of advising on the most appropriate techniques was probably greater than that of most general practitioners. She had to be invited through the general practitioner or through the health visitor or social worker and the parents must have agreed that they need her help. An initial doorstep visit of introduction is sometimes wise despite the time occupied. The facts are that one in two pregnancies is unplanned, one in five unwanted and one in ten ends in abortion. Had battering mothers requested termination? The Birmingham figure was 12 per cent. In Newcastle some who had actually written asking for termination, later denied having done so, so that hard data are difficult to find. Do parents ever want a baby even to the extent of requesting adoption in order to attack it? No supporting evidence in Birmingham. Nevertheless the unmet dependency need might come in here. Possibly family planning should be taught in schools as part of preparation for parenthood.

Was the Study Group suggesting too many workers to be involved in the family's life? Clearly one person would have to be selected with whom the family could establish and maintain confidence.

11. *A medical social worker's view*

Sally Beer

As a senior medical social worker I talk about my own experiences in the Paediatric Unit at University College Hospital, London. The hospital is situated at the southern end of the borough of Camden. Its specialist units cover a wide area of London, Hertfordshire and beyond, but although this applies to certain aspects of the Paediatric Unit, in fact the catchment area for most of the children who may come into the categories of 'non-accidental injuries' or 'at risk' is quite local, being mainly the boroughs of Camden and Islington. The area is very mixed, covering the wide extremes in living conditions from the expensive 'trendy' Hampstead households to the backstreets of Kentish Town. The borough is losing its middle-class inhabitants and therefore caters for two groups of families with differing needs and demands. The Hospital also offers a service both to intelligent, intellectual, well informed families and to less intelligent, multi-problem families who often function, emotionally, on a fairly primitive level. Experience of 'battering families' comes therefore from two very different backgrounds.

ACTION AT HOSPITAL

The hospital is often the source of primary intervention for the 'battering family'. The two main reasons are firstly that it is less threatening for the parents to present their child to the impersonal casualty department setting with the availability of the twenty-four-hour service, and secondly that these families are often isolated with no supportive general practitioner/health visitor contacts. It is vitally important that all casualty staff should be aware of the problems of the battered child, not only so as to look out for the injured child, but also to appreciate the special problem of parents who are often labelled as 'difficult' because of their obvious aggressive attitudes. At University College Hospital any child suspected of having non-accidental injuries is admitted to the ward. This achieves three things: the child is removed from a potentially dangerous situation, the immediate pressure is removed from the parents and the professional workers are allowed time to intervene. In my experience few parents have been unwilling for their child to be admitted, but on two occasions in the past year a place of safety order has been obtained in order to keep the child in hospital. Once the child has been admitted both the paediatric consultant and myself interview the parents. The usual pattern is for the consultant to hold the initial interview confronting the parents honestly with his assessment of the child's injuries and how they were sustained. He does not follow a line that a confession must be sought at all costs. The whole climate at the Hospital is a caring, treatment orientated approach, not a punitive aggressive one. Any social worker from another agency to whom the family is already known is contacted straight away.

The case conference

The immediate task is to call a case conference (see Appendix I, page 166). This is convened by the medical social worker and all the workers involved with the family are invited to attend. We have found that the most successful format for the conference seems to be for the medical and social history to be given by the relevant members and this is followed by general discussion when feelings are expressed about the existing situation. The aim of the discussion is to form a plan for future management, in terms both of the immediate future and the placing of the child, and of the long term as far as can be seen at this early stage. The two most important decisions are, firstly, the question of possible removal of the child and, secondly, a primary worker with the family must be established so that all involved should know who that main worker is to be. The decision on who this worker is to be may well influence action taken about the child. Where the child is to be removed from the parents for a period of time it is difficult for the person who is to work with the family to be the one seen to be responsible for the removal of the child. Another factor which may influence the decision on which worker should take on one of these families is that, although everyone agrees that 'battering families' are one of the highest priorities for the allocation of work time and resources, all social workers are under enormous pressures. There should be no set rule about which agency should carry the load of all these families but they should be distributed to the agency which seems appropriate for a particular case and which can offer the necessary skilled, available supportive service.

Removing the child

If the decision at the conference is to remove the child from the home, via the courts, there are several aspects to be considered. At present this has to be done either through the police or the local authority social services department, but I hope that in 1974 it will be unnecessary to call in another social worker just for a care order. It will be more satisfactory when the hospital based social worker can follow all stages, although I appreciate that there may be differing pressures when the hospital may be seen to be responsible for removal of the child. At the Hospital we have a very good relationship with the police at the local juvenile bureau. We often ask their advice on a situation and know that their concern, as much as ours, is for the good of the family as a whole. They have arranged a place of safety order for us in an emergency, but then have been quite willing to leave to us the decision about the future. We do not always invite them to the case conference but they have attended several. We have found their help very valuable, especially where there may have been difficulties about the giving of evidence by the medical staff. I have not experienced from this bureau any conflict over prosecution of parents, but there have been difficulties with police from another area, and several of my colleagues have found this can cause an extremely difficult situation.

The result of working in a well-informed supportive interdisciplinary team, which includes the nursing as well as medical staff, is that a bed is always available for the admission, if only for one night in an emergency, of a child that I feel might be 'at risk'. The anxious, tense mother who brings the baby to the out-patient clinic saying there is a feeding/sleeping/crying problem may be, especially in the more extreme cases, a potential battering parent. This is a warning that preventive work should be done.

THE RELATIONSHIP OF TRUST

It has sometimes been decided at the initial case conference that I should be the primary worker and take on the social work for a family. One of the very important initial objectives is to establish a relationship of trust. This is extremely difficult in many cases as the characteristics of these families seem to be their isolation, distrust and aggression. During the early stages they test you time and time again, especially when the injured child is at home with the parents. They will impart information to you in order to see what you will do with it. They will make arrangements for you to visit at home and be out when you call. The parents need practical demonstration of the fact that you care. They need the 'mothering' experience from you in order to allow them to mother their own children. They have to have their dependency needs met by you, in order that they will have reserves on which to draw when put under pressure. This can be illustrated best by a case example:

CASE EXAMPLE

Family   Mother—Jennifer, aged 23 years
            Boyfriend/cohabitee—Mr. S., aged 24 years
            Stephen—aged $2\frac{1}{2}$ years

Brief history
Stephen was $2\frac{1}{2}$ years old when he was admitted to hospital following fractured femur and bruising over his right eye. It is the typical history of delayed attendance at casualty— i.e. two days later. The story was that he had fallen from his cot catching his leg as he fell. The doctors were concerned and he was admitted. On investigating the social history we discovered that he had been admitted to a London children's hospital nine months previously with a severe burn on his back, for which an unsatisfactory explanation had been given. This was thought to have been inflicted by Jennifer's cohabitee, Mr. S. However, he left home a month following the previous injury and support being given to Jennifer by local authority social worker was stopped. When Stephen came to hospital Mr. S. and Jennifer were again cohabiting and, at this time, it was more obvious that Jennifer had in fact injured Stephen—the boyfriend having worked away from home for some days prior to the fractured leg.

At the case conference it was decided that I should be the primary worker as it appeared that Jennifer had established quite a good relationship with the Hospital and that local authority social worker felt she had not had a satisfactory working relationship when she had originally met Jennifer the year before.

My initial task was to form a trusting relationship with this aggressive, seemingly sullen girl. She had told her boyfriend to leave and was having considerable financial problems, rent arrears, electricity bills, etc. She is a girl of average intelligence but with a very low stress tolerance level, either of Stephen's demands or from her expectations of her ability to make and keep a home. She wanted and needed help with her budgeting. We spent hours each week, usually in the evenings after her work, trying to organise her finances. We planned menus for a week at a time and I helped her with her shopping once a week. She went through a difficult time of telephoning me twice daily and, at this stage, I consciously fostered this dependency. I felt she needed the intensive support. She is now, four months later, far less dependent. She contacts me approximately twice a week and sees me once a fortnight. We have admitted Stephen for one short period of three nights when Jennifer felt she could not cope with his demands during one weekend. Having got over the enormous hurdle of her belief that I wanted an opportunity to say that she was a bad mother, so that Stephen would be removed, we now work quite well together. She leaves Stephen with a child-minder near her work and, although she still finds it extremely difficult to control her feelings of exasperation, her expectations of him are far more realistic.

DIFFICULTIES FOR THE WORKER

The work with these families is often very difficult and usually exhausting. The strain of coping with their continual demands drains your own resources with small reward in some cases. The battering families with whom I have worked have often been initially very rejecting and aggressive.

The worker has to cope also with the conflict caused by reconciling the need for the protection of the child with the need to 'care' for the parents. It is sometimes very difficult to sustain your own decision that a child should be returned to its family for which you feel the responsibility, when you feel also that the child might as the result be 'at risk'. As recent press stories underline, it is a very big responsibility which may, in fact, involve the life of a child. It is not a decision that any social worker takes lightly.

SUMMARY

It is impossible to offer a solution to the problem of battering families. The NSPCC Battered Baby Research Unit is doing tremendous work and showing that, with enough of the right kind of resources, the incidence of re-battering could probably be eliminated. However, this can be very difficult—especially as shortage of social workers does not allow for the necessary amount of time to be spent on a relatively small group of families. Perhaps we should concentrate on forms of prevention, prior to the initial injuries. This would involve more support to groups acknowledged to be potential child batterers. For example there should be better services to support young mothers with several children born close together; and more health visitors, as well as social work support for a longer time, to mothers with premature or ill babies who have had a long period of early separation.

Shortly after I arrived at UCH, I realised that an increasing number of tense crying babies with tense crying mothers were being referred from the out-patient clinic. I felt that the best way to use my resources and perhaps a very valid form of support would be to start a group for these mothers. We hold it once a fortnight in the Paediatric Department. It is an informal, open-ended group to which I initially invited mothers, some who had gone through their difficulties, some who were at crisis point and others who were just beginning to feel the stress. This seems to have been a fairly successful venture. I was amazed at how easily many of them spoke of their aggressive feelings towards their children. Several described their desire to throw their baby across the room. I have not brought a parent who has actually battered into this group and am not at all sure that I should. I would be grateful to hear of the experiences of anybody running a group for parents in battering families.

The hospital has an important role in the supportive, safety network for children 'at risk' in the community. An 'at risk' list of families has now been introduced in UCH. This takes the form of an index kept in Sister's office in the casualty department and the Paediatric Unit also has a copy. The casualty records are marked so that any doctor seeing a child whose records show that he is on the list will go to the card and get a brief description of the reason for this. He will be given a name and telephone number to contact, either mine, the paediatrician's or the outside social worker involved. This list can be added to by any worker who feels that a particular child who is at risk may be brought to UCH. The casualty departments of hospitals are open 24 hours a day. They should be prepared to offer support or at least to open the way for support to be given in view of the fact that young doctors are educated not to admit a child to hospital unless the degree of illness makes it absolutely necessary.

DISCUSSION

Some concern was expressed about the future reorganisation of the social services departments which would be community oriented and might lose their direct links with the practice of medicine. The Home Office and child care officers used to have considerable knowledge and skill in managing families, and links with medical officers of health were strong. The family's first experience of care would often be when the injured child was admitted to hospital. Here the medical social worker had the great advantage of being recognisably a helping caring person rather than an uninvited visitor to the family's home. The question to be resolved in 1974 is where the power of decision and of action will lie. The social services departments have statutory authority and the duty to protect children. It is to be hoped that the unification of the services will not at first disturb the work but will improve the opportunities for liaison and communication between what are now hospital based social workers in direct touch with the doctor, those based in the community, the health visitor and those working in the voluntary societies.

Many questions were asked about the way in which local registers operated and who kept them. The social worker plays an important part in teaching medical students and student nurses.

12. A health visitor's viewpoint

J. M. Davies

There is probably no more emotive subject than that of 'the battered baby'. For this reason the term non-accidental injury is to be preferred as it enables a more balanced look to be taken at the situation. Obviously the safety and well-being of the child must be our first consideration, but as Miss Joan Court states (*Nursing Times*, June 3, 1971), 'we have to think of the child and its parents with equal concern'. The health visitor visits the homes of all children under 5 years of age, and continues to visit whenever help and support are needed. Thus she is in a unique position to detect early signs of injury and, just as important, to recognise the conditions that could lead to it. Should the parents be told of her suspicions? This must depend on the circumstances of each individual case. The health visitor can, under cover of normal routine visiting, observe without neighbours and relatives knowing that there is anything amiss. If she tells the parents of her suspicions she will almost certainly be refused admission to the house in the future. There can be no hard and fast rule about this, but the safety of the child must come first.

FRAMEWORK FOR DEALING WITH SUSPECTED BATTERING

There is no single pattern throughout the country, but each authority has developed its own policy. There must be effective co-operation between all concerned.

A typical set-up in one county is a central liaison committee with this composition:

Assistant director of social services
Area nursing officer (a health visitor)
Probation officer
Paediatrician
Medical social worker from hospital
Social worker from social services department
NSPCC officer
Police officer

This committee meets quarterly, reviews action and register and suggests future policy.

In each area there are local liaison committees with the following membership:

Social worker
Health visitor
NSPCC officer

Woman police officer from local force

Child guidance worker

Hospital representative

This committee meets whenever necessary and anyone can call for a meeting at any time. A register is kept of children at risk and action discussed. The police never take legal action without consulting the committee. For the composition and functions of area review committees and case conferences recommended by the Study Group see Appendices I and II, pages 165–7.

ACTION IN CASE OF SUSPECTED NON-ACCIDENTAL INJURY

The child should be removed to a place of safety, such as a hospital or nursery, whilst further investigations are made. This will need great tact and co-operation from the general practitioner.

No one person (health visitor or social worker) should attempt to carry the responsibility alone and work in isolation, but she should call the local liaison committee. The child must not be returned to its own home unless or until there is no danger of further injury.

RECOMMENDATIONS FOR FUTURE MANAGEMENT AND PREVENTION

Increase in the number of health visitors

With the widening of her sphere of work, the health visitor devotes less time to visiting the under fives. Often she will know the family background or will recognise signs of stress in the family. By showing her concern for the parents as well as the children, she can gain their confidence and give much needed support. Frequent changes of doctor or repeated failure to keep clinic appointments should be followed up.

In the DHSS circular of February 18, 1972, it is stated that whilst in some areas of the country one health visitor to 4,600 population is reasonable, a ratio of 1 to 3,000 population may be desirable in others, for example those with a highly developed system of attachment schemes or with a high immigrant population. This ratio would enable more supportive help to be given. It is essential that there is early diagnosis of non-accidental injury and recognition of factors increasing the likelihood of such injury.

Detailed ante-natal and post-natal supervision

Careful history taking should include details of any mental illness in either parents. We know that it is often the parents who have been deprived of affection in their own childhood who find it difficult to show affection to their offspring. Consequently their social history is as important as that of medical conditions. Repeated failures to attend ante-natal clinics should be followed up, and all expectant mothers should be visited in the ante-natal period. If a mother has to be separated from her new baby for any length of time because, for example, he needs to be in a special care unit, as much contact as possible should be maintained, and the mother be allowed to handle the baby as soon as possible.

Good teamwork between the health visitor and the midwife (domiciliary or hospital) is important in detecting those at risk and diagnosing injury early. This is one of the advantages of group attachment schemes.

Any tendency to puerperal depression needs to be carefully watched and treated.

Better preparation for parenthood

Whilst there is a certain amount of instruction given in secondary schools, it is mainly to the lower streams and then often to girls only. It is almost entirely neglected by grammar schools and the A streams, yet battering is *not* confined to the less intelligent.

Many young people set up home with no knowledge of how to adjust to their own relationships or to those with their children. This is often the start of stress.

More nursery or playgroup places

Where living conditions are poor, or the child isolated, these may be advisable. I personally do not favour special groups for children at risk as they soon gain a notoriety as something different and defeat their own object.

Family aids

These should be provided where necessary to support the parents at home.

Notification of injuries to children at home

The possibility of notifying the health visitor perhaps through the medical officer of health, or community physician of the future, of all home accidents to children resident in the area should be explored. Although there are immense clerical difficulties, particularly where large hospitals are concerned, this is surely too important a matter to be ignored.

Most accidents would be genuine and require no further action, but a child is not always taken to the same hospital for treatment and previous injuries may not be known. The health visitor could follow up repeated notifications and instigate action as necessary. It is not sufficient to inform the general practitioner, for there are still many practices who have not got attachment schemes or good liaison with health visitors or social workers.

Liaison with hospitals

Already with the 1974 reorganisation in mind there is much greater liaison between hospital and community staffs. This needs to be encouraged and extended. The ward sister and health visitor can then easily discuss the child and its background.

The appointment of a casualty sister to the liaison committee would help in promoting understanding of all the problems involved both at home and in hospital.

Placement of child after battering

This must be done with great care, understanding and affection if he is not to perpetuate the problem with his own children.

In the majority of cases the child will be able to return home but only if the parents are given the help they need. Our attitude must not be one of reproof and disapproval, but of concern, and if the parents know that we are concerned for them, they may begin to be concerned for their children. The battering parents need to establish a meaningful relationship with another adult. (She may even become a 'mother' figure.) This is often the health visitor, but may be the social worker. This is where good co-operation is essential.

Family planning facilities need to be extended. It is often necessary to bring up the subject with the parents without waiting for them to broach it.

Drugs

An increasing number of young parents are taking addictive drugs causing their behaviour to be unpredictable, a danger which should be borne in mind.

Communication

Last, but by no means least, there must be immediate and effective communication at field level. Only too often in the past this has broken down and action has been taken without consultation with the worker involved. This leads to resentment and misunderstanding and does nothing to help the child or its family. Workers are *not* in competition with each other but have the same goal of a happy child in a loving family.

Perhaps this symposium can show the way.

DISCUSSION

More use might well be made of the health visitor who should always know a great deal about her families. She could certainly help the case conference and also alert the general practitioner in a practice to which she was attached. While she has no legal right of entry and, as a 'friend of the family', does not wish to have one, she should report to the medical officer of health (community physician) or the social services department any family who refused her entry so that she was prevented from discharging her supervisory responsibility. The idea of the notification of all accidents to young children was welcomed, but the question 'notification to whom?' remained unanswered.

Part Two

The Social Service Element

13. The position of the local authority

Frances M. Drake

This paper is concerned with the need to maintain a creative tension between an individual social worker's personal responses to a situation on the one hand, and his or her functioning as an agent of the local authority on the other. The local authority has a statutory duty to act if certain conditions are found, and this inevitably limits the freedom of choice of its workers; secondly, its power may be perceived by clients and other professions both as a help and as a threat; finally, it may be under pressure from different groups to adopt a certain role which restricts its free functioning.

Spontaneity and creative response are essential in effective work with individual clients, implying sensitivity to and interaction with both environment and people. The local authority social services department faces the problems of maintaining the responsiveness of the staff and preventing itself from being thrust into a negative role while using its very extensive power.

We are no nearer to answering the question 'what is truth?' than was Pontius Pilate. The totality of facts present in any situation is beyond the power of any one person to apprehend, absorb and digest. To make any sense out of the multiplicity of phenomena that surrounds us, we consciously or unconsciously assemble the material into assimilable form and shape and we circumscribe and draw boundaries. Furthermore, we are selective, we put together certain facts according to our own particular purpose. Thus, to a degree, we see what we want to see or what we have been trained to see. As Oscar Wilde said—nature follows art, and art nature. This means that our apprehension of a situation is always an over-simplification, a selection of certain facts, and may indeed be a distortion which reflects not the truth, but only our particular requirements at that time. If we have to take some form of action, this process of over-simplification and the elimination of factors which appear inessential is intensified. We cannot move if the issues become too complex. To act, however, we must be motivated or compelled. There must be a desire to change to something other and presumably better, or a duty to take a prescribed course; consequently it is necessary to appreciate and judge what is good and what is bad both in the existing situation and in the future one. The impetus to act usually arises from strong feelings about the facts as seen and understood. This emotion could be roused by the unpleasantness of the existing situation and action spurred on by a feeling of revulsion and inability to tolerate it, or alternatively, by an appreciation of the very positive elements that could be seen in some new situation towards which one was working. To help the battered child, therefore, action could be taken because the position of the child was seen to be intolerable so that any alternative would be an improvement, or because the alternative offered such an improved position as to over-rule certain positive elements in the home situation. What is the application of this to the position of the local authority?

THE LOCAL AUTHORITY, ITS POWERS AND CONSTRAINTS

The local authority, acting through its social services committee, is called upon by statute to act, and to act in a certain prescribed way. It must carry out the protective functions of society towards all children in need of care. It is also charged with carrying out the community's parental responsibilities for all children deprived of a normal home. The local authority, however, is a composite body in one sense, an abstract conception in another, an instrument of legal power in a third, and a group of very diverse individuals in a fourth. Furthermore, it employs equally diverse individuals to act on its behalf. Who, or what, therefore, acts in this situation, what is the motivation for action, and whose is it? We could say that the personnel of the social services department are employed to carry out the terms of a statute which embodies society's perception of need and society's motivation to act, not necessarily their own. It must be assumed, however, that the persons so employed are broadly in agreement with the provisions of the statute, otherwise they would relinquish their employment. Even so the need to act means a concentration on certain elements, an over-simplification of the situation in which their own personal responses, motivation and perception may be far from uniform. On the other hand, while they must assume the role and carry out the legal duties entailed by their acceptance of employment by society for this purpose and to that extent must restrict their own freedom of action, they must also respond to the situation with sensitivity and intelligence if their own personal motivation to act to help the client in an effective way is to be aroused. Each person is different, and response may equally be different. From the point of view of the local authority worker there may be at times a conflict between the requirements of the statute, the role as perceived by the public and by other professions, and the personal and individual responses of social workers and administrators.

By statute the local authority has the power to remove a child and perhaps to break up a family. The powers and duties of parents may be vested in the local authority. The resources at its disposal are great. The authority which is given to the department and the power to act in a way which can completely alter the lives of many people is likely to give rise to considerable problems in itself. Officers of the department cannot opt out of the responsibilities placed upon them and must attempt to use their powers wisely. Nevertheless, whether wisely used or not, power and authority inspire very ambivalent feelings in other people, professional colleagues, other agencies and clients alike. There may be dislike, anxiety, fear, envy, irritation. Some people, both inside and outside the department, may wish the authority to act strongly and to use its powers boldly. Others, conversely, that it should not. Most people have developed their attitudes to authority as a result of their experience of their own parents. It is understandable, therefore, that the statutory parental role, together with the wide powers of the social services departments, may stir up in other people and agencies fantasies about their actions that are unconscious throwbacks to past infantile experience rather than realistic reactions to present circumstances, and the emotions so engendered will be at an infantile level. From time to time officers of the department will be the recipients of these emotions and subject to pressures to behave in ways that are not in keeping with their own perception of the situation. The conflicting needs of colleagues, other agencies or clients to see them sometimes as representing the caring, nurturing, protecting aspects of the mother, or conversely as the controlling, punishing aspects of the father, may make it possible to accuse workers, or indeed the whole department, of behaving irresponsibly in many situations, sometimes too weak, at other times too strong. These external and internal pressures, together with the training received by many social workers which has emphasised its concept of an enabling, non-punitive relationship, make it difficult for some trained workers to use authority constructively or readily. But genuine authority and power can give confidence and support to the client, the worker and other agencies, and should not be withheld if needed.

The word 'role' carries with it by definition an implication of artificiality. We can become imprisoned in stereotypes and roles which are thrust upon us by society. The extent to which we proceed to act out these roles in order to fulfil other people's expectations may limit our power to respond as human beings to the essential and changing reality of the situation with which we are confronted. Roles may, of course, be protective and enable us to function in pre-determined ways, which may avoid the need for thought, painful experience, personal involvement, or re-appraisal. As we are now aware, people live up to expectations of their behaviour; how far, therefore, do we rigidify a system and fossilise a department by unconsciously or consciously accepting someone else's definition of us, and to what extent do we also, as agencies, define ourselves in over-simplified stereotypes and then engage in a series of quite artificial encounters and movements with other bodies, which preclude real interaction? Furthermore, how far does the fact that we have identified parents as cruel or uncaring reinforce this behaviour? And do they then conform to our expectations? How many people are made miserable by trying to live up to the community's picture of a 'good parent' rather than examining their own personal reality?

To sum up, the local authority social services departments as entities and their workers individually are not free agents and must work within the statutory constraints placed upon them. In addition, they are subject to pressures deriving from the power they can exert and the role which they may perform.

THE BACKGROUND OF VIOLENCE

We are conditioned, as are our clients and colleagues, by the culture of our time. Violence is a pervasive undercurrent of our lives.

The Punch and Judy Show has been a popular comic entertainment for children and adults since its introduction to this country from Italy in the late 1700's. It has only recently been displaced by more sophisticated amusements. Most people would consider it rather juvenile knockabout farce, appropriate for the children's party or the sea-shore entertainment. How strange that its theme is child battering, wife murder, resisting arrest, haunting and struggling with the Devil (see page 93). Yet to his audience Mr. Punch remains a hero to the end, a roaring, merry fellow. What are we to infer from this? That the subject matter is unimportant, that violence relieves tensions, that the humour signifies anxiety, that Mr. Punch represents something in us all?

Our traditional pattern of child-rearing and education condones and justifies the beating of children—'Spare the rod and spoil the child'. The right to administer corporal punishment is a privilege strongly defended by large numbers of the teaching profession. Only recently the practice of physically chastising handicapped children was being justified by certain Members of Parliament. It is widely accepted that the word 'discipline' is synonymous with slapping, hitting and caning children and that this is a good thing if the child can thereby be made to comply with accepted social standards.

As there is no need to pass laws to prohibit what no one wants to do, we must accept that the re-enactment of legislation protecting children from neglect, ill-treatment and physical abuse implies a continuing significant proportion of the population who might behave in this way if not deterred. Indeed, most of us under prolonged stress would react violently in certain circumstances.

Against this background, it is not surprising that John and Elizabeth Newson, in their survey of child-caring practice, found that 60 per cent of the mothers interviewed were prepared to 'punish' a baby of 12 months and that many were concerned with teaching the concept of 'naughtiness' at this age.

Parents who ill-treat and batter their children are only at one end of a spectrum of what is accepted as normal behaviour in the culture of our society today. The public, which includes committee members, school teachers and magistrates, do not usually query the validity of the practice, but only the degree of intensity. Claims are frequently made that parents have a right to administer corporal punishment. These generally accepted attitudes and the child-rearing practices of large numbers of the population make it difficult for lay magistrates to accept that parents have ill-treated a child, unless some serious damage has been done. There is considerable ambivalence of feeling on the whole subject. The local authority worker represents the public conscience and must therefore take account of public attitudes.

POWER AND RESPONSIBILITY

The responsibilities of the local authorities in the field of child care have developed extremely rapidly in the last twenty years so that there is now a framework of legislation which allows a social services department to develop a very comprehensive child care service, incorporating preventive, protective, treatment, care and rehabilitative functions for all children in trouble. The extent of these powers may not be fully appreciated by workers in other professional fields, partly because the development has been so rapid and partly because some of the powers are normally exercised with children or adults not directly the concern of these other groups.

The local authorities' interpretation of their functions has not been a static one and experience gained as a result of work in one area of their responsibilities has led to re-thinking in other aspects of their work. The emphasis in the 1933 Children and Young Persons Act is firmly placed upon the protection of the child, but knowledge gained in the operation of the 1948 Children Act gave a better understanding of the problems of the long-term care of deprived children and led to a shift of emphasis towards preventive work with families which culminated in the 1963 Children and Young Persons Act. This Act, which had received good promotional support from social workers, placed a duty on local authorities to try to prevent the breakdown of families and the bringing of children before the courts by giving advice, guidance and assistance instead, and at an early stage. The whole of this process represented very clearly the progress made by individual workers and administrators responding directly to the needs of clients and groups and attempting, within the powers given by statute, to move forward to new methods and positions. The need to help a child in the context of his family and community continued to be emphasised during the '60's, but at the same time there arose an increasing desire to develop specialist residentail facilities for the treatment and intensive care of certain groups of types of children or families who could not easily be helped at home. Social workers therefore saw themselves as helpful and enabling—extending boundaries and providing treatment. They found the protective and the possibly punitive images difficult to reconcile.

The statutory duties and powers of the local authority to provide a preventive, protective, caring and rehabilitative service span and bridge the functions of the other professions and agencies concerned with these problems. In addition, other aspects of their work give an extremely wide communication network which is valuable for referral and treatment. They are centrally placed in that they share with the medical profession a remedial and treatment function; with the police the legal power and duty to instigate court action, and with the NSPCC powers to investigate, supervise and take legal action. However the NSPCC and the medical profession do not share the statutory accountability for carrying out protective functions in this field. What is often forgotten is that the powers of local authorities to provide community services for families and children are far greater than those of other groups, and their commitment is much longer. When a baby is committed to care, the local authority may be required to act as a parent and further his best interests for 18 or possibly 20 years. Should the child be severely damaged or handicapped, responsibility under other statutes may be for a lifetime. Social services departments are, or should be, concerned and involved in the process from the beginning to the end. It is essential that they and their social workers should try to think clearly about the policies that they pursue and that other departments and professions should not misunderstand their functions and their difficulties.

WORKING METHODS

Social work practices, methods of consultation and standards of work vary throughout the country as they have always done. Additionally, procedures and systems that have been built up over the years may have become eroded or lost sight of during the recent reorganisation of the personal social services, and the imminent reorganisation of both the health services and local government may bring similar problems in the future.

Child abuse, the battered baby, is not something that was never there before; what has happened is that a name has been given and a definable group identified. For many years, child care officers, health visitors and the NSPCC have been concerned with the protection and care of all neglected and ill-treated children as part of their normal work and consequently have necessarily been dealing with battered children within this overall pattern. As far back as 1951 particular attention was focused on the need for co-ordination of effort, information and action. Joint circulars from the Home Office, Department of Health and Department of Education made recommendations relating to the needs of children who were neglected or deprived in their own homes. As a result, most authorities appointed co-ordinating officers and instigated a system of meetings and case conferences to discuss methods of helping such children. The joint discussion between such people as social workers, health visitors, education welfare officers, housing officers, officers of the Department of Social Security, school teachers and general practitioners very successfully enabled joint programmes to be formulated or, if need be, recommendations to be made for removal of the children. Where removal was considered in the best interest of the child or children, the need for legal evidence was increasingly understood and a close watch was kept on the situation by a number of interested persons.

Even so, the problem of defining the situation, of identifying which elements required action, and what kind of action should be taken, of balancing the strengths and weaknesses of the existing situation against the problematical future gains, the power fantasies and the role distortion, all were already there, but multi-disciplinary discussions helped in their solution.

Recognition

The recognition of the battered child syndrome now more precisely defines a particular group of families and children and should therefore enable the decision to act and to give help to be taken more rapidly by eliminating areas of doubt. Unfortunately, the fact that the evidence of battering may now come to light in a hospital setting has sometimes led to the development of new procedures which may or may not take into account these previously developed systems and which, on the contrary, may delay investigation. We are all aware of the reluctance of some consultants and doctors to refer cases of battering to the local authority although this is advised by both the Standing Committee of the British Paediatric Association on Accidents in Childhood and the Department of Health and the Social Services in a more recent circular. Does this reluctance arise from the three areas we have been discussing and illustrate a failing to eliminate inessentials, a misunderstanding of the powers of the local authority and a stereotype image of the local authority and of the medical profession, or is it merely lack of knowledge of the existing systems?

The battered child may be discovered through a variety of channels and, unless effective means of communication and co-operation are devised and there is real interaction between staff members, there may well be a temptation for different professional groups to deal with the situation within their own closed circuit. It is quite possible for a child to be seen by a general practitioner, referred to a hospital, returned home and supervised by a health visitor, without involvement of a local authority social services department or the NSPCC. Similarly, a referral may go to the NSPCC, to be accepted on the same case-load of a worker of that organisation, and to be unknown to the local authority. On the other hand, the need for the local authority to work constructively with the family and try to safeguard the possibility of building up positive relationships, means that there are occasions when the activities of the social services department will be regarded with suspicion by the police, who may feel that the social services department's enquiries and actions interfere with, or make more difficult, their own investigations.

The register

Many people agree on the need for a central register, giving details of all families where abuse has or is thought to have taken place. In view of their central and long-term position, I would think that this register should be compiled by the social services department and should be available, with proper safeguards, to all those concerned with the prevention of battering. I share the view that there should be a statutory obligation to report abuse to the local authority in the same way that it is obligatory to notify certain illnesses and diseases to the health authority; this would relieve the doctor of the responsibility of deciding whether or not he was betraying a patient's confidence and would perhaps lessen delay. With goodwill and better understanding of the duties and attitudes of all concerned, adequate communication and consultation systems can be devised and set up, but not if we persist in seeing each other as stereotypes appropriate to the past.

Child protection

How does this affect the handling of a case? The local authority must first of all be concerned with the safety and well-being of the child and the worker must initially limit his consideration to those factors in the home which indicate or deny the existence of cruelty or assault. If there is clear evidence, his decision whether to remove or not must focus on whether adequate protection can be given in the home. For this decision he will require knowledge and will also need to assess the effectiveness of available skill and resources. If clear evidence exists and if there is doubt as to the effectiveness of protection in the home, the child should be removed whilst an assessment of the situation takes place.

The decision to work with a family with the child present should not be undertaken lightly; the full implications should be understood. Many social workers, anxious to avoid the authoritarian approach, aware of the problems of child care away from parents, and impressed with the idea of keeping families together, may, in their desire to help the parents and thus the child, attempt a programme of casework which cannot succeed, and in so doing may permanently injure the child either physically or emotionally.

Following the passing of the 1963 Act, considerable emphasis was placed by the then children's department upon intensive casework with families. This work, and its success, has never been systematically evaluated. The work carried out in America and in this country on family diagnosis and assessment became known to some more skilled workers, but was not in general use. There is real need for accurate family diagnosis to allow for more informed decisions to be taken. The very valuable research at present being carried out may enable real progress to be made here. It is considered inappropriate to place a child for adoption in order to help the neurotic symptoms of the adoptive mother; equally it is doubtful if the presence of a child should be used to improve the family functioning of a potentially battering family. The social worker's freedom of action and choice in these circumstances is restricted not only by professional opinion and lack of knowledge, but by the statutory duties of the authority. Without experiment no progress would be made either and we need to examine how the balance can be maintained.

The use of special family units, day or residential, is one possibility, and both the local authorities and voluntary bodies have power to establish them. A much wider use of day and domiciliary services to supplement the deficiencies of the home is another approach. Many of the factors which can cause breakdown are associated with low socio-economic status, poor housing and domestic equipment, lack of help with a large family, low wages or lack of employment, crowded, noisy conditions, no break from the children, and so on. A family in the higher income bracket can buy domestic assistance, an adequate house and equipment, send their children to nurseries and boarding schools, take holidays and obtain relief from stress in a variety of ways. A local authority social services department has the power to provide the equivalent help under a number of statutes as part of its combined powers. It can provide home helps, family aides, domestic equipment, furniture, intermediate housing, monetary assistance, grants, loans and rent guarantees. It can open day centres, play groups, provide holidays for children or families, set up holiday play schemes, support and help the psychiatrically disturbed in groups, clubs, day centres, or by casework. It can provide social centres and occupational therapy. There are powers to open training homes for mothers and babies or for entire families. In other words, social services departments, in conjunction with other agencies and departments, can give the sort of help and support to a unitary family in the lower income group that might be available to a middle-class home or an extended family.

All these possibilities exist with many of the resources for carrying them out. Although some of the statutory duties of the local authority may restrict the social worker's freedom of action, he is able to work within them in new experimental ways, retaining full protective functions and, at the same time, opening up new supportive and treatment possibilities.

Equally, the power of the local authority, which has been seen as a threat in the past, has at the same time, an expanding, supportive aspect, which should be more widely understood.

Social services departments should now be seeking how to use their statutory duties to afford protection in an effective and progressive way which allows for proper development of the child whilst giving every help to the parents and the family unit.

EXTRACT FROM 'LONDON LABOUR AND THE LONDON POOR'

By Henry Mayhew

Verbatim extract given by Proprietor of Punch and Judy Show in his own words.

Punch: We must have a Dance.

Judy: Agreed. (*They both dance.*)

Punch: Get out of the way! You don't dance well enough for me. (*He hits her on the nose.*) Go and fetch the baby, and mind and take care of it, and do not hurt it. (*Judy exaunts.*)

Judy (*returning back with baby*): Take care of the baby while I go and cook the dumplings.

Punch (*striking Judy with his right hand*): Get out of the way! I'll take care of the baby. (*Judy exaunts.*)

Punch (*sits down and sings to the baby*)—

'Hush-a-by baby, upon the tree top,
When the wind blows the cradle will rock,
When the bough breaks, the cradle will fall,
Down comes the baby, cradle and all.' (*Baby cries.*)

Punch (*shaking it*): What a cross boy! (*He lays it down on the playboard, and rolls it backwards and forwards, to rock it to sleep, and sings again*)—

'Oh slumber, my darling, they sire is a knight,
They mother's a lady so lovely and bright;
The hills and the dales and the to'rs which you see,
They all shall belong, my dear creature, to thee.'

(*Punch continues rocking the child. It still cries, and he takes it up in his arms saying*)—

What a cross child! I can't a-bear cross children. (*Then he vehemently shakes it, and knocks its head up against the side of the proceedings several times, representing to kill it, and then he throws it out of the winder.*) Enter Judy.

Judy: Where's the baby?

Punch (*in a lemoncholy tone*): I have had a misfortune; the child was so terribly cross, and I throwed it out of the winder. (*Lemontation of Judy for the loss of her dear child. She goes into asterisks and then excites and fetches a cudgel and commences beating Punch over the head.*)

Punch: Don't be cross my dear; I didn't go to do it.

Judy: I'll pay yer for throwing the child out of the winder. (*She keeps on giving him knocks on the head, but Punch snatches the stick away and commences an attack upon his wife, and beats her savagely.*)

Judy: I'll go to the Constable, and have you locked up.

Punch: Go to the Devil. I don't care where you go. Get out of my way! (*Judy exaunts.*)

DISCUSSION

Many important issues were raised by this somewhat philosophical presentation which dealt with some of the underlying reasons for difficulties in co-operation and for misunderstandings between the agencies concerned with caring, with punishing or with carrying out the law. The dangers that a hierarchical structure introduces into the conduct of caring social work were stressed.

The local authority has statutory duties and parental rights, but a balance must be struck between their exercise and the strengthening of the family. This strengthening outweighs considerations of dirt and poor hygiene. Before the Childrens and Young Persons Act of 1963 the emphasis was on protection of the child, now it is upon preserving the family and this has undoubtedly increased the difficulty of dealing with battering families. Fundamental to safe decision is the family diagnosis. The crux of the matter is, is good mothering possible? To leave the child in its family means the danger of further injury and of emotional and other deprivations while at the same time demanding an amount of support for which resources are often inadequate. On the other hand if the child is removed, what provision is available? A child left with its family is safer with a care order than a supervision order. This helps the immediate management, but it has to be remembered that the long-term programme may last for eighteen years.

14. The social worker's role

John Stroud

In this paper a description is attempted of the role of the local authority social worker when injury to a child is suspected of being 'non-accidental'.

It is well to remind ourselves at the outset of the wide range of situations in which the social worker may become involved. In my view the *majority* of adults pass through a phase in their development as parents when their children are at risk of injury, often through ineptitude, often because the emotions stirred up by the behaviour of the first-born are raw and crude and deep.

The majority of young parents come through this phase fairly quickly, the pace of their development seeming to depend in large part on the models of parental behaviour upon which they can base their own behaviour. When one or both of the young parents have themselves experienced poor parenting, their development as persons is much slower as they struggle to find their identities as mother/spouse/housewife or as father/husband/breadwinner. In a few cases deep feelings of inadequacy and revulsion are projected on to a particular child who remains 'fixed' as the scapegoat. In a very small number of cases, which unfortunately attract the maximum amount of publicity, one or other of the parents is psychotic or a psychopath, displaying 'indifference to life' or even 'hostility to life', or is so labile in personality as to have dangerously weak controls in times of stress.

If I may use the analogy of the spectrum in the present context, the psychotic parent lies in the 'infra-red' band: here the role of the social worker may be swiftly to provide protective custody for the child and the best available substitute family. At the 'ultra-violet' end lie families where social work intervention would be inappropriate—those where one error, one mishap, one panic, have in fact mobilised the personal resources of the parents and enabled them to develop rapidly. I wish to focus on the middle bands, where difficulties arise because one is uncertain if one is working in the orange or the yellow or the white.

A central dilemma exists for all practitioners. Clinical evidence led to the formulation of the so-called 'battered child syndrome' in the early and mid-'sixties; yet almost simultaneously further clinical evidence was accumulated for the traumatic effect of separation of the young child from his family and particularly from his mother. Concern about traumatic separation, the results of which were well observed by children's officers from 1948 onwards, was reflected in the wording of Section 1 of the Children and Young Persons Act 1963—an Act 'to diminish the need for children to come into care . . . or to be brought before the courts'. Furthermore the Children and Young Persons Act of 1969 stresses the need for the voluntary co-operation of parents and families by requiring that proof should be offered as to the necessity of court intervention and legal sanctions in order that a desirable objective may be reached. This wording may be contrasted with that of previous Acts, from about 1881 onwards, and in particular with the First Schedule to the 1933 Act.

The social worker—or perhaps more accurately the social services department—is therefore confronted by sets of clinical evidence which appear to be opposed to each other; by statutory duties which appear to be in conflict; and of course by the swirling uncertainties which surround the rights of parents to privacy and self-determination and the rights of statutory bodies to intervene in private affairs. It is only a few years ago that local authorities were accused of being too possessive of children in their care, and of resisting parental demands. Courts would often stress the importance of 'the blood tie'.

Incorporated in most recent (and indeed pending) child care legislation is the principle that the welfare of the child shall be the paramount consideration. The task of those concerned with child care is to attempt to assess how the welfare of the child can best be secured, given that much of the evidence collected, if not contradictory, will 'pull' in different directions. Strengths in the family situation may be revealed as well as risks; in most parents, perhaps more often in mothers, there will be a detectable emotional ambivalence; or, while the family circle may be fragile, there may be a known lack of viable and satisfying alternatives in the shape of adoptive or foster parents. Even where such resources exist, the experience of the children's departments in the 1950's indicates that there are risks in severing a child from his roots: we are still haunted by the concepts of 'genealogical bewilderment' and of 'children in limbo'. The short-term welfare of the child, placed in what is hoped to be short-term protective custody, may have to be set against his long-term welfare and his need 'to belong'.

Nor must we be exclusively concerned with the welfare of *this* child at *this* moment in time. There is also the welfare of children as yet unborn. If children are hastily removed from parental care and no attempt is made to treat or modify the parents' problems, not only may those problems discharge themselves on the next baby, but the parents may carry forward, on their emotional profit-and-loss account, hostility to and suspicion of social workers, health visitors and so on. Anger is sometimes expressed about the social worker's concern to 'preserve a relationship' with parents, a relationship often woolly and purposeless, yet the social worker's preservation of this trusting relationship may be the only lifeline to the child still in the womb.

Given all these doubts and uncertainties, and given that families as units, and parents as parents, grow and develop, it is clear that the role of the social worker should not be too precisely defined. It may even change in the course of one particular case. What is first needed is the mechanism which will help the worker to perceive what the role is at a particular time in a particular case.

Because we are focusing upon the under-fives, at the stage when parental inadequacies are most severely tested, the health visitor is also involved. Sometimes, following a big row, the health visitor has been excluded, just as sometimes it has been the social worker. With these exceptions, the social worker is never working single-handed. This means that we are thinking in terms of a socio-medical approach. It also means that the roles of *both* visitors to the family have to be defined.

In Hertfordshire, health visitors are based on general practices; but they also relate to the community health teams. They therefore have access to resources through their GP's and through their medical-officers-in-department and nursing officers. The 'corporate management' of child abuse cases is built in at three levels: health visitor/social worker; divisional medical/divisional social services officers; and centrally at the level of assistant director/deputy county medical officer (soon to be community physician child health). It is with this concept of 'corporate management' in mind that we can turn to examine the role of the social worker.

THE CHILD IN THE SPECTRUM

There are cases where at the point of first professional contact the child is, in the analogy of the spectrum, clearly 'in the red': the child has facial injuries, there have been delays in seeking treatment, there is evidence of more than one injury over a period of time, a place of safety order must be obtained. The essence of all procedures must be their speed and thoroughness and the 'openness' of lines of communication. This means local activity and no long lines of hierarchical command, and depends on the patient and vigilant preparatory fostering of good and trustful relationships within the socio-medical team. The social worker has to perform a skilful task under pressure of time. She has on the one hand to draw out from the parents as much relevant information as possible in order to reach a reasonably accurate diagnosis of 'the welfare of the child', and this usually means an exploration of their backgrounds, their life-experiences, the models on which they have formed themselves as parents. This is the exploration of the past.

Yet at the same time the parents are in 'the here and now': they are fearful, angry, guilty, they are having to face serious and urgent issues about themselves as parents, as marriage-partners, as mature or immature personalities. Often the situation is open and undefended, and, as studies of 'crisis casework' teach, sometimes more can be achieved over a short period than over long years of more diluted activity during which attitudes and defences may harden. The amount of time and skill demanded in capitalising on a crisis situation is such, however, that social workers sometimes seek refuge in their 'record-taking' activity. 'Let's be surer before we make a move' is an understandable reaction to crisis not exclusive to the social work profession.

Let us now focus on an 'orange alert' which might equally be a 'pale yellow alert': a baby is observed with a fading bruise over one eye, the mother seems scared, and there is nothing more to go on than that. The first stage must be the systematic collection of all available data. Given all the pressures and conflicting priorities with which social services departments have to contend, it may not be necessary to allocate a social worker to the case at this stage. One of the discoveries of the last year's work has been the amount of fragmented information—'little bits of information'—in the possession of so many people who did not know others were involved. It is important to establish first of all who is responsible for collecting and collating 'the little bits' and this is likely to be a senior officer of one or other of the departments, usually a senior medical officer.

On the record-taking activity itself, much has been written and information abounds. One recalls, for instance, the forms used by children's assessment centres and the former classifying approved schools; the work done by family service units, and research projects on the prediction of delinquency and the identification of families at risk. It is not difficult to draw from this information forms or check-lists of almost infinite sophistication. The danger is that of 'information overload', the relentless pursuit of minutiae which may come perilously close to inquisition and may scare the living daylights out of the parents and deprive them of what rags of self-esteem they may possess; which may take up too much professional time over too long a period; and which may result in a report so long that nobody can see the wood for the trees.

THE RECORD FORM

There is perhaps no perfect model for a form which will help to secure the vital information while avoiding overload, but as an example rather than a model I give below the headings which might appear on a form which a health visitor might reasonably be asked to complete in the case of a 'bruised baby'. Much of the information will already have become known to her:

1 Child's surname, forenames, date of birth, address
2 Details of the household—names, ages and occupations of all occupants and their relationship to the child
3 General condition of this child
4 Detailed notes of observed injury
5 Parental explanation of injury
6 Have there been recent visits to general practitioner, clinic or yourself with anxiety expressed about apparently trivial problems or complaints? (If yes, give details)
7 Give details of all references in medical records to any previous injury, bruising, failure to thrive, gross mishandling or rejection *of this child or any sibling*
8 Has any sibling died? If so when and what was the cause?
9 Is there any record of abnormal ante-natal or peri-natal circumstances regarding this child? e.g. was the child born prematurely, did he/she enter a special care unit? Was this child wanted and planned for?
10 Is the child presenting problems of rearing, e.g. is he a sickly baby with a nagging cry, or is he forward and demanding?

11 Is there to your knowledge any record of mental illness, instability or anti-social behaviour in either parent?

12 Are the parents socially isolated and in particular isolated from their own parents and other relatives?

13 Does the general appearance of the house suggest that there may be problems of household management, financial stress or obsessional levels of cleanliness?

14 Are there such housing problems as shared accommodation, overcrowding, serious disrepair, etc.?

15 Have the family moved house frequently?

16 To your knowledge, from what backgrounds do the parents come—e.g., is there any history of deprivation or of erratic upbringing?

17 What do you observe of the parents' attitude to the child and the child's reactions to them?

It is on the 'score' of risk factors which this type of enquiry brings out that a decision has to be taken as to whether a social worker should be allocated to the case and if so what her role should be. In a certain number of cases it may be decided that the health visitor will remain as the *only* worker actively in contact with the family with a named social worker in a 'stand-by' role in case of a deterioration in family functioning. In some cases the health visitor may be the *primary* worker to the family with the social worker focusing perhaps on the factor of social isolation, or, where the child may have been admitted to a day nursery, acting as a child care officer. There have been cases of *two-handed* working where the health visitor has been focusing on the mother and a male social worker on the father. Where, on initial appraisal, the family have multiple problems and the risk-factors are numerous, the social worker may become the *primary* worker because swift protective action may well become necessary and 'continuity of contact' may be important.

Broadly speaking the social worker will be focusing on the adults in the situation with a view to assessing their functioning, their potential for positive development and the effect of this or that type of intervention. Social workers have sometimes been criticised for looking through blinkers at the adults and failing to notice overt signs of distress amongst the children. I believe this may occur because roles and lines of communication and review have not been laid down clearly at the outset so that each worker 'assumes' that the other is watching the children and partly perhaps because social workers may have assumed too readily that they are working 'through' the parents to effect change without seeing the family as a complex and ever-changing whole. Sometimes children are 'labelled' at a particular time as though the label were an eternal truth, and so changes are assumed not to be taking place.

FAMILIES AT RISK

Again for purposes of discussion rather than as presenting a model guide-line, I give below an extract from my own department's Guide to Procedure addressed to social workers involved with 'families at risk'. On this I would say first that there is a long tradition in Hertfordshire, in both children's and social services departments, of using narrative reports rather than report forms. Provided that proper guidance is given as to the areas to be covered, the narrative report permits the social worker to expand on areas of concern, whether the subject is a family at risk, a foster-child or an application by would-be adopters. Secondly, I must mention that this particular guideline was devised as long ago as 1964 when child care officers were in touch with many hundreds of families. Clearly there is a need for revision if this were to be used for the purpose under discussion. There would be a need perhaps to report on the adults' background, the circumstances of the formation of the marriage, the extended family and the significant points about the conception and carrying of the child now at risk; but a social worker who conscientiously enquired into these areas and reported in the form shown, would be able to contribute much to the understanding of the family dynamics.

'Every six months a review report should be completed in duplicate, following discussion with the senior social worker (team leader). One copy of the agreed Review should be sent to County Hall. These reports are made in narrative form on Form SS220. While the contents of the report, and its length, are a matter for the social worker's judgement, it is suggested that the following points should be covered:

1 *Any change in circumstances.* This will include any change from the information given in the original report, including any change in the problem presented, and also any important events in the period under review.
2 *The home.* Description of dwelling, standards of comfort.
3 *The parents.* How are they performing their different roles, e.g., as mother, wife and neighbour, or as father, wage-earner and husband?
4 *The children.* It would be wise to devote a sub-paragraph to every child in the family, noting as far as possible school performance, health, emotional development and social behaviour. What are they at risk of?
5 *Finance.* Is finance a burden? Is the 'rent' paid? Is the housekeeping budget sensible? Is positive action being taken to deal with these problems, e.g. by collecting rent?
6 *Evaluation and plan.* This may prove to be a difficult section to write, and it is suggested that social workers think in terms of four sub-sections:

(a) *Assessment*: how in general are this family making out, both internally (in their relationship with one another) and externally (in their dealings with the community)?
(b) *Diagnosis*: what seems to be preventing them reaching a more acceptable standard?
(c) *Response*: how have the family responded to the caseworker so far, and how do they see him?
(d) *Plan*: what does the caseworker see as his objective over the next six months?'

I would particularly mention the section dealing with financial matters. This form was devised when social workers were particularly concerned with families at risk of eviction with a focus on payment or non-payment of rent. Within marriage money is not only fiscal currency, it is emotional currency as well. The wife kept short of housekeeping money is likely to be starved too of other forms of affection. In several recent cases of child abuse handled by my department, the mishandling of money, in one form or another, gave the clue to a matrimonial problem which in turn, when brought out into the open, gave the clue as to why a child had become the scapegoat.

In the early stages of active involvement in a case, a social worker may well need to continue the process of diagnostic history-taking. In trying to establish what is in the best long-term interests of 'the bruised baby', the cause of her involvement in the case, she must try to explore the subject of 'the parental model', mentioned earlier. What can be gleaned of the parents' childhood experiences? Did this restless young man have a father at all upon whom to model himself? Was he brought up in a home or an institution run by rules and regulations, so that he cannot understand why a baby should not understand and obey his own? Has this depressed young wife escaped into marriage from a home where her own mother was mentally ill? In a recent case the mother was reared in an old-fashioned 'colonial' setting, not by one beloved ayah but by a succession of native girls: she has no understanding of how a mother is expected to behave in an English setting.

The gathering of this type of information is not easy. These areas of childhood experience, courtship and marriage may be painful and therefore heavily defended; or the parents' motivation may be unconscious; or sometimes parents may be so worried about the 'here and now' that they grow impatient of enquiries which appear to be irrelevant. At other times parents may be so relieved to be able to talk about bottled-up problems that information comes in a great gush. We are considering a spectrum of human action, reaction and interaction; and while some parents mature as individuals in an upward curve of varying steepness, others proceed by a series of lurches and regressions, forwards, backwards and even sideways. The social worker's tasks, having established what sort of parental model exists, are to try to compensate for its deficiences, perhaps to substitute a better model ('parenting the parents' may be important to arrange) and to monitor the results.

THE CASE CONFERENCE AND THE COURTS

In cases where the needle may be trembling towards the deep orange or the red—and this may not be at the point of initial appraisal but because of a deteriorating situation—it may be necessary to consider whether juvenile court action should be initiated. By this time the social services department has moved into a central role. This will be the agency which brings the case (or takes responsibility for not bringing it) and this is the agency which must summon the case conference. Unless the situation is deteriorating so sharply that immediate action to protect the child is called for, it is essential that the conference is called. There are other people who may have to face repercussions in their professional relationships—the GP, the psychiatrist who may be treating the mother, the health visitor with responsibilities to other children in the family and so on. There are all those 'little bits of information' which tend to be overlooked, and there is always the problem of staff changeover.

A discussion of the criteria to be applied when deciding on case-management and on whether or not to seek court orders would be too extensive for our present purposes, and it could lead us into multidisciplinary ramifications such as the use of authority in casework, the style and functioning of juvenile courts, the realities of the doctor/patient relationship and so on. Often the decision can only be made in terms of the available resources in that particular place at that particular time. Each participant in a case conference must be able freely to talk about the constraints and limitations placed upon him—for each participant is probably accredited by the others with various magical and superhuman powers. In very general terms, however, I would hope that, having balanced up as accurately as possible the pros and cons of alternative forms of action, case conferences would lean towards the most positive action to help the family as a unit rather than towards helping the child in isolation. In other words, the removal of the child from the family circle needs stronger justification than protecting him within it. I say this not from a sentimental attachment to 'the sanctity of the family' but from the experience of watching over two generations of children in care and observing what happens to parents whose children are lightly removed.

Without venturing further into these troubled waters, there are two points I would like to make in connection with supervision, whether voluntary or under a court order. The first is that it is unrealistic to expect a social worker undertaking this duty to be able to provide a daily pair of eyes to watch the child and indeed, even were she able to pay daily visits, I would regard this as a misuse of an expensive skill. The social worker should be standing further away from the trees so that she can see more of the wood. Her task is more to appraise and reappraise the functioning of the family, to try to encourage the growth of the family towards the objectives set by the case conference, to try to relieve environmental stresses such as bad housing, and to try to promote the confidence and self-esteem of the parents which in the long run may be the major safety measure for children born and unborn. This is not a policing job, it is a casework job, and when a supervision order is made it should be with this in mind. Where a daily pair of eyes is required, this might well be provided by a dayminder, day nursery staff, a special home help or perhaps a selected playgroup, and it is interesting to note an increased use of these facilities by supervising social workers.

Under a court order a supervising officer does have a greater power to issue directives than is generally used. The extent of these powers has not yet been tested in the courts, and there is always the problem of knowing what directives to issue. One can scarcely direct a parent to be less inept, or to have a higher flashpoint, but a supervisor could direct a parent to report every week to an nfant welfare or out-patient clinic. In this context I would make my second point, which is that perhaps a fruitful field for further development lies in the concept of 'intermediate treatment'. This is a colloquial expression for schemes ecently introduced under the 1969 Act, and so far the schemes have been geared towards dealing with older, delinquent children with much talk of clubs, adventure schemes and so on. Intermediate treatment requirements may be applied for in respect of any child under supervision, whatever his age. Much nteresting work could be pioneered under this statutory provision. The whole problem of *compulsion* remains a delicate one. A parent directed to a clinic could scarcely be expected to arrive in a co-operative frame of mind.

In any case where there is ongoing supervision of a child at risk, whether voluntarily or under a court order, it is tempting to suggest that regulations hould be devised to lay down some duties for supervising officers—as to frequency of visitation, for instance, as in the case of foster-children, or as to the enquiries to be made such as are required of the guardian *ad litem* in adoption work. There are, however, some dangers in applying rigid rules, bearing in mind the spectrum of behaviour encountered and the fact that many families pass through a 'risk zone'. In the early days of supervision, visits to a family two or three times a week might not be too frequent when a situation is 'open' and movement is taking place; but later such intensity of visitation might be unproductive in terms of the social worker's time and even threatening to the continued growth of the parents.

More important than limiting regulations is the continuing appraisal and reappraisal of the situation—the case review. On what does a supervising officer report? How often? And to whom? And this brings me back to my major point, which is that three heads are better than one. There is need of a 'third man'.

THE THIRD MAN

Structures in social services departments vary, as do the responsibilities carried at different levels, but the levels I am discussing are those of social worker, senior social worker and a senior and centrally placed officer who might be a principal caseworker or assistant director or child care specialist. As far as the first two are concerned, it is normal practice for a social worker to be under the supervision of a senior. Casework supervision is an elaborate subject, and it involves elements of staff-development, but it focuses on case-management and in discussion the skilled senior may be able to help the social worker to see, for example, where one form of intervention is proving ineffective, or where the assessment of a client has been based on a doubtful premise, or where a significant area has been overlooked. Essentially it is the senior's responsibility to see that his scarce social worker resource is being used to maximum effectiveness. In the present context, when the intial case conference has set down certain objectives—to protect a child, to relieve a source of stress, to heal a disturbed marriage—it is for the senior to establish whether the objectives have changed, whether they are being reached quickly enough, whether there may be a more effective form of help available and so on. This form of case-management is usually competently done except that pressures at all social work levels are such that it is rarely ideally well done.

Unfortunately, once such a case-review has been carried out, I suspect that there the matter rests; or that the report with its recommendations goes but one stage higher in the hierarchy, to an area or divisional 'reviewing officer' who may comment and countersign. In most social services departments there has been since 1971 a distinct trend in delegating power down from central office, to take decision-making 'closer to the client', a trend of which in general terms I approve. It may be, however, that the baby has gone down with the bathwater.

It has been estimated that on average a general practitioner will encounter a 'battered child' case only once every five years. Much depends on the definition of that term, but a senior social worker may encounter only two or three cases a year and a social worker will obviously be involved even less frequently. Expertise takes a long time to grow in a small 'patch'. Given that many of the situations are complex and uncertain and that the clues presented are often subtle and elusive, expertise is necessary for their interpretation, and that expertise may be more quickly developed if the 'catchment area' is larger. There is an abvious analogy with the role of the consultant in medical practice.

I reach this judgement after long years of experience of acting as 'third man' in respect of boarded-out children in Hertfordshire. I found that although child care officers and senior child care officers, as they were then called, were admirably competent in the production of review reports, there was usually some helpful comment I could make simply because my horizons were wider. For example, I might know that a case which was unique and puzzling to the West Herts team was paralleled in, say, East Herts where some effective form of treatment has been devised, and I could put one isolated worker in touch with another.

The procedure I am advocating, therefore, in supervision cases is that there should first be a statutory requirement that a review report should be completed, not less frequently than once in three months. As to the form of the review, I would suggest that the guideline reproduced above gives a basis, but only a basis, for it obviously requires modification and improvement. Clearly, for example, there should be room for the health visitor's comments. Sometimes the report may be completed immediately after a reviewing case conference, and sometimes after discussion between social worker and senior, but in either case the senior social worker should countersign the document and the proposals it contains for the ongoing management of the case. The review report should then be forwarded to the central office of the department and marked for the attention of the nominated consultant; who in turn, on behalf of the department but principally, let me emphasise, on behalf of a child who cannot speak for himself, issues such directives, suggestions or approvals as seem fit.

I have given some thought to as to whether the consultancy role might be played by a case committee, either of magistrates or of elected members; but while there is a value in the case committee, and it may provide an extra safeguard, I come down firmly on advocating that this is a professional task. It should be undertaken by a professional social worker of sufficient stature to be able to call in medical, psychiatric or legal advice as required.

The introduction of a statutory review would, I believe, require legislative action. Any regulation on the form of the review would best be drawn in very broad terms, permitting local authorities to develop their own styles subject to the guidance of DHSS advisers. It would, however, be difficult to draw up a regulation governing the appointment of the consultant, and perhaps again this matter could best be dealt with by the DHSS advisory service.

We must remember that supervision orders can be made in respect of children of all ages up to 17. Clearly the handling of the case, say, of a turbulent teenage girl under supervision poses quite different problems from those presented by an inarticulate infant. Regulations appropriate to the one may be nonsense to the other. It may therefore be worth considering whether a new form of order—called, perhaps, a protection order—might be needed in respect of children under 5; and if Parliament would consider this in the form of an Amending Act to the Act of 1969, perhaps consideration could also be given to an extension of the concept of intermediate treatment to which I have referred.

WHAT THE COMMUNITY WANTS

Finally, any spokesman from the social services departments—even an entirely unofficial spokesman, as I am—must include a reference to the demands which the community now places upon its social workers. There is always a danger of sounding too defensive about this matter and of appearing to whine too much; but the truth is that the experienced, qualified, committed social worker, perceiving all that is needed in a case, sensitive to risks and dangers, can still find herself engaged in what has aptly been described as 'too much dabbling and too little dealing'. What society wants for its battered children depends on what society wants for its frail elderly people or its mentally handicapped people or its disabled people or its drug addicts. A department which allocates top priority to child abuse cases, as my department has done, has clearly and consciously to allocate low priority to other groups, and then to face the consequences. And battered children have no votes.

15. Nurture and nature: the nurturing problem

Joan Court

It seems that in modern society the stresses on the family and on parental capacity render mothering quite a hazardous and anxiety provoking event. Many professional workers are aware that even normal and comfortably-off parents have on occasion a need for counselling and support. We can understand this and it does not cause us discomfort, but if there is a serious break in nurturing care and a small child is injured the natural response in all of us is one of extreme anxiety and denial. We are likely to be less angry with the mother who actually kills her baby than we are with the battering mother: 'poor soul', we think, 'she must have been out of her mind'. Yet it is likely that the origins of both disasters are similar.

In devising a foolproof system to protect the children and treat their parents questions of management and control, the setting up of committees and agreement about procedures are all vital activities. It is equally important to understand why children are sometimes injured and to come to terms with the disturbance it arouses in our own hearts. In time we may learn to understand the suicidal impulses in a depressive illness. Twenty years ago doctors and social workers would have hesitated to encourage a depressed patient to talk about her suicidal preoccupations. Now this is a routine procedure. Perhaps it will become increasingly acceptable for mothers to talk about the angry feelings they have towards their infants and, as with suicidal thoughts, once these are put into words and shared with a sympathetic listener the danger of violence may be diminished.

PREPARATION FOR PARENTHOOD AND ANTE-NATAL CARE

The physical care of pregnant women in this country is of a very high order, but less professional attention is directed to understanding the pregnant woman's social and psychological background and in particular to evaluating her own experiences of being mothered, even though this may be of vital importance to her psychic development and to her capacity to nurture babies. Indeed some women are quite unsuited to the role of motherhood, but cultural expectations and other factors give such women little real choice in the matter. A girl may drift into marriage and pregnancy, although not always in that order, because she does not understand that there is any real alternative. Women who express a dislike of babies are likely to be reassured that they will feel differently when they have their own child. In a minority of cases this may prove to be tragically incorrect.

The results of predictive studies in Aberdeen based on an analysis of questionnaires may lead to the possibility of identifying pre-natal mothers who are potentially likely to injure their children. The researchers hope that by developing such a measurement it may become feasible to offer mothers at risk extra support in their maternal role. It would of course be even more helpful if we could identify women, before they become pregnant, who for one reason or another have limited maternal ability. Some might be glad of family planning advice to avoid pregnancy altogether, others if they were treated sympathetically might be willing to postpone having babies until they reached a greater emotional maturity. A girl of 19, who has injured her child several times, explained:

> I've got years of anger to take out on Penny. When I get at anyone I take it out of Penny. I've got too many problems, she's not behaving, she's provocative, I lose my patience and get carried away. When she screams bloody murder you don't know what to do. I bumped her head on the sink. Young people having a baby today are supposed to be perfect when the baby is born. I didn't know about staying up at nights and the in-laws interfering. Everything I do is wrong.

CHILDBIRTH AND PRE-NATAL EXPERIENCE

In spite of increasing interest in the matter, direct observational studies of the interaction between the human mother and her infant lag behind animal studies of the same period in the life cycle. Consider for example the maternal pattern of the tree shrew. Until recently all the baby tree shrews born in captivity were promptly killed by their mothers, and it was thought they could not breed outside their natural habitat. During a long period of patient observational study in the London zoo an ethologist discovered the cause of the mother tree shrew's unnatural behaviour. This happened when by mistake two nests instead of one were left in the breeding cage, so giving the mother tree shrew, who by good fortune was at term, the chance to follow her innate behavioural pattern of delivering her baby in one nest and then promptly returning to the second nest, which appeared to be the matrimonial home. She returned to feed her baby and to empty its bladder every 48 hours, mother and infant thrived, and the delighted ethologist was able to record a new discovery to the scientific world.

Women vary in the resources and handicaps they bring to mothering, in part dependent on their own experience of being mothered but also on a variety of other factors, including emotional maturity and the support they may or may not receive from their husbands. But all mothers need very sensitive care during childbirth and in the vitally important neonatal period. Research has shown that premature babies are at particular risk of injury (Elmer, 1967; Skinner and Castle, 1969). As Winnicott once remarked, 'Premature babies are cared for mechanically, the mother takes over a baby who has learnt to respond to mechanical care taking'. For an immature mother, who may not have wanted a child in the first place, traditional obstetric practices may further impede the communicative attachment of the mother to her newborn. Researchers have discovered that the human baby can respond to a soft voice and follow the movement of a human face within 24 hours of birth (Wolfe, 1959; Robson, 1967). In all cases then, whether or not the baby is premature, we need to do everything we can to increase the possibility that mother and baby will form a bond. Many mothers who subsequently injure their infants look back with negative feelings to their confinement experiences and, although this is likely to be only one facet of the problem, it is one deserving careful study. Abnormalities in the infant, disturbance in the parents and environmental factors are important variables in the battered child syndrome, but psychological studies and the recent work of ethologists (Richards and Bernal, 1972) describe how the mother may experience a series of frustrations in her instinctive acts of mothering which may undermine her sense of competence and initial responses. If this is so with normal mothers and infants, how much more vulnerable is the immature woman and her newborn.

FAMILY PLANNING

A number of studies have shown that abuse is associated with an accumulation of stress in the family, and that the most common type of stress is the birth of several children close together, often less than one year apart (Elmer, 1965; Skinner and Castle, 1969). These studies report that at the time of the battering episode at least 40 per cent of the mothers were pregnant or had delivered an infant in the past year. Regardless of parental pathology, frequent childbearing exhausts physical and emotional energy. Interrupted nights upset natural rhythm and lead to increased irritability. Strained marital relationships and additional economic stress enhance the possibility of loss of control in parents who are vulnerable to such disturbances.

Abusing parents, with their grievously unmet needs to be dependent, may have an unconscious drive to have babies in the hope that they will give them the love they have lacked in their own childhood, and may resist family planning advice unless the worker is sufficiently empathetic to enable them to appreciate her deep concern. Premature advice on this subject may be seen as yet another authoritarian interference, but once a trusting relationship is established between the professional worker and the parents it may be possible to give helpful guidance.

ENVIRONMENTAL STRESS

The role of crisis and stress in the lives of these parents needs careful evaluation. Childbearing as a crisis is well documented. Less well appreciated perhaps is the stress caused by such events as the loss of a job, bereavement, illness in the family and moving house. Many abusive parents will say, 'everything has gone wrong this year, it's been one thing after another'. Unemployment and ill health are obvious hazards. But rehousing is less often perceived as a source of stress, when for instance, the family have moved to worse or even better accommodation. Yet moving house always involves considerable stress. It is likely to add to financial worries and fatigue and to separate the family from familiar sources of support. Parents who injure their children are in any case intensely lonely people; they seldom have deep and sustaining relationships and may depend on quite casual encounters to alleviate feelings of isolation. One mother who attacked her 3-week baby said:

> To begin with he was born a week too early, so my cousin wasn't able to get down from Scotland in time to help me out. Then we were rehoused just before the baby was born so I couldn't see my friend from next door any more. She's only a school-girl, but she used to drop in for tea and sometimes did her homework in my kitchen and we'd have a bit of a gossip. I got to look forward to it. And then because we moved I had to change my doctor and that was the last straw. Nothing seems to have gone right since we left the old place, and I miss it though I know it was a dump and we had to move.

Rehousing then may bring a sense of loss and, however necessary it may be to get the family into better accommodation and it is of course often essential to do this, we should be aware of the stress it involves, its meaning to the individual parent, and do all we can to avoid what Winnicott described as 'unfortunate coincidences'. These might be for example a change of worker, or a lessening of casework support, or the return of a child who has been in care. Changes which may further disturb the parents' precarious balance should be postponed as far as possible until the family has become rooted in its new home.

INTER-GENERATIONAL ASPECTS OF CHILD ABUSE

Donald Winnicott once commented at a seminar (July 9, 1969): 'There are parents who are sensitive to their baby's screaming because they have a scream inside which they have never screamed. In momentarily losing their temper, these people become possessed by a disassociated part of themselves, or by an introjected parent figure. This has been called identification with the aggressor. The event has its place in the individual economy of that person. The husband's jealousy of a new baby may be extreme if he has not finished using his wife as a corrective for his own deprivation.'

There is evidence to indicate that some violent parents have experienced physical abuse in their own childhood (Scott, 1973). Without long-term prospective follow up studies we cannot be sure how frequently this occurs, but recent research supports the view that violence is a self perpetuating style of life, and in some instances this can be traced through three or four generations (Martin, 1972; Oliver and Taylor, 1971). These parents often deny the hardship in their own background or do not recognise its significance. Mrs. G., who disliked babies and inflicted severe injuries on her 3-year-old daughter, said her own childhood was quite normal:

> Our mother was always good to us, though she disliked children and never liked to touch us. But father was Victorian and made us do everything properly. I was always in trouble and in tears, though my sister got off lightly. Mind you, I think it's right to be strict, you've got show them who is boss, and the sooner the better. It's funny but I find myself shouting at the child like my father used to shout at me. I think I was brought up to believe all babies are wicked.

In addition to a possible history of abuse in the parental background, there is often a story of being the family scapegoat, the least favoured child, or the little mother who had to look after the younger children at the expense of her own unmet dependency needs. Not infrequently there is a history of alcoholism and disruption in early family relationships, or a reversal of roles causing the young child to feel responsible for its parents' well being.

If child abuse is an inter-generational problem this obviously has many implications for treatment and prevention. For instance it may be unwise to remove a child from the parental home and place him with his grandparents although in the course of care proceedings one is frequently urged to do so by the family. Increased understanding of the extended family's dynamics may reveal unresolved hostilities which are inimical to the child's well being.

TREATMENT AND PROTECTION OF THE ABUSED CHILD

In a number of cases the parents of abused children are deeply disturbed with marked psychopathic or psychotic disorders. It is usually recognised that an injured child should not be left in the care of psychopathic parents. If the parents are not married and the abusive adult is an elusive figure in the home, difficulties may arise even in these cases. In the case of mentally disturbed parents decisions are more difficult and careful psychiatric assessment is essential. If the infant is involved in the delusional system of its parent or parents, he is obviously at much greater risk. In other instances, although the parents are not psychotic or psychopathic, they may regard the child in such a negative way that there is a delusional quality in the relationship. The child caught up in this web of hostile unreality is likely to need skilled care and treatment, if he is to survive unscathed physically and mentally.

The treatment of children subjected to abuse, whether this takes the form of assault, severe neglect or failure to thrive, has tended in the past to be concentrated primarily on medical care and on ensuring physical survival. Recent studies examine in greater depth what the child needs to enable him to develop without the handicap of retardation, inadequacy, dependency and loneliness (Martin, 1972; Pavenstedt and Bernard, 1971). In the USA excellent work has been done with abused children in a few day nurseries where specialised care for such children has been provided. A high staff ratio, great emphasis on mothering and much physical comforting combined with skilled, psychiatric advice and supervision have produced a remarkable response in the children (Galston, 1973). Similar methods are being used by the NSPCC in a day nursery attached to the Society's Battered Child Research Department. Many of the children, institutionalised in their own homes, retarded in speech, inhibited in play and frozen in their relationships with other people, respond to a remarkable degree if placed in a benign atmosphere. The change in the children may well spark off a change in their parents who may be haunted by sado-masochistic fantasies, and infuriated by the dependence of a young child. As one mother explained:

I keep hitting her because of the way she keeps watching with those big sad eyes. I can't stand the way she looks at me and acts like she was helpless. If only she'd learn to talk and stick up for herself. But she keeps wanting to hold on to me and it gets me down.

The role of fear in the lives of these children and its repercussions in later life has not been sufficiently studied. It has been suggested that some children survive unscathed, but it seems more likely that their problems do not come to the notice of social and medical agencies. Another neglected area of study is the effect of parental violence on the brothers and sisters of the abused child. In some families one child only is the victim of abuse. In such cases very careful attention should be given not only to the mental health of the scapegoat child but also to the others. It is bad enough to be the focus of negative parental objection. It may be equally harmful to be seen as the good child, who may indeed feel very guilty about this. He may be filled with mixed feelings because of his inability to cope with his parents' disturbance, or at least live with it unharmed. Observers have noted that some children seem able from a remarkably early age to act in a therapeutic way towards their anxious and angry parents, and it has been suggested that these children are not in danger. It might be as well to be less sanguine about the long term effects of such reversals of the natural order.

SUMMARY

The nurturing of young children is a complex phenomenon dependent in part on the mothering experience and maturity of the parents and their ability to empathise with the infant's needs and respond to his dependency. This in turn is likely to be affected by the degree to which they are emotionally prepared for the parental role and the extent to which the helping professions and the community can respond to the relative isolation and loneliness of the nuclear family.

Early attachment between mother and infant is a theme of primary importance in good obstetric practice. The part played by stress and crisis, particularly when there is frequent childbearing and premature births, emphasises the need for skilled preventive services.

The possibility of identifying parents with diminished nurturing capacity is likely to emerge from current studies, which may in time lead to a more general recognition of the problems of emotional deprivation in parents, and the inter-generational implications of such deprivation. This in turn may help in the development of better services for abusive parents and their children.

DISCUSSION

The discussion took the Study Group deeply into relationships within the family, stressing especially the two bonds, that between husband and wife and that between mother and baby. The passive introverted husband from whom the wife, as mother of the family, can get little or no response, can drive her to desperation. Many factors damage the mother/baby bonding. Psychosis makes perhaps 10 per cent of mothers who damage their children not amenable to treatment or help. Obstetric and labour ward techniques need re-examination and to be judged in the light of their liability to weaken or to prevent bonding through physical separation and in other ways. A baby damped down by drugs fails to elicit the normal response from its mother. The whole apparatus of premature baby care frightens some mothers. The development of a normal, healthy relationship between mother and her new baby is too much taken for granted and if this be true for a normal mother and a normal baby, how much more important it is in the presence of abnormality or extra stress. Ultimately behavioural studies may reveal especially vulnerable mothers for whom the risk of neglect or abuse of a child is high. This discussion led to the resolution that the British Paediatric Association and the Royal College of Obstetricians and Gynaecologists should be asked together to survey current labour ward and perinatal practices giving the opportunity and the need for bonding its proper importance and examining especially anything which might interfere with its development.

6. Providing a service

Raymond L. Castle

> Every year in Britain 300 babies are battered to death by their
> parents and the number is increasing; of 500,000 babies born
> each year, 3,000 are beaten by their parents.
> Report in *Evening News*, 27.11.72

The above is one of several recent educated estimates made by concerned medical
consultants and others, probably based on cases they are seeing in their own
hospitals and regions.

Although there are no accurate figures available for the United Kingdom as a
whole, the National Society for the Prevention of Cruelty to Children has been
keeping a national registry of cases concerning children under the age of 4 years
suffering from non-accidental injury, and our most recent study (Castle and Kerr,
1972) showed that three times as many cases of suspected child abuse were being
referred to the agency in September 1969, as when the research department
published its first report (Skinner and Castle, 1969). This does not indicate an
increase in incidence but is rather an illustration of a growing recognition of the
problem and of better medical diagnosis in some areas. If we accept that this is
essentially a socio-medical problem which in a large number of instances could
be prevented, we should also recognise that growing awareness and better
medical diagnosis alone cannot resolve the problem but will merely serve to
bring it to our attention.

This paper examines some of the myths and realities of the battered child
syndrome and attempts to highlight some of the problems relevant to diagnosis,
management and treatment in this country at the present time.

RECOGNITION OF THE BATTERED CHILD

Among the many definitions made within the last few years, the most widely
accepted is that of Professor Henry Kempe who recently re-defined a battered
child as 'any child who received non-accidental physical injury (or injuries)
as a result of acts (or omissions) on the part of his parents or guardians'.

Let us now examine and hopefully dispel some of the current myths surround-
ing this problem.

The first suggests that this is a completely new phenomenon manifesting the
upsurge of violence in our present day society. The following examples illustrate
that, although the syndrome went unrecognised until quite recently, it has existed
for many years.

Dr. Samuel West, writing in the *British Medical Journal* of April 1, 1888, described acute swellings in several young infants of the same family. The matter came to his attention when a mother brought her 5-week-old baby to his surgery saying that for no reason his left arm had dropped and it appeared to be very painful. Examination showed that there were similar swellings on the right arm, left leg and ribs. It was suggested at the time that the infant had been the subject of intrauterine rickets, possibly caused by poor nutrition of the mother during pregnancy.

The second example is taken from an early edition of the National Society for the Prevention of Cruelty to Children's publication *The Child's Guardian*.

A young baby was seen by an Officer in Leicester in the year 1890 suffering from injuries to the face and mouth. Further medical examination revealed old injuries. This is a particularly interesting case as both the nature of the injuries and the comments of the mother, that she never wanted the baby and could not bear to look at it from the time it was born, are frequently encountered in our work today.

Another popular misconception is that parents who batter their children come exclusively from the lower socio-economic groups. We know from our own work and from research carried out in other countries that the syndrome is not confined to any one social class or socio-economic group but is present in all strata of society. It is probable that more cases come to our attention in the poorer sections of the community because these parents have fewer avenues of relief and in many instances tend to be under greater social stress occasioned by homelessness, bad housing or unemployment.

A third false assumption presupposes that all parents who batter their children must be psychopathic. An examination of the facts reveals that, at most, no more than 10 per cent could be diagnosed as actually suffering from any form of serious mental illness.

One of the most misleading myths is the assumption that all women want and will be able to accept the role of motherhood naturally. Very often attempts to help mothers under stress fail because it is so difficult to acknowledge that this is not the case.

THE BATTERED CHILD RESEARCH DEPARTMENT

Efforts are now in progress to examine the syndrome in a scientific manner. By 1967 the National Society for the Prevention of Cruelty to Children, together with certain members of the medical and legal professions, were becoming increasingly concerned at the number of very young children coming to notice with serious physical injuries for which there appeared to be no adequate explanation. In keeping with its pioneering tradition of service in this field, the Society decided to set up its own Battered Child Research project. It was to be the first of its kind in the country and would examine this complex problem in some depth using clinical research methods. The Research Department was established in October 1968 and is aided by a Scientific Advisory Committee, chaired by Professor Thomas Oppé, Director of the Paediatric Unit, St. Mary's Hospital Medical School. Very strong links have been formed with Professor Henry Kempe and his medical team in the United States and several exchange visits have been made. The knowledge accumulated by the Department has enabled its members to provide educative and consultative facilities to many agencies and bodies.

Two major research reports have already been produced, *78 Battered Children: a Retrospective Study* and *A Study of Suspected Child Abuse*. Both studies were carried out with the full co-operation of the Society's officers and the Department was fortunate in having nationwide information to call upon. Some of the more important findings are worthy of note.

Each study has emphasised the very young age at which the child of a battering parent is at risk. Over 50 per cent of children up to the age of 4 years were under 1 year of age. The younger the child, the more likely is it to be injured and the more serious is the injury likely to be. The high risk to a subsequent child in families where a first-born has been battered is a finding of particular importance. Records showed that in families where the first child was battered there was a 13 to 1 chance that a subsequent child would be injured. Another finding was a *re-battering instance of 60 per cent* for those children who remained at home after referral. In weighing the risks of supervised home care for the battered child against an alternative protective course of action, these factors should be borne in mind.

There are strong indications that bruises and injuries of a minor nature, particularly to the face and mouth of very young children, may signify the beginning of increasingly violent forms of injury. Trauma to the face may allow early diagnosis of a nurturing problem, modification of which might avert serious injury.

In both studies there have been very low rates of referral from general practitioners (3·87 of all referrals in the initial report and only 2·39 in the most recent). 2 out of every 5 children in our sample admitted to hospital because of injury had previously been injured to an extent sufficient to warrant medical attention which has invariably been given by the family doctor.

As part of its clinical programme, a 24-hour service is provided to the hospitals and community of three London boroughs. Families are referred for help at any time of the day or night when a child under the age of 4 years has received injuries serious enough to require medical attention and inflicted injury is suspected. The facilities include a therapeutic day nursery where, in addition to the special needs of the children, some of the needs of the parents are met by encouraging their informal attendance. A regular group meeting for some of the mothers has arisen from this. The on-call service, which is also available to parents, underlines a flexibility and availability which experience has shown is of major importance in treatment, particularly at times of stress and crisis.

Close contact with the families reveals that in many cases the parents themselves were subjected to a consistent experience of disapproval and rejection from early childhood. Whatever they did was never enough to gratify their own parents and they have grown up feeling denigrated and worthless. It has been said that 'throughout life they have pathetically yearned for good mothering, returning again and again to their mother, seeking for it but not finding it and ending up with disappointment, disillusionment, lowered self-esteem and anger' (Anthony and Benedek, 1970). Because of their unmet dependency needs, they are acutely vulnerable to anything they perceive as being critical and have extremely low tolerance of any form of rejection. Unfortunately instances are frequently seen where stress is considerably roused in the parents, to the detriment of the child, when the person trying to assist the family is insensitive to this particularly dangerous area.

If prevention of injury or of re-injury is the aim, the parents must be given, within the context of a professional relationship, some of the emotional nurturing that has been so sadly lacking. They should be helped to feel that they can turn to someone in periods of crisis and that at these times, in contrast to their earlier experiences, uncritical support and practical help will be offered.

SOME PRACTICAL DIFFICULTIES

Taking the foregoing factors into consideration, some of the difficulties that arise within the community regarding diagnosis, management and treatment can now be considered.

Delays in referral

Despite some regional improvements and the wide distribution of a memorandum prepared by the Department of Health and Social Security (DHSS, 1970) aimed at increasing the awareness of the battered child syndrome and giving advice to hospital staff on the steps that should be taken, there continue to be long delays before referrals are made to the appropriate authorities. In the case from the Research Department, described on page 118, not only was there a delay of nearly three months between injury and referral to a social work agency, but no attempt was made to call a case conference in order to discuss the family's needs.

Problems of co-ordination

Very often there is a failure to recognise that effective treatment can only be achieved by a multi-disciplinary approach and co-ordinated plans for management. The case conference could fulfil this function but can only work effectively if members are able to see themselves as part of a team and are prepared to recognise each other's professional expertise.

Communication difficulties

Frequently communication breaks down because clearly defined, easy to follow procedures do not exist. In the case described, the casualty officer had no knowledge of previous injury to the child and no way of finding this information easily even though the hospital had been involved with the family over a long period.

INADEQUACIES IN THE PROVISION OF COMMUNITY SOCIAL SERVICES

At present there continues to be a high rate of re-injury to children originally referred to both statutory and independent agencies after medical diagnosis of inflicted injury. An alarming number of these children subsequently die as a result of their injuries and others suffer permanent brain damage. There is still a lack of recognition of the needs of the families involved and a failure to provide the kind of service which can be meaningful to the parents and can effectively prevent a recurrence of injury. The situation is further confused by the effects of reorganisation in local authority social service departments and the shortage of social workers with adequate training and specialised skills in child care to work with clients or to supervise volunteers.

The NSPCC has recognised the great need for skilled specialised social work assistance in dealing with this problem, and is prepared to set up specialised treatment units. However, an organisation which depends on voluntary contributions from the public can only make this kind of provision if adequate funds are made available from official sources.

The difficulties of management and treatment require a brief look at the parts played by juvenile court magistrates and the police.

The role of the juvenile court

Accepting that our primary concern must be the welfare and continued safety of the child at risk, the juvenile court magistrates will often be involved during the initial stages of treatment. As was pointed out in a recent research report (Castle et al., 1972), 'Some of the records studied indicated that use of the juvenile court, which could offer protection to both the child and the parents from their own actions, was sometimes delayed, occasionally with tragic results'. Even when cases are brought before the courts, many children are not offered the protection they require and are returned home because the court feels that there is insufficient evidence to fulfil the requirements of the law. Such children often reappear before the court within a short time, following a more serious re-injury.

Sometimes decisions are made and the child is sent home under supervision without the magistrates realising the full implications for both the child and the family. The present legislation concerned with the protection of children needs to be reviewed and possibly revised to cover the points mentioned. More should be done to help magistrates take advantage of the increased knowledge about this syndrome, so that they are more aware of significant features when they make legal decisions. Perhaps, too, some guide-lines, similar to those sent out by the Department of Health and Social Security in their memorandum on the subject to hospitals, could be prepared and sent to juvenile court panels.

The role of the police

This is probably the most difficult and sensitive area when it comes to co-ordination and co-operation. In a few regions enlightened senior police officers have done much to foster co-operation. In the majority of areas, co-ordination has not been possible because police officers take the view that if information is placed before them at a review committee, case conference or in any other professional situation, which leads them to suspect that a criminal offence has been committed, they must investigate the matter immediately. This means that quite often bringing a case before a juvenile court as part of a co-ordinated plan is followed by a police investigation with the possibility that criminal sanctions are applied to the parents with all the resultant trauma. Little change can be expected in this sphere without some guidance from the Home Office to senior police officers. There is a need, too, to train specially selected police officers to work in co-ordination with review committees and case conferences.

Effective treatment and prevention rests on the mutual recognition of professional expertise and the maintenance of communication. A co-ordinated team can do much to break down the artificial barriers that sometimes inhibit the provision of service to these families.

A CASE REPORT

Parents: Father aged 20, unemployed labourer
  Mother aged 19, housewife (pregnant at time of marriage)

Child: Male, born 30.12.71

Date of referral: 20.3.72

Child's medical history prior to referral

(a) First admitted to hospital at two weeks of age—diagnosis 'failure to thrive'. No attempt was made to ascertain if there were any social difficulties and child discharged home to parents after four days with no follow-up.

(b) Re-admitted to hospital at seven weeks of age with severe bruising. Explanation that child had fallen out of cot. This explanation was apparently accepted.

(c) At 11 weeks of age child suffered severe bruising to head, said to have been caused 'possibly by rough handling'.

(d) Two or three days later the child was seen with further injuries to the head. Father said he had caught the child's head accidentally on a door whilst carrying him.

(e) A week later the baby suffered yet another injury to the head. On this occasion (17.3.72) he was admitted to hospital and the paediatrician ordered full skeletal X-rays. These showed that, in addition to bruising on his face, the baby had old healing fractures of the fifth, sixth and seventh ribs. Parents' explanation was that he had fallen from a low settee to a carpeted floor.

Three days later, on 20.3.72, it was decided by the hospital to refer the matter to a community agency, in this case the National Society for the Prevention of Cruelty to Children.

The Society initiated care proceedings and after a long hearing the juvenile court decided that a two year supervision order should be made to the local authority and that the child should be returned to the care of his parents.

Child's medical history subsequent to juvenile court proceedings and supervision order

May 1. Child admitted to hospital after having convulsions. A tentative diagnosis of meningitis was made. Shortly afterwards child restored to parents' care.

May 22. Health visitor making routine visit, having been advised by hospital that child had been discharged home, saw that child had severe bruising to face and mouth. Persuaded parents to go with her to welfare clinic where doctor advised immediate visit to casualty department. Child said to be drowsy. Physical examination in casualty showed no bone injury. The casualty officer, having no knowledge of child's history, advised parents to return in 24 hours for X-rays.

Fortunately, the health visitor had alerted the social worker concerned, who in turn contacted the paediatrician at his home.

The paediatrician was able to reach the hospital just as the parents were about to leave and ordered the child's immediate admission. Medical investigation showed a subdural haematoma and further injuries to the ribs.

June 8. The parents removed the child against the advice of the doctor, saying that they did not like either the hospital or the paediatrician.

The NSPCC was again called on, this time the officer having to search the streets for the family because they had 'taken flight'.

He found them and persuaded them to allow him to return the child to hospital. A place of safety order was obtained and the matter brought before the juvenile. court. On this occasion a care order was made.

In this paper the author is expressing his own views and his opinions based on personal experiences. They are not necessarily the official views of the National Society for the Prevention of Cruelty to Children.

DISCUSSION

Ray Castle's paper and that of Joan Court were taken together. A wide-ranging discussion followed, but in this presentation the comments and questions directed to Ray Castle have been transferred to the discussions about identification of families, about their management in casualty departments, about the legal problems and about reporting. The special units of the NSPCC were recognised as setting an excellent example and as performing an invaluable function in the community. Much guidance for both primary and secondary prevention is anticipated from the research studies now in progress.

Part Three

Two Views from the Police

17. *The police role*

James Collie

When a social problem involves more than one discipline there can be a tendency for the services involved, all of whom are trying to achieve the same end, to pull in different directions. This may be so in 'battered baby' cases. The end to be achieved is a happy healthy child. The different professional workers involved are the medical profession, social workers working for the local authorities, the medical services and the NSPCC and the police.

THE BATTERED CHILD SYNDROME

The phrase 'battered child syndrome' was probably intended by Dr. Kempe to be highly emotive so as to draw the attention of the medical and allied professions to the condition where young children have suffered serious physical abuse at the hands of their parents or from parental substitutes. These children, usually between a few weeks and 3 years old, are incapable of speaking for themselves.

The attacks may occur at frequent or infrequent intervals, and an estimate of between three and four times a year in some cases is given. Recent studies in this country and in America estimate that at least 10 per cent and possibly even 20 per cent of the babies who are attacked die; and about 30 per cent sustain permanent brain damage or physical injury which cripples them for life.

The condition is not easy to diagnose. Very often the injuries are consistent with the explanation given by the parents. Understandably it is difficult to believe that a parent would deliberately physically attack a young baby. A doctor not only faces the difficulty of diagnosis. He may find the explanation given by the parent difficult to believe. He may have suspicions but he has nothing in the way of proof and no means of establishing proof. The danger of rebattering arises when a child, who has been treated for, say, an alleged fall downstairs or a fall from a pram, is returned home.

Doctors find their difficulty with confidentiality made all the more difficult in cases where there is no proof that the child has been assaulted but only grave suspicion; or where it is not clear who within the family may be responsible.

In the majority of cases suspicion is first aroused when a child is taken to hospital for treatment. A great deal of attention has been given to the syndrome by hospital paediatric departments, and social workers have contributed much to the management of the condition. It is depressing that some of the experts in this disorder are forensic pathologists. Procedures must be devised to remedy or reduce the syndrome so that the number of cases available to pathologists will show a steady decline.

Many doctors call in the medical social worker at the hospital to make background reports. These enquiries are usually delicate and may prove ineffectual because the parents are not prepared to co-operate. When the child is ready for discharge the social work department of the local authority, which has a statutory responsibility for the welfare of the child, should be informed so that a decision can be made about the future custody of the child. Their workers have to decide whether the child may be safely returned home or whether he should be placed in the care of the local authority, either by an order of the Juvenile Court or by informal arrangement under Section 1 of the Children Act, 1948. In some cases the NSPCC is informed so that supervision may be given on a voluntary basis.

The NSPCC in its study entitled *78 Battered Children* (1969) commented 'The unsatisfactory aftercare arrangements made by many hospitals despite the evidence of repeated unexplained injury is disturbing. Two out of every five children admitted because of injury had previously been injured to an extent sufficient to warrant medical attention. Three out of every five who were discharged home after hospital treatment had to be re-admitted on account of subsequent injury', and 'The efficacy of investigation procedures frequently described in the records is questionable.' (Page 20.)

In an article in the *British Medical Journal* of March 5, 1966, it was considered that the decision whether the police should be informed of cases was ethically very difficult, but acknowledged at the same time that doctors have a duty as citizens as well as medical advisers. One example was given in which the doctor might inform the police so as to obtain a place of safety warrant when parents insisted on removing from hospital a child whose injuries gave rise to suspicions that the injury was deliberately inflicted by the parents. In general it was suggested that the children's department might be the more appropriate body to be informed and to inform the police.

THE POLICE

The extent to which the police should be informed has generated considerable heat. The situation is widely polarised: on the one hand there are those who maintain that under no cicumstances whatsoever should the police ever become involved; at the other extreme there are police forces who insist that since physical injury of a child is a crime, the concealment of these cases is unlawful, and all injuries to children should be reported to them.

The police are not opposed to the general desire to preserve the family as a unit into which the child can be happily integrated, and to avoid prosecution where guidance or supervision is sufficient. The police have, however, a clear responsibility to investigate assaults and woundings, and any delay in the commencement of an investigation is likely to lead to the loss or even suppression of essential evidence. It has to be remembered that the law is primarily for the protection of society and not merely for punishment. Indeed a child who has been assaulted is entitled to an even greater protection since in addition to the Offences Against the Person Act, 1861, the Children and Young Persons Act, 1933, made it a specific offence for anyone over the age of 16 years having custody, charge, control or care of a child under that age to assault, ill-treat or neglect him.

The most important factor, which must outweigh all other considerations however valid, is the protection of children from serious maiming of mind and/or body or from the loss of life. This issue is often lost sight of by those reluctant to notify the police. The police have the facilities, training and experience for verifying the accounts given by parents, but it is essential that the cases are reported at an early stage so that the truth of the matter can be reached. Delay may deprive police of the opportunity to gather important evidence, which could well be to the advantage of the parent. For to leave a parent under a grave and undeserved suspicion is doing him intolerable injustice.

Delay in notification to the police may also result in the unavailability of adequate evidence to present at any subsequent trial and in the acquittal of a parent when, in all the circumstances, conviction might have been in the best interests of the child and his family. Courts of law not only consider punishment, but after the establishment of the facts, are just as concerned as any of the social agencies with the help, support and the psychological condition of the offender.

Cases reported to the police are treated in every way as seriously by them as by the medical profession. A senior CID officer will be in charge of the case, and officers qualified by training, with experience and an understanding of cases of this type are deputed to investigate them. Indeed they are recognised as difficult cases and the resources applied to their investigation would do justice to murder enquiries. Should there be evidence against a parent the decision to prosecute will be taken either at a senior police level or by the Director of Public Prosecutions, and then only after careful consideration of all relevant issues.

CONCLUSIONS

The crux of the difficulties may be a lack of appropriate arrangements for communication between the various professional staff, including the police, who are involved with child abuse. There is an obvious need for an agreed system for early notification of suspected cases. The doctors ought to have available such information as may be in the possession of the police and social workers, instead of having to act, as it sometimes appears, as investigator, judge, jury and even reformer.

The police, the doctors and the social workers should be involved together and the best decision is likely to be reached when there is understanding and co-operation between them. This understanding clearly depends on close consultation and, following the recommendation in the joint Home Office and Department of Health and Social Security circular (32/70), the majority of review committees now include police representation at senior level, but few case conferences ever include a police representative.

SUMMARY

The police view is that it is essential:

1 For police to be informed of 'suspected battered child' cases at an early stage through an accepted and adequately known system of reporting.

2 For only experienced, trained officers with an understanding of these cases to be appointed to investigate them, and

3 For the establishment of recognised and open consultation between all the disciplines concerned.

4 The decision as to proceedings must remain with the police at a senior level in cases not dealt with by the Director of Public Prosecutions, but account should be taken of all the attendant circumstances, and police of senior rank should attend at review committees.

18. Offences of criminal violence, cruelty and neglect against children in Lancashire

Joseph Mounsey

What this Seminar is pleased to call 'non-accidental injuries' to children are usually crimes classified by the law of this land under one of the following headings:

murder	child destruction
attempted murder	wounding
manslaughter	assaults
infanticide	cruelty to children and young persons

I believe that we are only aware of the tip of the iceberg. Large numbers of medical practitioners, social workers, and others similarly and devotedly dealing with 'non-accidental injury' to children fail in an important citizen's duty. To call the police is more often than not a last resort.

Last year in Lancashire our first sight of 22 of these innocent and vulnerable victims was on the mortuary slab. Doctors are bothered about their medical ethics and social workers are troubled that the policeman's size 12 boots and philistine approach to life will disrupt the delicate business of rehabilitation. Policemen are not unsympathetic to the cause of those who have difficulty in coping with the stresses of their particular environment. We all know and sometimes have been able to help the woman struggling to bring up a large family with the splendid and sole support of a drunken thief as her helpmate. We are well aware that environmental stress can be a primary cause of the commission of this type of crime by 'inadequates' and the last thing we want to do is to interfere with the work done by the social agencies to enable these folk to cope with ordinary life. However, we also know about cruelty, and in my view it is still a sad fact that there is too much regard for the offender and too little for the victim. My duties as a policeman include, as a high priority, the protection of life and the prevention of crime. There should never be a case where an abused child, whose condition has been brought to the notice of any medical/social agency, is returned to the same domestic environment for further punishment. This happens all too frequently. I would like to stress that we believe that communication between all the agencies involved in dealing with this problem is a matter of tremendous importance. Of all the variety of crimes in the UK, those involving the 'non-accidental injury' to children are surely those most worthy of urgent preventive measures.

We have made a survey of the cases brought to police notice in Lancashire during 1972. I do not know what percentage this comprises of the true total. The survey included all cases of injury, no matter how slight, cases of neglect or where children were felt to be at risk from birth up to and including the age of 13 years.

Variously we received information of 105 suspected cases of child abuse, which concerned 166 children. The first consideration in the survey was the age of the child in relation to the degree of injury or neglect, and of the 166 children involved 22 of the 26 fatal cases resulted in someone appearing before a court. 36 had serious injuries whilst 13 were injured slightly, 75 children were neglected and the remaining 16 were considered to be at risk. The majority of the fatality and injury cases involved children within the first two or three years of their life.

The age of the persons responsible was analysed and the danger ages appeared to be up to 26 and over 35 years.

The marital status of the mother was considered and this analysis first showed what appeared to be an unusual trend in that of the 105 cases almost half were in families where the mother was married to and living with her husband. A further check was made on the incidence of domestic unrest within the various units, and when this was superimposed on the previously mentioned figures the picture became somewhat clearer. Our enquiries showed that of the 35 'no domestic unrest' cases there were only 21 where there was reasonable evidence to prove this fact. In 14 cases it was impossible to get a 'yea' or a 'nay' to the question. It would perhaps be of assistance if I explained the term 'domestic unrest' in this context. These were cases of domestic disputes which have come to the notice of the police and are the subject of a report. They were not the minor altercations which serve to add spice to normal marital relationships.

The sources of reference to the police were investigated and showed that by far the majority were from neighbours and close relations. A very small proportion were referred by social agencies and of the 19 cases referred by doctors, no less than 16 were made by Dr. Hall of Preston Royal Infirmary, and this perhaps indicates more than any other fact the crying need for co-operation and communication between organisations having to deal with the problem.

The foregoing facts paint a gloomy picture of the situation as it prevails today and it would be of great assistance to compare these figures with statistics for previous years. Unfortunately, we are precluded from doing this, as the information available regarding past years is insufficient to provide a comparable study. One area which can be compared relates to the death of young children. To go back but one decade, in 1962 the police in Lancashire had reported to them 6 cases of homicide, of which one related to a child. Five years later in 1967, the figures were 21 homicides reported, 6 relating to children; and for 1972, 49 homicides were reported, 22 of which related to children. Although allowances must be made for the reorganisation of police boundaries in 1969 whereby the Lancashire Constabulary area was increased, these cold hard facts accurately portray the alarming increase in death by violence, particularly in relation to children.

These are the only figures we have available, but it is a safe assumption that 'non-accidental' injuries to children and the other categories analysed in the survey have shown a comparable increase. During the same ten-year period crimes and other forms of lawlessness have shown a marked increase but the rise in crimes against children has been little less than meteoric. It is obvious from all this that the preventive measures being taken at present are inadequate. Surely the time is right for an overhaul of the systems employed by everyone concerned. One of the main problems in the past has been the lack of communication and consultation between the social, medical and police organisations involved, and there is an overwhelming need for all disciplines to break down the conventional barriers of confidentiality, and combine in a concerted effort to protect the innocent victims.

I would reiterate that we appreciate that there are many sociological and environmental factors which affect the actions of persons who commit this type of offence against young children, but the protection of the child must nevertheless always be paramount. In some, if not most, cases this must inevitably lead to the prosecution of the offender; indeed, in my view in many cases this is the only form of action which will ensure that the necessary attention and treatment will be given to the offender, whether it be by imprisonment or medical/social agency help. I make a plea that the police should not be looked upon as merely prosecutors to be called in when all else has failed. We should be informed of all cases of apparent 'non-accidental' injury to children, so that a thorough investigation can be made into the case. Ideally this involves full consultation with any other agency able to assist in building up a full picture of all the relevant information which will ensure that the correct action is taken in the best interests of the child. I am afraid that at present in many areas this close co-operation and consultation does not exist. Only in extreme cases of serious injury, or as all too often happens, in the case of death, are the police brought into the matter.

Faced with a similar problem I understand that the United States has introduced laws requiring that every physician, medical worker, or social worker, having reason to believe that a child has serious injury or injuries inflicted upon him as a result of abuse or neglect, must report such cases to one of the law enforcement or one of the social agencies. Such reporting is mandatory in all but four states and some states impose a penalty for non-compliance. If co-operation is not forthcoming for the voluntary reporting of such cases, it may be that the time will arrive in this country when similar legislation will have to be enacted, but we hope that such compulsion will not be necessary and that satisfactory results can be achieved on a voluntary basis. All too often unilateral action has to be taken by the police, simply because other agencies involved are not prepared to co-operate.

Looking to the future, we in the Lancashire Police Force have realised that there should be a focal point, within the service, having special responsibility for such cases. We are using our Juvenile Liaison Department, the personnel of which are already involved with many of the organisations concerned with the problem of the 'battered baby' and the 'abused child'. This branch has recently been given responsibility for collating and assessing information on all cases brought to our notice. We are building up a comprehensive index; I hope it will not only be policemen who will use it or make useful contributions. The members of Juvenile Liaison have also the responsibility to act as liaison officers between the police and any outside body involved in the care and treatment of victims and offenders.

We promise tact, understanding and communication. Perhaps one day our combined efforts may achieve a measure of prevention.

DISCUSSION

Free communication with the police is one of the most sensitive areas in management and the Study Group listened attentively to the statements of the police point of view so ably and so genially given in these two talks. Those who favoured a total collaboration were heartened and those who did not were compelled to think again. Collaboration was manifestly impossible if the police were punitive in outlook and inflexible in interrogation. It appeared that discussions with the Home Office might help to soften attitudes in relation to the agreed aims, namely to protect the child and the siblings, to rehabilitate the family whenever this seemed possible, and only at the bottom of the list to prosecute.

Further education of the policeman is desirable. Already the CID is trained in recognising non-accidental injury, but in general the young constable in the sensitive age period 18 to 20 years is not. He could be the first man called in to the family. The police often hold valuable information in their files especially about 'families come to notice', that would help the decision-making. The question of when to involve the police remained unanswered, but the need to explore the question was recognised in a resolution to approach the Home Office and possibly later some of the police associations.

Part Four

Legal Aspects

19. Should reporting be mandatory?

Hugh Bevan

Professor Bevan spoke as an academic lawyer and acknowledged his debt to Jean Stark.

The problems that mandatory reporting has produced in the United States should not deter us from seriously considering statutory reporting in the United Kingdom. There were five questions to be asked:

1 Should there be a legal duty to report?
2 What should be the scope of the reporting?
3 On whom would the duty fall to report?
4 How may this duty be discharged?
5 What would be the object of reporting?

The interests of the child should be paramount and the object of reporting would be detection followed by promotion of the interests of the child, the reduction of the risk of re-battering and in a few cases the securing of a conviction. There was no legal duty on a citizen to report a crime with the exception of treason.

In discussing the scope he asked whether the person with the duty of reporting, when he suspected injury, should confine his thoughts to clinical injury and if so how much injury should there be before a report was made. Should it be on reasonable grounds or on some degree of suspicion? If the child's interests were paramount, any suspicion should be enough. There would have to be some sanction for failure to report and also an immunity from legal liability. The only exception, if reporting were made statutory on rather tenuous grounds, would be where there was a malicious reporting. He thought that mental cruelty should be included. There would need to be some guidance as to what constituted suspicious circumstances.

As regards the agency reporting, this would primarily be the medical profession, but it could be wider and include other agencies such as the coroner. Reporting should be to both the law enforcement (police) and the child protection (local authority) agency.

Professor Bevan then put forward the suggestion that there should be a new office of 'children's guardian'. The guardian would stand up for children's rights and attempt to protect their interests as his primary duty. The other agencies tend to be too involved in what is going on, since they have the double duty of recommending and providing the service. The guardian should be a social worker of experience who had some legal training. Possibly he might act as the chairman of the committee that safeguards the family when discussions of management were being held. Clearly there would need to be a mutual sharing of information and the closest touch with the social services and the police. His office could be used as the registry.

As regards the technique of reporting there might be a national adoption of the voluntary arrangement that exists in Preston. Other possibilities would be Ministerial circulars or making it a statutory duty.

A NOTE BY SUPERINTENDENT INGRAM

Two possible solutions exist to the problem of incomplete co-operation between professional bodies in notifying information. These are mandatory notification and mutual trust. The former raises difficult problems of enforcement, of punishment for failure to notify and of professional fees. Mutual trust, on the lines of the Preston liaison, is the only alternative and would need guaranteed continuity.

All professionals concerned would have to understand why the information was required and the purposes for which it would be used. The type of information to be notified could not be defined. The common sense of the professional body involved would settle whether notification should rest on suspicion or on anything more definite.

With statutory notification the number of known cases would undoubtedly increase. What the Superintendent favours is a reiteration of the guidance contained in Home Office Circular number 32/1970 which encouraged discussions to be initiated by medical officers of health and children's officers when the question arises of injury of young children by their parents. These duties would in future fall on community physicians and the directors of social services departments.

DISCUSSION

No decision was reached on the question of mandatory reporting. On the one hand some felt that this would improve the prospects of proper communication between the professionals involved in a case. Others believed that notification by itself unsupported by action accomplished nothing. It might indeed place obstacles in the way of good management. Medical freedom of action would be impeded. Families might be even more afraid of the consequences of seeking help or might panic and leave the area. The essentials were the case conference at which information would be exchanged and the growth of trust between the individual workers and the agencies which they represented. There were difficult problems of who should report what to whom.

A local register was a different matter. Experiences were exchanged between those who already used such registers all of whom found them helpful. Questions to be resolved were where the register should be kept, in medical or in social service hands, who would have access to it, how would in- and out-patient services in hospital make use of it and who would be responsible for keeping it up-to-date. It was decided to form a sub-committee which continues to study the whole matter.

Reporting or notification, central or local, raised questions of confidentiality and the following legal opinion was quoted.

'On the narrow legal issue about confidentiality, you can take it that in practical terms there is really no possibility of the parent of any injured child obtaining any remedy against the doctor who participated in consultations of this kind. The confidential relationship as between doctor and patient is, according to the law, not an absolute one and a doctor is entitled to break the confidence in certain circumstances; one of these is where he feels under a social obligation to do so. There is the additional point that in these cases the practitioner also owes a duty of care to his patient (i.e. the child) and, by failing to participate in the consultation, he may be in breach of that duty of care.'

20. Court proceedings

Jean Graham-Hall

This paper sets out the types of court procedure now available in cases of non-accidental injury to children, deals with their jurisdiction or relevance, and discusses whether or not more suitable procedures could be devised.

PRE-COURT CONSIDERATIONS

The battered child syndrome is first of all a medical occurrence, and is part of a much wider spectrum of non-accidental injury to children including physical, mental and psychological injury. The phenomenon has many social overtones. The fact must be faced that medical and social welfare considerations on the one hand, and legal rights and safeguards on the other, do not always appear to have a mutually satisfactory solution.

Before any case comes to court, whether as a criminal charge against an adult and/or a care or control case of the child, the police or other authorised prosecuting authority exercises a discretion whether to bring proceedings. When they have ascertained all the relevant facts, they decide what action is appropriate. In exercising this discretion, the seriousness of the allegations, the likelihood of recurrence, the probability of the case being proved are, *inter alia*, taken into account.

Sometimes doctors and social workers appear reluctant to notify any authority if they consider this might result in the parent being prosecuted. They do not want to leave this discretion to the police, and wish to keep the matter in their own hands. By reserving to themselves this discretion of whether to pass on any information, they may thereby deprive the child of his legal rights of protection.

THE CURRENT SYSTEM OF JURISDICTION

Two separate types of proceedings can result from the investigation of the alleged non-accidental injury to children:

1 Criminal proceedings against one or both parents or guardians in the adult courts;
2 Care proceedings in respect of the child, in the juvenile courts.

Each court has a different jurisdiction and a different basis for trial and disposal. There is a clear distinction between the rights and legal safeguards of a person accused of a criminal offence and welfare considerations for the care of the child. The legal rights, the high burden of proof on the prosecution to prove their case, the right of the accused to remain silent, the right to have certain prejudicial evidence excluded—these are the same whatever type of case is brought in an adult criminal court.

Criminal proceedings commence in the magistrates' court for the area in which the alleged offence occurred. The majority of cases are completed in the magistrates' courts. Most of the cases of non-accidental injury to children are brought under the Children and Young Persons Act 1933.

By The Children and Young Persons Act, 1933, Section 1, any person who has attained the age of 16 years and has the custody, charge or care of any child or young person under that age and wilfully assaults, ill-treats, neglects, abandons or exposes him or causes or procures him to be assaulted, ill-treated, abandoned or exposed in a manner likely to cause him unnecessary suffering or injury to health (including injury to or loss of sight or hearing or limb or organ of the body) shall be guilty of an offence. The maximum penalty on summary conviction is £100 fine and/or six months' imprisonment. On indictment, i.e., trial by jury in the Crown Court, the maximum penalty is £100 fine and/or two years' imprisonment. The accused person has this right of trial by jury. If the charge is brought under Section 18 of The Offences against the Person Act, 1861 of grievous bodily harm with intent to injury (a charge not confined to such harm to children) the magistrates' court cannot try the case.

In sentencing the parents, the criminal courts have the same wide powers as they have for all those found guilty of criminal offences. By the Criminal Justice Act, 1972, Section 14 there are now restrictions on imprisonment of a person who has not previously served prison sentences. The court must be of the opinion that no other method of dealing with him is appropriate and, for the purpose of determining this, must obtain and consider information about the circumstances and also any information which is relevant to his character and his physical and mental condition.

At the same time as the criminal proceedings are taking place against the adult, the child is brought before the juvenile court for the same area, under the Children and Young Persons Act, 1969. If the juvenile court is of the opinion:

1 That the proper development of the child is being avoidably prevented or neglected or his health is being avoidably impaired or neglected or he is being ill-treated, and also
2 That he is need of care or control which he is unlikely to receive unless the court makes an order, then the court may make a court order or supervision order for the child.

SOME CRITICISMS OF THE CURRENT JURISDICTION

There often appears to be an unfortunate lack of liaison between the adult and juvenile courts. Unless specific enquiries are made, it frequently happens that the bench of one court has no idea what is happening or has happened in the other. The authorities usually preserve a discreet silence in the apparent belief that it would be improper to mention any other proceedings in connection with the same set of facts.

Difficulties also arise on disposal. A care or supervision order of the child in the juvenile court is made to the local authority, which has no responsibility to the court. A supervision order in the magistrates' court or Crown Court is made in the form of a probation order.

Whichever type of supervision order is in existence, the court which made it does not have any power unless the supervisor takes the case back to it. When an order is made in care proceedings, the supervisor can go back to the juvenile court and suggest that, in the light of events which have occurred since the order was made, a care order should be substituted. Where a probation order is made, the supervisor has to prove a breach and then the parents can be dealt with in any way in which they could have been dealt with on conviction.

Should it be made legally possible to have one supervision order of both parents and the child, with the same supervisor? This would remedy the situation in which otherwise there may be two different authorities supervising the home under two different court orders. It would not solve the difficulty which is inherent in all supervision orders, namely that no supervisor can be with the child and the family for more than a fraction of the time. A supervision order, therefore, must take the parents on trust a good deal.

Should medical supervision of the child not be able to be made part of the court order? It is a pre-requisite to the making of a probation order that the adult agrees to keep the term of the order. Considering the frequency with which non-accidental injury to children is said to recur, the child might be better protected if the parents were required to take him at regular intervals to a named medical practitioner for examination and assessment.

WOULD A 'FAMILY COURT' OFFER ANY SOLUTION?

Could all proceedings be conducted in the same court? Can the two distinct types of procedure be reconciled? At first glance an attractive solution appears to be that all proceedings be merged in a 'family court'. This begs the question: What is a family court and what should be its jurisdiction?

On August 4, 1971, the Lord Chancellor announced the setting up by the Law Commission of a Working Party to consider what kind of court, below the level of High Court, should deal with family matters. The Working Party, of which I am a member, continues its deliberations.

At the beginning of 1972, the Working Party stated that it had made a tentative and somewhat arbitrary classification of the expression 'family matters', i.e. 'Our present thinking is that the expression should include consents to marry, divorce, nullity, judicial separation and ancillary relief; presumption of death and dissolution of marriage; declaration of status (legitimacy, legitimation and validity of marriage); magistrates' matrimonial orders; maintenance during marriage; occupation of the matrimonial home; wardship; guardianship; adoption, affiliation. It should not include any criminal proceedings or proceedings arising from offences by children and young persons. No view has yet been formed as to whether it should include certain other matters such as: care proceedings, summonses under the Ministry of Social Security Act 1966; torts between members of a family. This classification is by no means final.'

Any criminal proceedings against adults are clearly excluded by the Working Party's definition of 'family matters'. Further, there has been a repeated and strong plea to remove family matters from the criminal atmosphere of magistrates courts.

The primary object of the Working Party may be seen in the light of recent words by the Lord Chancellor. At the opening of the Wandsworth County Court on March 2, 1973, he said, 'Though it is not, and in this Parliament is unlikely to become, Government policy, I would personally like to rationalise the jurisdictional jungle in the matrimonial and family fields which covers the civil jurisdiction of the magistrates', the county court and the High Court.'

The transfer to any family court of the whole of the jurisdiction of the juvenile court would include both its criminal and civil jurisdiction. Unless one contemplated a special juvenile division in the pattern of some fully comprehensive family court, this would be open to the same criticism to which I have already referred, i.e. of permitting criminal proceedings in a court specifically committed to a non-criminal atmosphere.

A transfer to family courts of all care proceedings might leave our present juvenile courts sadly truncated. A particular case could be made out for including all cases of children under 10 years to be dealt with in a family court. This would include all children under the age of criminal responsibility, Proceedings in juvenile courts in respect of children under 10 years are exclusively civil proceedings.

SUMMARY

One must decide what kind of court proceedings are necessary in the case of non-accidental injury to children.

Criminal proceedings should and must follow in certain cases and the discretion whether or not to prosecute should be fully exercised by the police.

The child needs some protection. In some cases, this can be given by the action of the local authority in taking the child into care under Section 1 of The Children Act, 1948, without any court action. In other cases, legal protection of the child will require care proceedings. Within the present constitution of our courts, this can be done in the juvenile court.

Doubts may be entertained as to whether a finalised juvenile court order is necessary where criminal proceedings, successful or not, are instituted against the adult. One could contemplate the possibility of an interim order being made by the juvenile court when the matter first arises, and the finalised order being eventually made by the adult court. This would avoid the duplication of court proceedings, but it would require fresh legislation.

21. Battered children cases in the courts

Winifred Cavenagh

'We could not get the local authority *or the court* (italics ours) to take out a care order. The parents insisted on having him back.' This remark by a hospital doctor is quoted in the *Birmingham Post* of November 21, 1973, and refers to a case in which a child was eventually taken into care under a court order but only after the third of three siblings had died 'in mysterious circumstances'. Without knowing anything of the particular case under discussion these remarks do seem to embody some misunderstanding about the role of a court (which in fact has no power to take the initiative in proceedings) and also something of the anxiety and frustration which is being widely felt in relation to the powers available in so-called battered children cases at all stages. The intention in this article is to look at the problem from the point of view of the lay magistrates' court, with reference to other aspects only as they relate to the question of court proceedings.

From the point of view of the courts the subject does not bulk large, numerically speaking. For example, in Birmingham where between seven and ten adult plus one or two juvenile courts sit daily it appears that something between one and two dozen only of such cases are brought annually. An enquiry in London suggests that the incidence there may be somewhat greater. The number of court cases in any area is likely to be influenced by factors such as the policy of the agencies concerned locally, but enquiry in the less densely populated parts of the country suggests that in terms of petty sessional divisions the vast majority of magistrates have no court experience of these cases whatsoever and are quite likely never to have any. This low incidence compared, for instance, with shoplifting, soliciting for prostitution, and on the juvenile side truancy or care cases generally, points to the difficulty of expecting much instruction specifically on this matter to be included in the basic training of magistrates. It is, as in any other case, for the parties to draw the court's attention to the meaning and significance of particular points in the evidence. A lay bench is in a particularly good position to insist on the explanation of jargon or technical phrases and terms in ordinary language which both they and the defendant or respondent can understand. It is also probably unnecessary to point out that the term 'battered baby' is unknown to the law, yet the writer has heard an expert giving evidence ask the court to 'accept that we have here a battered baby *syndrome*'.

CRIMINAL PROCEEDINGS

Grounds for legal action may result in either civil or criminal proceedings and sometimes both. The criminal case is brought in the adult court since the point at issue is whether or not the adult has rendered himself liable to be dealt with under the criminal law. The case is usually brought under the Children and Young Persons Act, 1933, Section 1, on the ground of cruelty of a specified kind, and is usually completed in the magistrates' court. In a very few cases and where there is a definite wound the charge is brought under the Offences Against the Person Act, 1861, Section 18, and this must be heard in the higher court. In either event the prosecution must, if it is to succeed, have evidence which pins the responsibility on to one or more specified individuals, usually the parent or the guardian. The sentencing powers of the court include imprisonment.

The criminal procedure is not, in practice, quite as useful as might at first sight be expected. In the first place it may turn out to be impossible to secure a conviction because there are often no witnesses to the acts alleged and the accused persons refuse to incriminate themselves. For this reason some police, understandably, feel that the ends of justice are likely to be defeated if they, as expert interrogators of suspects in criminal cases, are (as often happens) not brought on to the scene until after questioning by doctors and/or social workers has alerted the suspect to possible lines of defence. Secondly, if the defence is 'accident', it may be impossible to prove the *mens rea* required for a conviction. Thirdly, the trend of social policy and social work training today seems to support the view that the family must be kept together or restored almost at all costs and that its offending members and their victims can best, or can only, be rehabilitated *in situ* so to speak, and as part of a family re-education. The criminal jurisdiction, however, is geared to penal sanctions imposed upon an offending individual. It is most appropriate in cases where it is felt by the police on grounds of social policy, ordinary justice, and common peacekeeping that the need is for a criminal conviction followed by deterrent or even exemplary punishment. The court has also its usual power to make a probation order, thus providing a situation in which it is sometimes possible for reform to take place. What the court cannot do is to make an order relating to the juvenile victim. Since 1969 it has had no power to order that he be brought before the juvenile court since it was thought that the possibility of bringing care proceedings will normally have been considered already. There is thus no statutory machinery by which the court must draw the attention of the social services to the situation, but it may of course do so informally if it is thought necessary, and there is established procedure under which the police are required to notify the social services departments of the circumstances of convictions for offences against children.

CARE PROCEEDINGS

The case in the juvenile court is under its civil jurisdiction and the point at issue is the quality of care being received by the juvenile and likely to be received in the future. Proceedings are brought under the Children and Young Persons Act, 1969, Section 1 (2) on the ground that 'his proper development is being avoidably prevented or neglected or his health is being avoidably impaired or

neglected or he is being ill-treated'; and also that he is in need of care and
control which he is unlikely to receive unless the court makes an order. Care
proceedings may be brought only by a local authority, the police or the National
Society for the Prevention of Cruelty to Children. In most instances they are
brought by one of the first two. The weight of proof required is not, as in a
criminal case, such as places the matter beyond a reasonable doubt but is the
lower civil standard of proof which enables issues to be decided upon the
balance of probabilities.

The conviction in the adult court can shorten and simplify proceedings in
the juvenile court since it provides part of the evidence required. For this
reason if proceedings in the juvenile court are contemplated it is advisable for
these to be held back pending the outcome in the adult court. The parent is
usually on bail in the meantime and the child in the care of the social services
department on an interim order or in hospital. No final assessment of the child's
needs and no definite plans for his future can be made nor can serious rehabilitative work with the family begin until it is known whether the parent is
or is not to be removed from the scene by a prison sentence. Prolonged delay
can disastrously increase the effects on the emotional side of whatever damage
has already been suffered by the child. A good child care department can do
much to minimise the probable impact of this situation by various means, but
it is of the highest importance that the criminal case is brought on with no
avoidable delay whatever and that every individual who has a part in the process,
including the justices to whom repeated applications for interim orders are
made, should feel a personal responsibility to do what he can to bring this about.

An acquittal in the adult court does not necessarily mean that the juvenile
court case will fail. The essential matters to be proved in that court are the facts
of the child's situation and not necessarily who is responsible for causing it.
Thus the allegations may be proved without the court necessarily being certain
as to whether it was the father, the mother, another child, or the neighbour
who was the culprit. Again, a case may be proved to the court's satisfaction
although it has not been shown that the damage was non-accidental in the sense
of being intended or due to conscious recklessness, since the point at issue is
the child's actual situation now and probable situation in the future, not the
culpability *per se* of whoever did the damage. This is exceedingly important
since it enables a successful case to be brought and the child to be protected
even though the culprit cannot be brought to justice through lack of evidence.

ADMISSIBILITY OF EVIDENCE

On another important point, i.e., as to what is admissible in evidence, practice
seems to vary from one juvenile court to another. Doctors who have appeared
in the juvenile court as witnesses for the complainant sometimes protest very
strongly afterwards that a case has been lost because they were prevented by
the clerk, or even by the complainant's lawyer, from including in their evidence
material which they see as highly significant in relation to the general picture.
It must be rememberd that the allegation is twofold and relates on the one hand

to the child's condition now, and on the other to the need for the court to make an order if adequate care is to be ensured in the future. We suggest that these are to be treated as two aspects of the case rather than two distinct stages. If this view is accepted then much relevant family history can be heard from the social worker, the doctor, or the teacher in evidence before the finding instead of only in the social background report after, and if, the case is found proved. The door is opened to factual evidence about relevant behaviour as observed by the witness and the conclusions he bases on it as to personalities involved and in relation to the likelihood of adequate care in the future. Such evidence must, however, be either clearly fact or clearly opinion. It must not be hearsay. There may, for example, have been a conviction of the relevant adult for an offence indicating violence to someone other than the child, or observed outbursts of irrational or unpredictable behaviour under the influence of drugs or mental ill-health, or cruel treatment of an animal. An unfortunate aspect of these cases, even in the juvenile court, is that it is not always possible to prove non-accidental or even avoidable injury plus the expectation of inadequate care in the future if there is only one instance and the parents provide an adequate explanation the truth of which only they can know. Many juvenile court cases answer simply to an aggregation of minor injuries and there is often no known significant history of violence and cruelty in the parental histories. However, injury on more than one occasion is more likely to tip the balance and to be accepted by the court as evidence of the child's endangered situation within the requirements of the law. But on even a first appearance in court there may already be a history of accumulation of smaller incidents which have put the social services on the alert. It is essential that the expert witness especially, e.g. a doctor, should say clearly what the significane is of even very slight bruising if this in his view indicates very violent shaking or banging with consequent risk to the brain or sight, or is sited in a position where it could well have set up internal damage.

DIFFICULTIES OF WITNESSES

Since so few of these cases come to court the expert witnesses are quite likely never to have been there before. Like many other witnesses and defendants they can feel baffled by the procedure and afraid of being made to look foolish. Doctors in this situation particularly seem sometimes to have assumed until they got into court that the procedure would be inquisitorial and are upset and even affronted by an attacking manner on the part of the defence lawyer. Questions based upon the concept of 'certainty' also seem to present them with special difficulties. The court can help by explaining the procedure beforehand, but a heavy burden may rest on the complainant's counsel if the case is not to be lost in a semantic tangle.

The social worker giving evidence may be struggling with some of the same feelings and difficulties. In the new general social services departments, social workers are likely to be carrying mixed case-loads which include the aged, the handicapped, the mentally and physically sick, and only a few children, most of whom will never come into court. He or she may never have been in court before, or at least for a number of years. Though cases of this precise nature are comparatively rare in the court, care cases of a more general kind can amount to between one-fifth and one-sixth of the total business of the juvenile court and there would seem to be an advantage if the social services departments in busy areas have some member of staff who is familiar with the procedure and its pitfalls and can act as a 'court officer' for the purpose of liaison with the social workers concerned.

WHAT KIND OF ORDER?

The choice of order can be a major problem. The grounds of complaint are so defined in the 1969 Act that it is rather difficult to envisage the complaint being brought at all, and following the sort of investigation which must have been made without consideration of the question as to what order is required. These are surely cases in which the social services departments should state clearly, on the basis of their examination of the situation and their expertise in child welfare, what order is in their view required to ensure that the child gets the care he needs. This does not mean that the court in deciding upon the order will simply rubber stamp the department's view. As arrangements for care have not been made on a voluntary basis and it has been thought necessary to bring the child before the court at all, it may be assumed that a state of conflict either exists or is regarded as more than a possibility. There may therefore be two points of view as to whether an order—and if so what order—should be made. The choice is almost always between a supervision order, which does not give the local authority power to remove the child, and a care order which does. A court will not usually make a less weighty order than is being asked for without very solid reasons for doing so, but it is absolutely vital that the social enquiry and any medical evidence shall have made out their case for the order they are recommending with all the relevant material at their disposal. In present circumstances the quality of the investigation and advice, and of the supervision or accommodation available if such an order is made, must be an especially important factor. Many social workers are young, inexperienced and not fully trained. Although the recommendation decision may be taken expertly by a fully trained worker further up the hierarchy it can rest on an inexpert selection of factual material by the field worker. Where a care order is being strenuously opposed it may be helpful to the court if the defence lawyer questions the department as to what they have in mind in the way of provision.

Care orders may well be made because supervision alone is likely to be sparse and inadequate to pick up and act promptly enough upon indications of present or impending danger. In some cases the court or the social services department itself may wish the latter to have in reserve power to remove a child at a moment's notice at any time, without argument or effective opposition, on even the suspicion of danger if they feel this to be necessary. A court making a care order usually assumes that the child will be removed at once. But the order is not a removal order. It simply confers powers on the local authority which the latter will exercise or not at its own discretion and entirely on its own responsibility. The quality of expertise and decision-making in the local authority is therefore crucial.

Justices sometimes wonder whether the position would be improved if they had power to order removal, i.e. set the terms of a care order on their own initiative. We do not think it would. There are glaring inadequacies in the social services but these are not likely to be remedied by putting on to the court the duty of making welfare decisions *out of its own knowledge*. Lay justices do not become experts by being appointed justices, and there is no occupational or professional qualification for appointment. They cannot investigate cases themselves in the field, nor can they personally supervise the application of remedies. In deciding on the order to be made they must rely on the arguments advanced pro and con by the parties. Some justices do have considerable welfare experience but the fact that they sit on the bench is not *per se* a reason for supposing them more expert in welfare than the welfare authorities, though it may make them more alert, and able to alert their colleagues to the need for clarification of some points and issues, and may give them a fuller grasp of the implications of situations revealed in evidence or expert reports. But extra care is also needed to ensure that decisions are not taken on the basis of mere suppositions which have not been put in issue before the court and for which there are in fact no grounds in the evidence.

Is there a case for a special panel, perhaps as part of a special panel for domestic cases? If there is, what does it rest on? For example, the nature of the case (assault)? The fact that family relationships are involved? A need for special knowledge of social conditions? Or for some awareness of the pathology of injury? Should an offender and his victim be tried by the same panel—the former being deprived of his right to meet and refute a criminal charge under the safeguards provided by the criminal jurisdiction and bringing the criminal atmosphere of the ordinary court into the domestic or family panel hearings? Where, for example, would charges of wife-battering fit into the pattern? Or cases where the child batterer is not a relative? In a few divisions the justices have elected special panels to deal with domestic cases, though as far as we are aware most have not and there are some who may be said to have done so only by default, as it were, in that some male justices very much dislike this part of a justice's duty and prefer only to sit to deal with what is sometimes in contrast described as 'good clean crime'.

The present situation as far as the victim is concerned is that battered children cases are already heard by specially selected justices in the shape of the juvenile court panel. Would a 'family court' be better able to deal with 'the family as a unit'—to use a somewhat hackneyed phrase? And would that be an improvement if it could? As far as the law is concerned the child, as much as any other victim of assault, is entitled to the protection of the criminal court. In another sense, and as already pointed out, so is the offender, even if he is a member of the same family. If the rights of all the parties concerned in these cases are to be safeguarded and the public peace preserved it may be thought that the unitary or 'family' approach most appropriately operates in the social background report to the juvenile court. The exact form of the court is less important than the quality of the social services investigating the background and offering recommendations. This is also the experience of family courts in America.

HOLES IN THE NET

This is not to say that there are not gaps in the present situation. One of these appears to us to be that since they are not themselves before the court there is no power in juvenile court proceedings to require the parents to submit themselves to psychiatric examination in order to help the court to decide on the appropriate order (or the social services to make an appropriate recommendation) although they may presumably be 'blackmailed,' so to speak, into doing this.

Another gap seems to be not so much in the powers of the adult or juvenile courts as in the provisions of the social services. One of the most difficult types of case is the one in which there has been a short history of several accidental injuries at different times in the first six to nine months of life, from which the child has made an excellent recovery and is now before the court on a further allegation of injury, which is proved. In a recent case the parents appeared as a capable and loving 20-year-old mother with a husband of similar age, but completely unused to handling any little animal. It was he who had 'accidentally' caused a further fracture. Though extraordinarily clumsy he appeared well-intentioned and loving. This injury had also healed well. All parties agreed that the child was now in excellent condition and appeared also to have suffered no emotional damage whatever by the two spells in hospital. The injuries so far had not been serious and had never been shown to be wilfully inflicted. Should the child now be taken into care with the risk of emotional damage, since 24-hour minute-by-minute supervision is otherwise impossible? In cases of this kind could there not be provision for training for fathers which courts could require to be undertaken as an alternative to prison or otherwise?

Recent cases suggest three further points. First it may well be that whenever a child is brought before the court as in need of care, or on an application that a care order be revoked or a supervision order discharged, that child's interests ought to be watched over by an independent person as in adoption cases. In these cases the court appoints an independent guardian *ad litem* to represent his interests to the court even though the adoption application is unopposed and has the blessing of the social services department who may indeed themselves have made the placement. Secondly, it is probably unwise even for unopposed applications for revocation of care orders to be heard in the absence of the child concerned, and perhaps other persons such as foster parents who have been immediately concerned in his care should be notified and have a right to appear and to be heard. Thirdly, though consultation and co-operation between doctors, police, local authority and NSPCC are greatly to be encouraged yet it is our view that the possibility of unilateral action should continue to exist. Too much interdisciplinary brainwashing can bring its own dangers. *Sed quis custodiet ipsos custodes?* There is a need for safeguards at longstop.

Part Five

Education

22. Notes on education

THE DOCTORS *by Ronald Mac Keith*

Doctors need to learn something about both treatment and prevention.

Treatment calls for a general knowledge about the non-accidental injury, the recognition and immediate management of the acute episode and the continuing co-operative team management of the chronic problem. Such knowledge is essential for all doctors who deal with children, including ENT, orthopaedic and eye specialists, as well as general practitioners, hospital and community paediatricians. The teaching should be part of routine undergraduate, vocational and continuing education. The continuing co-operative team management of the chronic situation will be briefly discussed but knowledge in depth is a specialist area of knowledge needed only by the doctors specialising in paediatrics or consultant casualty work.

Identification depends on recognising a small number of *danger signals*, which include:

1 Discrepant or incompatible histories, such as 'he pulled the saucepan over himself' when the child is scalded in the back or 'he fell off the divan', when he has a fractured skull.
2 Characteristic injuries include facial injuries, especially black eyes, finger bruises without damage of cuticle or swelling of skin, gripping injuries of trunk, slapping and beating injuries of buttocks, cigarette burns, swollen joints, scalds and burns, retinal haemorrhages which often accompany intra-cranial damage and signs of intracranial injury or of subdural bleeding.
3 A suggestive social situation.

Differential diagnosis includes bruising in purpura, with an excessive reaction to minimal trauma, and in other bleeding disorders. The patient must always be examined totally undressed. Mongolian blue spots are seen in normal dark skinned babies including Italians and Spaniards.

In immediate management the designated area consultant should be summoned to all suspicious cases and the following steps taken:

Photograph in colour and in black and white
Full blood count to exclude bleeding disorders
Height and weight and head circumference measured
X-ray 1, affected joints and bones
       2, skeletal survey
NB repeat X-rays two to three weeks later.

The total continuing team management is done by a designated consultant, but all paediatric and orthopaedic surgeons should be informed of the plan. As this is a post-graduate specialist topic, details are not given at this stage. Essentially it involves collaboration between medical, social and police services of the area with quick consultation and discussion and allocation of responsibility at each step.

Prevention is primary, secondary and tertiary.

Primary prevention prevents it from happening and might be assisted by formal instruction of school children between 7 and 17 years about family relationships, marriage and parenthood.

In the ante-natal clinic the recognition of mothers at risk could lead to the giving of special guidance and support. In the management of all labours, good mother-child relationship should be promoted if mothers are treated as sensible and sentient people and allowed to enjoy their babies. In the first six weeks of motherhood, guidance and help should be immediately available.

Secondary prevention, once injury has occurred, depends on the early awareness of a deteriorating social situation and the recognition of minor but highly significant injury.

Tertiary prevention takes the form of the total continuing team management referred to above.

Malcolm Hall demonstrated part of a tape-recording of an interview with a mother. Such material together with photographs and lantern slides should be publicised and at least shown to doctors, social workers, police and magistrates. In this way the teaching of some of the warning danger signs and of the way in which a situation is built up could be made more effective.

THE SOCIAL WORKERS *by Edward Higgins*

Social workers in their formal training study human growth and development, marital and inter-familial relationships and deviancy. They are aware that non-accidental injury, neglect and other forms of deprivation exist. Most will have come across an instance in a social work department. The many untrained social workers, social work assistants or aides now being used in social service departments should receive in-service training, first to fill in gaps in formal training and secondly to relate theoretical training (whether professional or in-service) to the local organisation, local practices and policies. Their awareness of the general circumstances in which neglect occurs needs reinforcement in relation to local conditions.

They must understand the role of the local authority and of its social workers, the provisions of the law and its apparent ambivalence, on the one hand requiring the local authority to bring a child before the court in certain circumstances, and on the other requiring it to do all it can to avoid such action. They must be prepared to exercise the authority that the law gives them and to take the consequences of exceeding that authority, a difficult concept to accept and to work with, but a necessary one.

They must learn the local management system for such cases, and this must be laid down precisely both as to the agencies to be consulted and involved and as to the time scale in which consultation and action must be accomplished. They must know and exercise the role of the local authority in this management system and they must know and respect the role of the other agencies which may be or must be involved depending on the policies and practices agreed by the local authority or any review committee. Particular attention must be paid to the need for case conferences and also to the recording process. They must also learn the attitudes, policies and practices of the other agencies, best taught by visits to paediatric departments, local health visitors, local police etc. They should be aware of the symptoms of non-accidental injury, neglect etc., seeking the help of paediatricians whose wards they should visit.

They must realise where their own individual responsibilities cease, where delegation ends in cases of this kind and where consultation with senior colleagues is essential. They must understand the place of residential or day care, the likely emotions and reactions of the staff concerned, and the need for sympathetic handling and encouragement of parents, and for co-operation between field and residential staff. They need to know when to decide that parental contact is appropriate, to what extent and in what circumstances and to discuss this with the staff of the homes.

They should be made aware of the complexity of court procedures, and in what circumstances to obtain place of safety orders, care orders (interim or otherwise) or supervision orders, and of what action is possible in the adult courts against the parent or parents. This information can be given in lectures by the local clerk of the juvenile court, who will deal with the difficulties of presentation of evidence, and with the differences between civil and criminal proceedings with their two sets of rules of evidence. As these cases, involved and serious as they are, arise rarely in the experience of individual case workers, they come most appropriately as part of in-service training, when a case arises.

The staff should understand something of the motivation of the parents and of what other helping agencies and services are available to reduce stress, so that they may help the parents to deal with the hostility of neighbours and sometimes of workers in other agencies.

They must learn always to act in the best interests of the children at the time and in the future. The local authority is the body authorised under statute to take action. It is acting in a quasi parental role and making decisions that go far beyond the incident in question and may involve the tragedy of a childhood spent in care.

THE POLICE *by James Collie*

Police education is conducted in three main stages. The basic or initial course lasts 17 weeks and is continued by 'release' from duties for two days a month augmented by short residential courses during the two years of probationary service. There follows continuation training which includes field training, refresher training and pre-promotion courses. Lastly comes specialist training which covers a very wide field, CID, women police, communications, traffic patrol, forensic science etc.

During the initial training the policeman studies society and learns about social problems. As he progresses through his service, what he learns from his experiences on the beat will be augmented by informal seminars in Divisions and by lectures from experts in the various branches of sociology at continuation and specialist courses. The Criminal Investigation Department, among other things, examines the causes of violence, and in recent years it has given special attention to non-accidental injury to children.

At present no special instruction is given to the junior officers of the Force on this particular subject, although it is most often the young constable who is first on the scene when a non-accidental injury has been inflicted in a child or is suspected. The first officer on the scene will glean much useful information from talking with those present; and this information, if passed to the right quarter and correctly analysed, could often lead to a much earlier identification of the syndrome. Perhaps a tape-recording of the kind which Dr. Hall demonstrated to the Study Group would be useful in the training of police officers.

With regard to the enlightenment of senior officers I pride myself that they are reasonably well informed. They still, however, need to be brought up to date with the latest information concerning non-accidental injury to children and the current views of doctors and social workers. This can best be achieved by close personal contact rather than impersonal circular instruction.

23. A report on the teaching of legal studies on social work courses

Submitted by *Winifred Cavenagh*

GENERAL CONSIDERATIONS

The questions to be considered are what knowledge of law and procedure the fully trained professional social worker should have attained and what the best method is of acquiring it. We look at both from the point of view of effectiveness on the job. The overall feasible length of such courses limits the time which can be spent on any one aspect, and legal studies will not be regarded as of equal importance with, for instance, the study of human growth and development. In a one-year course legal studies *as such* may have to be limited to a maximum of say 20 to 25 hours, though much knowledge of law and procedure will be taught and acquired incidentally through studies in other parts of the course. As with the training of magistrates, a problem exists in that the training is required for effective functioning right at the start, yet much can only really be grasped whilst doing the job.

Although the students will be working in practical placements alternating or concurrent with attendance at the training institution, and many will also have had one or two years of trainee experience, these may not involve court appearances. It is all the more important therefore that the legal studies course should be taught by using active participant methods, especially case studies, mock courts and interviews, small group seminars etc. Placements should include some court experience including if at all possible discussions with clerk and magistrates relating to points and principles arising in cases which have just been heard. Straight lectures should be avoided altogether if possible.

THE CONTENT OF THE TEACHING

The areas which need to be covered would appear to be mainly two. The first relates to the legal aspects of problems and difficulties most commonly found amongst the social workers' clients. The teaching should enable the worker to recognise situations in which there is a legal remedy and to advise clients up to the point where professional legal aid and advice would normally be sought. These will include subjects such as debt, landlord and tenant, hire purchase, crime, husband and wife, parental rights and responsibilities, adoption, state benefits and assistance, the enforcement of rights and claims against the state, the powers of police and bailiffs, legal aid, bail. Teaching in these areas would appear to lend itself particularly well to case study methods.

The second area is that connected with the social workers' role in relation to the court. Social workers, some much more than others, need to know what would be expected of them as prosecution witnesses or complainants, reconciliation agents, guardians *ad litem*, expert advisers and social investigators to the court, and as officers supervising under a court order. This entails understanding the nature and purpose of the procedures in civil and criminal courts, the standards of proof required, the rule that innocence is presumed, the nature of evidence and rules relating to hearsay. These matters are best taught in a court or mock trial situation. Social workers require to have a firm grasp of the rules of natural justice and in particular the injunctions to hear the other side and that no man should be a judge in his own cause. These important rules are best elicited, pointed out, and hammered home during case-study and participant teaching of the subjects listed in the previous paragraph. Similarly, the roles respectively of the judges, magistrates, clerks, and of courts and tribunals in our society should be discussed in conjunction with case and court illustrations and, in so far as they have not already been dealt with *en route*, towards the end of the course.

Finally, the making and changing of laws by Parliament and judges, by statutes and cases, can be taught in discussions of the means and limitations of social action and the uses and methods of pressure groups. These are subjects in which many of the students will already be actively involved and be able to play a dynamic part in a seminar.

Some workers need more preparation for court work, for example intending probation officers obviously require at least one month's intensive court experience in either in-service or full-time training. But as workers in social service departments now carry very mixed caseloads, including few children and perhaps no cases which involve reports or appearance in court, many will never go into court. Or in many areas they may go no more than once or twice in a matter of years. When they do, a detailed coaching by an experienced departmental court officer on the day before a court hearing may well be what helps most. If the legal studies during training have been taught by case studies and mock trial situations, the basics of the court procedure should be familiar.

24. Problems of communication and co-ordination

Thomas E. Oppé

A consensus view of the objectives in management of the battered child might be summarised simply as: prevention, early detection and comprehensive diagnosis, skilled medical care, protection from further injuries and restoration to a family which has been fashioned into a safe, secure environment. It is more difficult to obtain agreement about the objectives of the management of the battering or potentially battering adult because of the need to take into account: the rights of parents to rear their children without unjustified interference, the ethical rules forbidding the disclosure of confidential information, the necessity to enforce criminal law, and uncertainty regarding the effectiveness of efforts to make beneficial changes in adult behaviour.

In practice conflicting views emerge regarding matters of policy, rightness of decisions in individual cases, and the effectiveness of different types of remedial actions. Disagreements appear between major institutions which determine policy, professional agencies which attempt to implement them, and individual workers who participate in the care of abused children and their families.

INTERACTION BETWEEN SURFACES

It is helpful to analyse the problems peculiar to the battered child syndrome into: the tribological* associations between institutions, agencies and workers and those related to the nature of adult aggression toward babies and young children.

The law

The interacting institutional surfaces are the law, medicine and the social services. A prominent area of friction relates to the criminal aspects of child abuse. When the battered child is viewed as the victim of a serious criminal offence it is unavoidable that on information being received a criminal investigation must be undertaken. Criminal investigation 'successfully' concluded results in prosecution, conviction and sentencing of the offender which in the case of battered children is usually a parent. Many doctors and social workers believe that this sequence is incompatible with good management, but the arguments that existing law should be enforced, severe sentences have deterrent value and

* Tribology is the science and technology of interacting surfaces and includes the design of bearings, the application of lubricants and the environment in which surfaces interact.

the actions of the police and the criminal courts can be positively beneficial, cannot be rejected until the criminal law has been changed or better methods have been unequivocally demonstrated. Meanwhile it is not surprising that some doctors and social workers hesitate to facilitate criminal investigation procedures and become liable to the criticism that they are denying to children the protection currently afforded by the criminal law. Not only is the principle disputed but it is also contended that in practice the machinery of the law enforcement is harmful to the management of the battering parent, and that the widespread variations in judicial sentencing have brought the law into disrepute.

Perhaps of greater importance is the operation of civil and statute law regarding parental rights and duties, and the obligations of local authorities to ensure the protection and well-being of children and young persons. There is general agreement that in certain circumstances it is necessary to transfer custody of children from their parents to the care of the local authority. In giving powers to local authorities to initiate proceedings and to provide resources for this, present statutes make it clear that the aim should be to prevent children being taken into care and to return them to parental care as soon as it is safe to do so. In the context of the battered child the weight of this is clearly against the protection of the battered or vulnerable child unless the parents agree to a care order being made and maintained. Much dissatisfaction is at present felt among doctors and social workers that the burden of evidence required by some juvenile courts before granting care orders is too great for them to carry out either their preventive or protective functions adequately. Furthermore the local authority social worker is often placed at a disadvantage in simultaneously having to appear to the parents as the person making application for the deprivation of their rights, and attempting to create and pursue an understanding, therapeutic relationship with them.

A somewhat uneasy but generally harmonious relationship exists between medicine and the law, disturbed sometimes by issues of confidentiality and negligence. The institution of medicine has at this time an abrasive relationship with that of social service. Custom in Britain accepts the medical principle of total individual responsibility for the clinical welfare of the patient. This is best seen in the power of the consultant who, in fact, if not in law, can admit and retain patients in hospital, order any form of treatment, and refer or communicate according to his personal wishes. He is in effect subject only to the criticism of his colleagues and possible legal action for negligence.

The social work service

It is the emergent institution of social work which is most disturbed by these medical attributes because it regards itself as having care of the whole person (as distinct from medicine's involvement with diseased parts), and directing the resources required to deal with all social problems. Social workers do not deny, and may even admire, the technical skills and expertise of medicine and surgery but would regard them as just one of the resources available to their profession in its comprehensive approach. This attitude is demonstrated rather more explicitly by local authority social service departments who do indeed command many resources and hold statutory powers, than by voluntary organisations.

The doctor

Institutional attitudes are encoded within the professional conduct of the workers involved and much of the overt and occult conflict existing in the handling of battered children can be traced to them. The doctor is trained to wield extraordinary individual power and responsibility, and to shrug off failure with a dirty joke and a glass of beer. He is, however, used to the support on request, and at all times, of more senior or experienced colleagues. He is clinically accountable only to himself and to his patient and is extremely adverse to interference with what he regards as his clinical sphere. He will, of course, utilise the results of investigations obtained by X-rays, chemistry or a social history in forming his clinical judgement, but in clinical matters he expects to have the final word. This attitude would probably not be greatly disputed in matters of specific medical or surgical treatment but they are less acceptable when social, legal or educational issues are involved. Social workers think and act rather differently. Within local authorities they do not have individual responsibility and are not accountable to their clients, but function as agents of the social services committee. At present they often do not have immediately available support, and their resources are limited in practice to those provided by their employing authority, to which they are expected to be loyal.

The health visitor

Between these two professional attitudes the health visitor is particularly privileged and particularly vulnerable. She has statutory powers to visit families in which there is a young child and an ill-defined obligation to ensure the child's wellbeing; often she is also expected to supervise families in which a child is at special risk of disease, deprivation or abuse.

All professional workers in the so-called caring or helping professions serve individuals and must often act in the interests of the patients or client on information and evidence which is insubstantial. They also recognise that with many of the problems with which they deal a successful solution cannot always be expected. One would hope that these common factors would lead to mutual tolerance, respect and confidence but unfortunately this is not always so, partly because of the separateness of training and now the divorce in management between the health and social services.

The courts

The police, magistrates and justices are primarily concerned with the enforcement of the law and the administration of justice. The key to the adequate performance of these necessary tasks is factual, objective evidence. When professional workers such as doctors and social workers fail to provide, or deny to others the opportunity to obtain, evidence which might lead to prosecution the police are critical; on the other hand it is not unusual for magistrates to be criticised (privately) when they appear to pay insufficient heed to the pleas of social workers or their legal representatives seeking a care order for the protection of a child. It is not only differences in professional procedure which perpetuate these frictions but also attitudes towards fundamental principles. There is some irony in the fact that juvenile court magistrates are now sometimes castigated for inflexibly upholding the view, vigorously propounded only a few years ago by social workers and some child psychiatrists, that residential care was almost always worse for a child than remaining in an unsatisfactory home!

The media

The battered child syndrome is undoubtedly a subject of national concern and public interest. It is therefore a legitimate area for journalistic activity and the threat of, or actual publicity in, the mass media can have adverse effects on decision making and judgement; while premature or uncritical publication of results or opinions may lead to loss of confidence or demands for services of unproven value. Journalistic interest, unless sensitive to the interests of the persons involved rather than the pursuit of news or entertainment, is a barrier to proper management of cases. At the same time it is important that public opinion as well as professional knowledge about battered children should be utilised, and this can only be attained if the public is well-informed about the nature of the problem.

MANAGEMENT

Identification

The majority of battered children are first seen by doctors and their initial management of the problem is crucial. Prevalent allegations of imperfect handling are: failure of diagnosis; failure to refer and communicate; failure to gather or support evidence necessary for the protection of the child; undertaking aspects of treatment which is beyond their competence or resources; and behaving in an unwarrantably authoritative, judgemental and dictatorial fashion towards the parents and workers concerned.

Poor diagnosis is due to ignorance, difficulty or denial. Often all three factors are operative. The chances of an individual doctor or health visitor encountering a battered child are small, although the condition appears common to those with a special interest. There are good reasons for ensuring that the clinical conditions arising from insufficient parenting are taught to doctors, social workers and nurses.

The identification of the battered child as opposed to the accidentally injured or naturally diseased infant is at times difficult and hindsight does not always make allowances for initial uncertainties. Particular difficulties do arise because of the widespread belief that only the manifestly 'abnormal' adult is capable of violence towards a child and the conditioning of doctors to the understanding that interrogative questions asked during history taking are usually answered truthfully. Non-recognition or denial is likely to occur when the battering adult is like the physician in appearance, speech, intelligence and demeanour. These difficulties will tend to limit the completeness of reporting.

After identification

Once battering has been recognised the subsequent management has three main aspects: specific medical treatment, protection from further injury, and identification of the family problems and remedial intervention. Little criticism or even questioning arises in matters of specific medical treatment although it is by no means always successful as both case fatality and permanent morbidity rates testify. It would be considered naive, if not impertinent, for a social worker, magistrate, or Member of Parliament to ask, except in exceptional circumstances, why medical treatment had failed. The limits to the efficiency of medicine and surgery are generally recognised, as also is the supposition that doctors treat their patients to the best of their ability.

Other professions do not enjoy this confidence and understanding. A tolerant view is not always taken of failure to protect a child from re-battering. The individual responsible for misjudgement is held to be incompetent or inadequate, and similar criticism is levelled at the social worker who fails to rehabilitate a family thereby allowing further episodes of injury to the original victim or sibling. This unreal expectancy of the quality of judgement and efficiency of practice in social work is reminiscent of the battering parents' distorted expectations of the behaviour of their children, and is an important factor in creating anxiety in personnel working with battered children.

These workers have already a high level of anxiety because decision making generally involves hurting either the parent or the child, and intervention is both unwelcome and unrewarded. It is not therefore surprising that the tendency now is for decisions regarding care and protection of the child to be made by committees (case conferences) rather than by individuals. Many doctors trained and experienced in individual responsibility dislike case committees and are often reluctant or ineffective participants. This creates friction and misunderstanding.

Although collective responsibility may be desirable for decision making concerning the plans for protecting the child and later for restoring the child to his family, it is no means of providing therapy. A committee can suggest action to individuals and mobilise a number of resources, e.g. rehousing, day nursery placement, health visitor supervision, but it cannot initiate and maintain the 'parenting' relationship with the hitherto 'unloved' adult which is said to be the key to successful therapy.

The social worker

Case work agencies whose workers provide such treatment point out the stressful nature of the task of working with clients who are immature, suspicious, ungrateful and hostile. It is easier for a social worker to adopt a supervisory, authoritarian attitude than to undertake the deep involvement with the client which appears to be required. The ability to work in depth requires special aptitudes and experience, not least of which is a willingness to accept failure.

We do not yet know whether battering parents can be successfully nurtured into normal parenting. If not, the more superficial approach may be effective in tiding the family through periods when the child is most vulnerable. Until the question is settled it is clear that authorities and workers providing only a limited service will feel insecure and threatened by those who claim better results from more intensive methods.

Whatever the merits of various approaches it is undeniable that unspecialised, inadequately trained and inexperienced social workers are ill-equipped for the task of providing therapeutic intervention. There seems a good case for setting up within social service departments, specialised teams, not necessarily exclusively concerned with battered children, of workers who have an interes and experience in the work.

Voluntary societies

It has happened in Britain that the development of the specialised team approach has been pursued not by statutory authorities but by a voluntary organisation—the National Society for the Prevention of Cruelty to Children. In many ways the roles of voluntary bodies and statutory authorities are happily complementary, but in certain aspects there is rivalry and mutual suspicion. Nowadays voluntary organisations exist to detect, to define and publicise deficiencies, to provide, if only temporarily, missing services, to exert pressure to emphasise the importance of a particular subject and to promote research. To be effective they must expose inadequacies, mobilise public opinion and support, and overemphasise their particular causes. It is not surprising that the victims of their campaigns sometimes find the behaviour of voluntary organisations arrogant, hypercritical, unbalanced and strident. At the same time a voluntary organisation by utilising substantial resources on model projects can create envy in those struggling with lesser resources to cope with the same problems. One of the causes of friction in the management of battering families is that the hard pressed, generic, local authority social worker feels threatened and despised by the voluntary organisation worker who not only has greater expertise derived from specialisation and a smaller case load, but also enjoys greater autonomy and freedom from the rigid, hierarchical structure of the local authority. In response the local authority worker can flaunt his command of wider resources and attempt to exert his statutory powers in an interfering or obstructive fashion.

These factors seem to be unduly prominent in the context of the battered child, and one may speculate as to the underlying influence of the problem's special nature. Cruelty to children, especially when inflicted by parents, is a violation of the ethos to which the majority of doctors and social workers subscribe. It is suggested that the worker may be as 'sick' as the battering parent and the abused child in that he or she may have great difficulties in maintaining defences against personal aggressive feelings and that confrontation with battering parents reveals unconsciously the flimsy nature of the defensive façade. It can hardly be doubted that the temperament, personality and attitudes (conscious and unconscious) of the decision maker and the therapist are of importance in determining both the outcome of a child abuse case and the nature of the relationships of the involved personnel. These factors are at present neither measurable nor predictable; they are, however, recognisable and understandable.

CONCLUSIONS

The battered child syndrome presents problems of recognition, judgement (decision making) and action, which involve concurrently and sequentially workers in a number of disciplines and several professions.

It is likely that the outcome in a particular case depends upon the communicating and co-ordinating skills of the workers as much as the technical expertise.

The nature of the syndrome presents various barriers to good communication and co-ordination, and it is important that these are understood.

Appendices

Appendices

Local arrangements for the management of individual cases and for the planning of policy were the subjects of much discussion by the Study Group. The methods to be examined and adopted in different parts of the United Kingdom must vary. A stereotype cannot provide the proper solution everywhere. Nevertheless the Study Group came to certain generally agreed conclusions which were incorporated in the report that was circulated by the Department of Health and Social Security, from whom copies may still be obtained. The conclusions relate to the functions and the composition of area review committees and case conferences. Because the Study Group attaches such importance to them as being the one way to secure full co-operation between the various professions, the recommendations are published here as Appendices I and II.

What was not discussed in detail was something, well known at least to the medical members, which has assumed a greater importance in the light of some recent tragedies brought before the courts. On what basis should an answer be found to the question—'Is this baby or this child thriving in the place where it is, whether with its own parents, step-parent, foster or adopting parent or in a home or institution?' What data should be known on which an answer can safely be based? Appendix III attempts an outline of the general principles to be applied.

Appendix I: The area review committee

The DHSS has recommended the establishment of area review committees. Many already exist, but the Study Group did not know whether they yet cover the whole country, nor exactly how they are composed nor their exact functions. The Study Group felt that these committees have a vital part to play and made the following suggestions about function and composition. The committees should be set up at area health authority and local authority level with appropriate administrative and secretarial services. Meetings should be held quarterly.

The functions of the area review committee:

1 To act as a forum where the widest possible consultation can be held between all professions who play any part in managing the problem;
2 To take responsibility for formulating policy and procedures;
3 To review the work of the case conferences in its area;
4 To ensure that long-term plans, whether with the child at home or placed either in a Home or with foster parents, is being satisfactorily carried out;
5 To promote the spread of knowledge;
6 To encourage research;
7 To co-operate in epidemiological studies;
8 To be in touch with review committees in adjacent areas;
9 To submit an annual report to the DHSS and the Home Office.

The composition of the area review committee. The area review committee should include at least the following:
Medical personnel: a senior community physician, a senior paediatrician, a senior community physician with a special interest in child health, an accident consultant, a psychiatrist, a general practitioner.
Other professionals include a senior nursing officer from the community services, a casualty department and a paediatric department sister, the director of social services, a probation officer, a representative of the social welfare service of the DHSS regional office and of the NSPCC; a magistrate's clerk and a senior police officer.
The latest DHSS document [LASSL (74) 13, CMO (74) 8] stresses the management and educational functions of these committees. Among 20 representatives listed, to which one district nursing officer for each district is to be added there is no link with the legal profession. The Study Group, welcoming the Department's fresh stimulus, hopes that each health area will be able to modify the general principles according to the needs of geography and time. Even if the minimum prevalence suggested is accepted, the necessity, mentioned

in para 24 of the Report and Resolutions of The Tunbridge Wells Study Group, for a suitable secretariat to conduct the business of these committees must lead to considerable expense. Monitoring the success of plans adopted, an absolute essential, will also need paid personnel. Services cannot function without finance.

Appendix II: The case conference

The Study Group takes the view that collaboration between the hospital service, the social services and the police is essential for the proper management of families caught up in this problem. The management of an individual case should be discussed at a case conference, convened soon after admission so that a preliminary plan can be made.

The functions of the case conference. The task of this case conference is to bring together all those who can provide information about the family, those who make decisions and those who provide services. Responsibility for co-ordinating the details of treatment has to be delegated to one person, but it is necessary for the case conference to retain an overall responsibility for each step that is taken. This responsibility continues at least until after the child has returned to the care of his own family at home and therefore, even if no actual meeting is convened, every member must be informed when the child leaves hospital wherever he is sent, and, very importantly, when the child returns home. No child under suspicion should leave hospital without the agreement of the social services. Plenty of warning should always be given to members of the case conference, possibly by the probation officer, when a parent is to be discharged home from prison. Many tragedies that might have been prevented have occurred because of failure to inform and consult with colleagues. The making of a plan by this team is one thing, the carrying out another. The case conference should have the power to put its plan into operation or to modify it according to events or the development of some fresh crisis.

The composition of the case conference. The following is the suggested composition of the case conference. The named members provide the minimum requirements: the senior paediatrician with members of his staff, the psychiatrist, the ward sister or the senior nurse concerned with the child, the senior member of the social service staff concerned with the child, the health visitor and the representative of any voluntary social agency such as the NSPCC who may have been already involved. The family's general practitioner should be invited to attend. With regard to the police, a superintendent or chief superintendent, either of whom are able to make decisions, should be given the opportunity to attend. The police can then use their discretion about the need to attend and will no doubt be influenced by the seriousness of the situation and the degree of suspicion.

The meaning of team-work. Underlying these questions is the special role of the different members of the team. The *doctor's* duty is, if possible, to save life or to preserve or restore health. The *social services* have a statutory duty to protect children and, where possible, to keep the child as part of its family. The *police* have a legal obligation to detect crime, to try to arrive at the truth, to decide whether or not to bring proceedings and if so to present evidence before the court. The *law* defines crime and regulates sanctions or the appropriate form of control. *The court* makes a judgement and applies the law. What constitutes criminal action is influenced by *public opinion* which progressively liberalises concepts. From all these elements a system is compounded. If the best long-term interests of society as a whole and of the family in particular are to be served, no one part of the team can profitably act on its own. Statutory and legal obligations must, however, be given due weight. The question to be decided is whether and how far the problems raised by non-accidental injury to children within the family are accepted as community problems always to be settled by team decision and action. Should one element ever act without due regard to the other elements? There may sometimes be occasions for unilateral action. The legal obligations of the police as well as the statutory obligations of the social services and of the NSPCC under its constitution, like the clinical responsibility of the doctor, must be recognised and respected. Could there be a general agreement that unilateral action is undesirable and that the maintenance of mutual confidence and respect is paramount? Therefore could each party agree that if ever unilateral action is taken in opposition to the majority view, the other parties should have the right to be informed both of the action taken and of the reason that led to it? The Study Group was disturbed by stories of the tragedies that had followed when unilateral action had been taken by doctors, by social services or by the police.

Appendix III: A note on the assessment of thriving

The assessment of children's progress presents the doctor, the health visitor, the educational welfare officer and the social worker with a number of problems. These vary with the age of the child and have become increasingly complicated in recent years. When interest centred on physical growth, height and weight were religiously measured at frequent intervals, but with a diminishing frequency as the infant passed through the toddler and school ages on the way to adolescence. Although the Department of Education and Science has now advised that the routine termly measurement of the height and weight of school children is unnecessary, weights are still recorded regularly in child health centres. And it is essential that children whose progress requires periodic assessment should be accurately measured under standard conditions. The charts reproduced in Figures 9 to 18 are commonly used. Weight should match height for sex and age. A disparity between weight and height or a change of centile line is significant. For reasons of space the charts available for older children are omitted. The point needs stressing that deprivation, abuse and non-accidental injury may all be sustained by children in the older age-groups.

These basic measurements should be obligatory, but there are others of equal importance. Routine surveillance of infants with special reference to neurological development requires medical expertise. The old-fashioned milestones which were not so much milestones as stages, each occupying a number of weeks, have given place to periodic detailed surveys of function. These too make possible objective measurement of progress. Movement, communication, speech, dexterity, the alertness of responses provide not only clues to intellectual development but also some indication of the success or failure of emotional adjustment. Physical growth, emotional adjustment and intellectual development are inextricably mixed in the early years of life.

During school years, learning motivation and ability as well as behaviour, whether erring towards the aggressive or the withdrawn, give further information to the experienced school teacher and educational welfare officer. If the child is being properly cared for, he should be thriving at school as well as at home.

Those charged with the responsibility of supervising and summarising the progress of children, especially children under court orders, can no longer rely on conversations with parents or foster parents and a periodic look at the child at play. Such subjective data are, of course, of value and experience increases their value, but the periods of observation are necessarily limited both in frequency and duration. Even the most harshly treated child can have moments of laughter and happiness. Objective measurements of greater or less sophistication and requiring training in method are available and should be used. Assessment of progress is a skilled professional exercise and added importance attaches to its accuracy now that the specialised children's service has been discarded in favour of generic social work. Such assessments are essential when decisions about the care of children are being reached, whether the responsibility lies with courts or social workers. No doctor can give his opinion as an expert without them.

BOYS 0-1

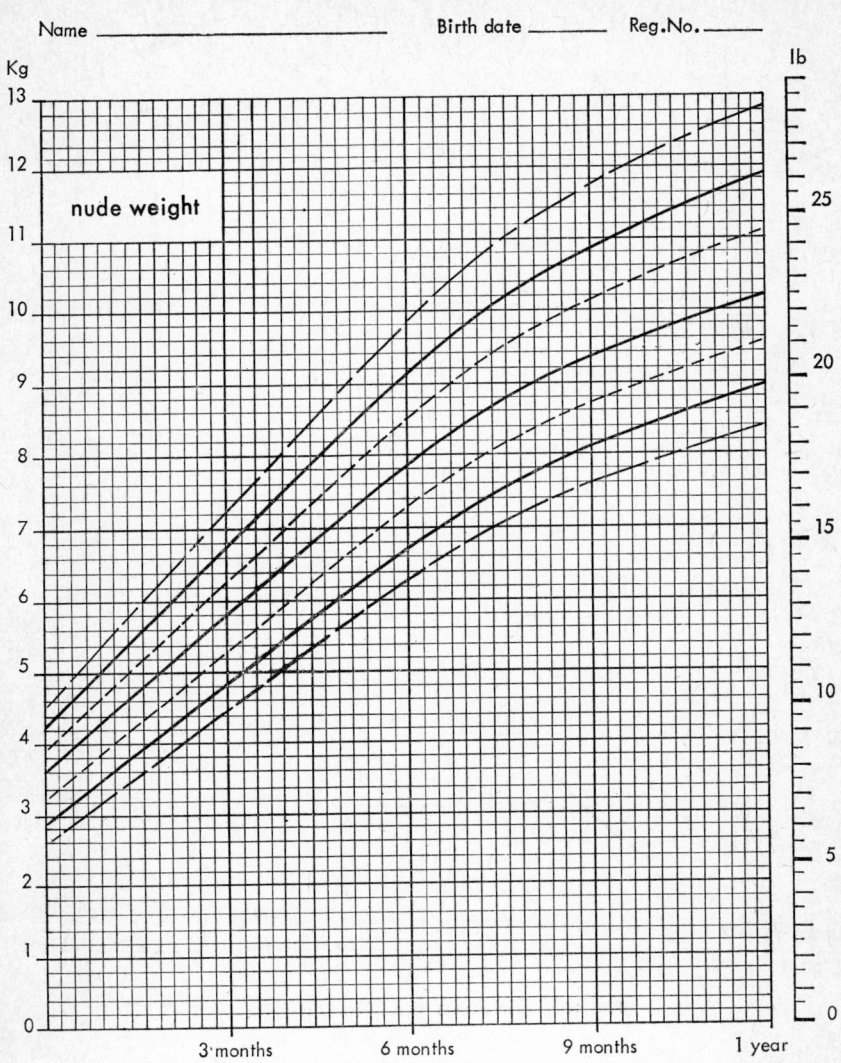

FIG. 9. Boys 0–1 year. Nude weight.

GIRLS 0-1

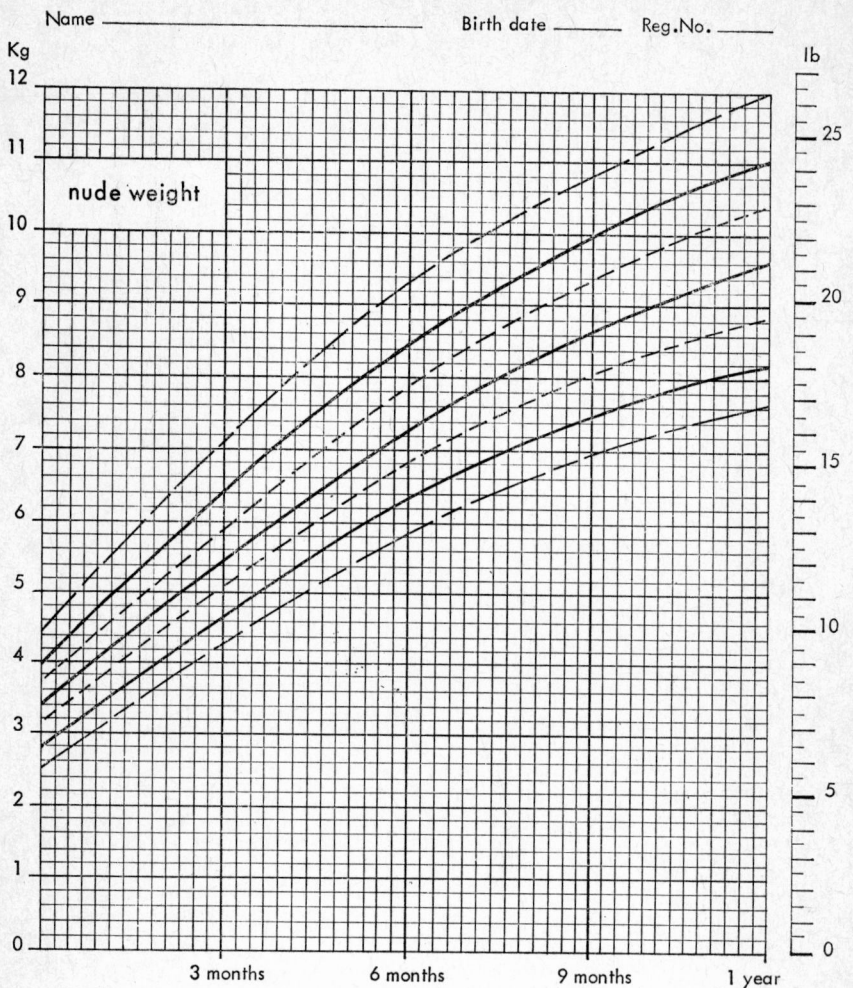

FIG. 10.   Girls 0—1 year. Nude weight.

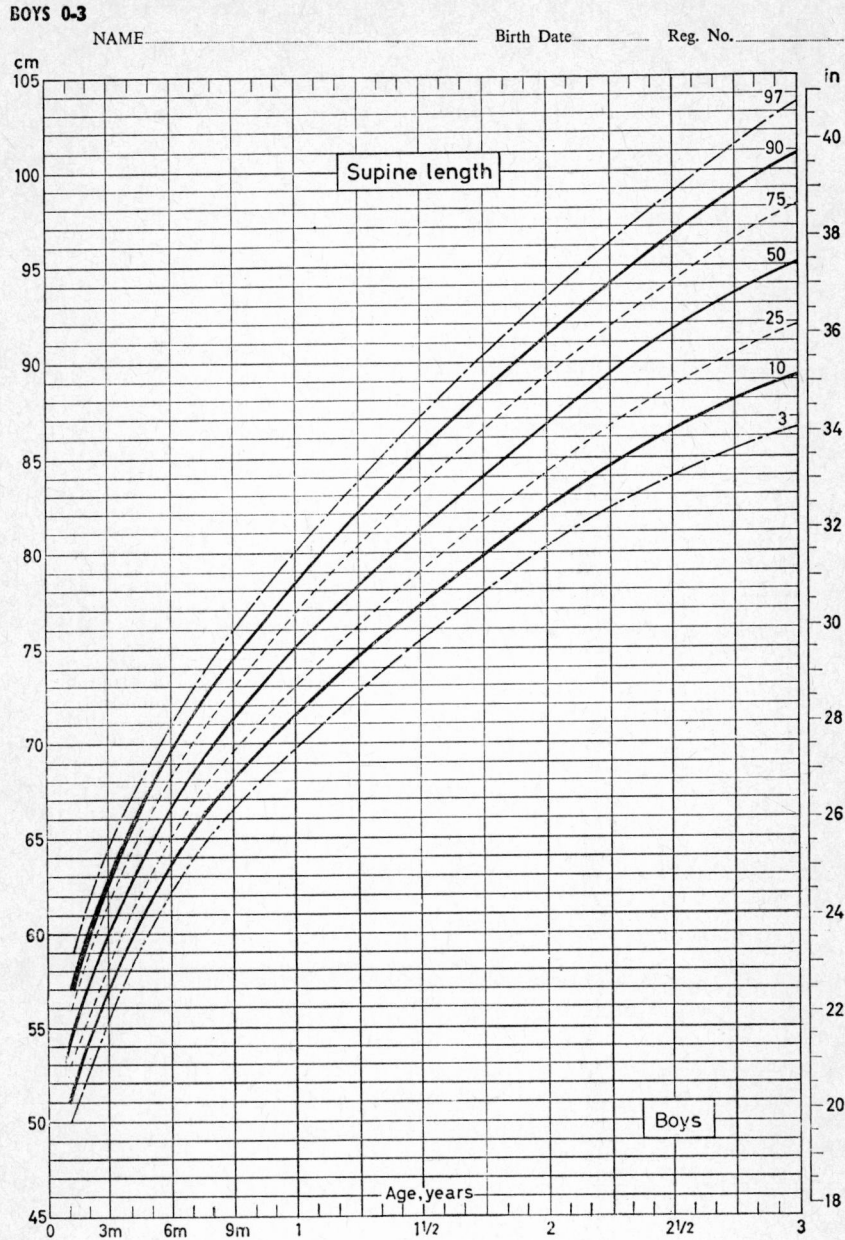

FIG. II. Boys 0—3 years. Supine length.

NAME.., Birth Date.................. Reg. No.........................

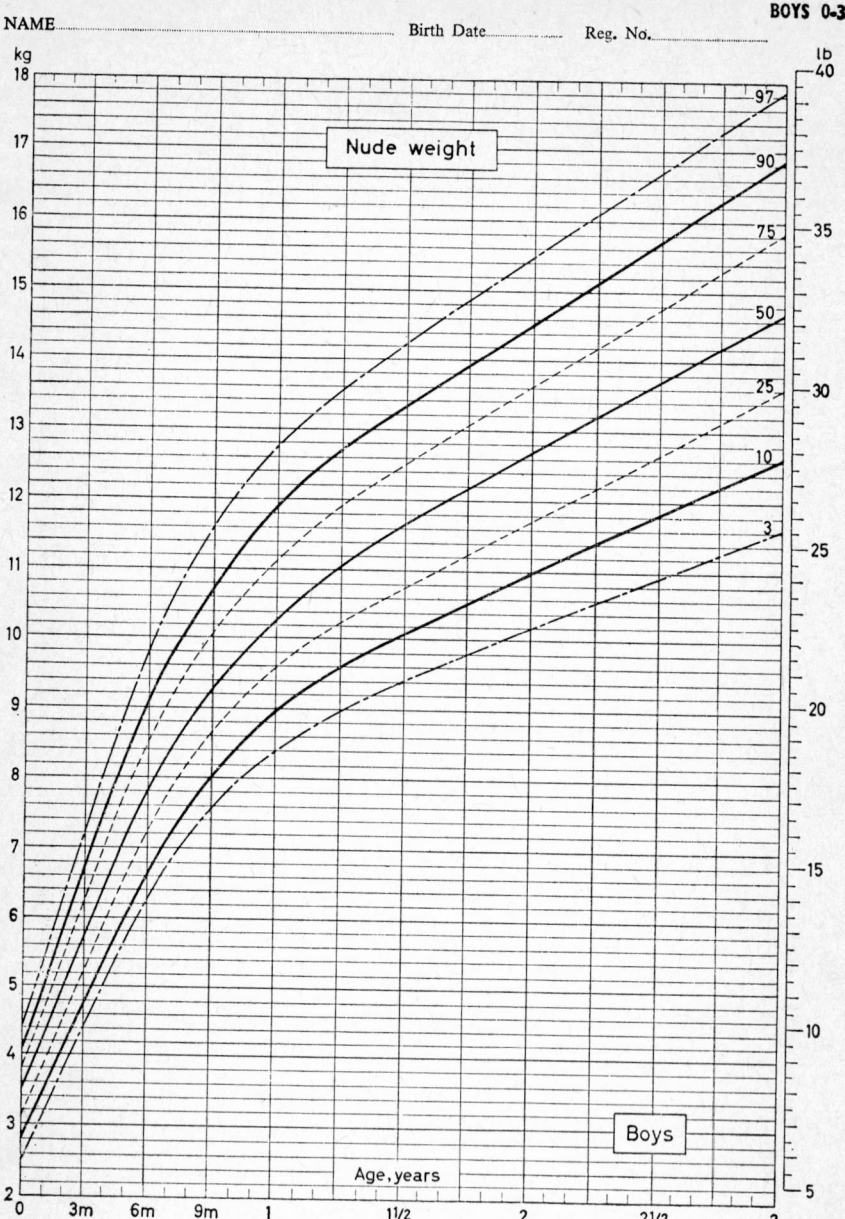

FIG. 12. Boys 0–3 years. Nude weight.

GIRLS 0-3

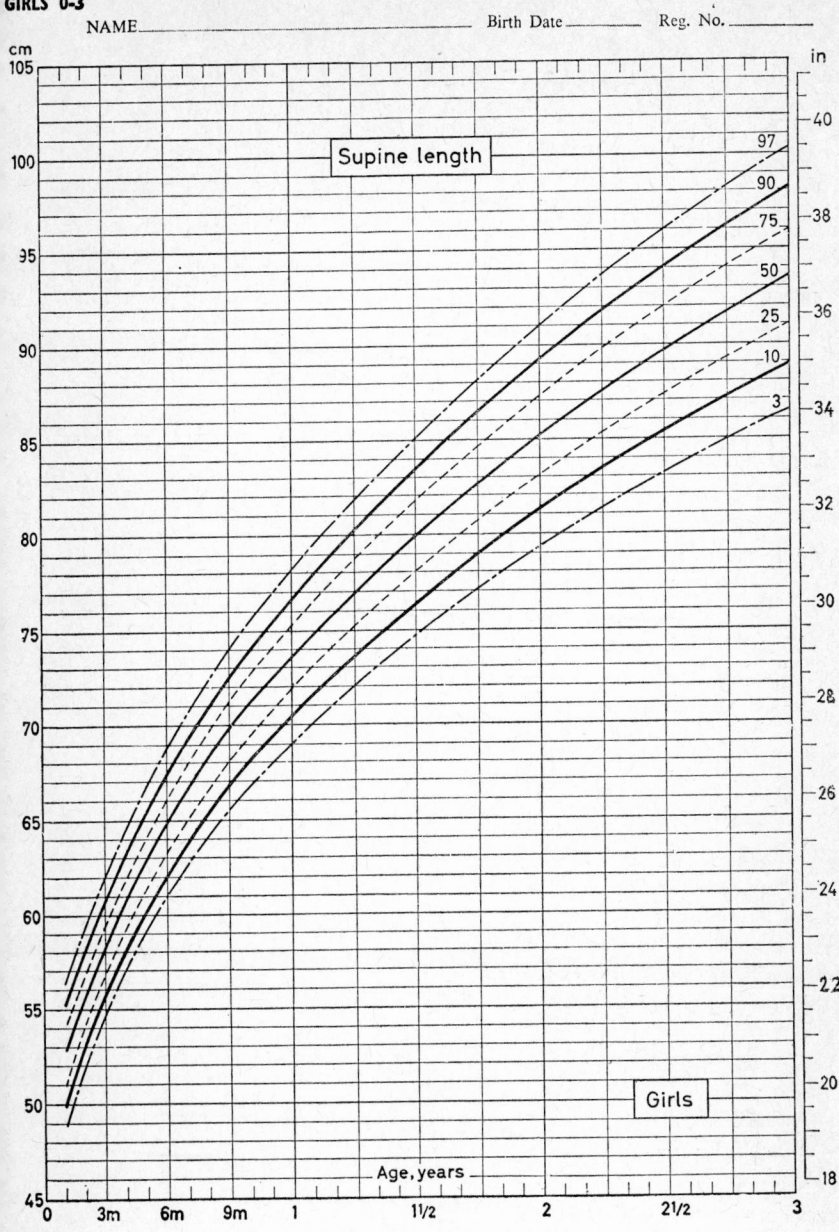

FIG. 13. Girls 0–3 years. Supine length.

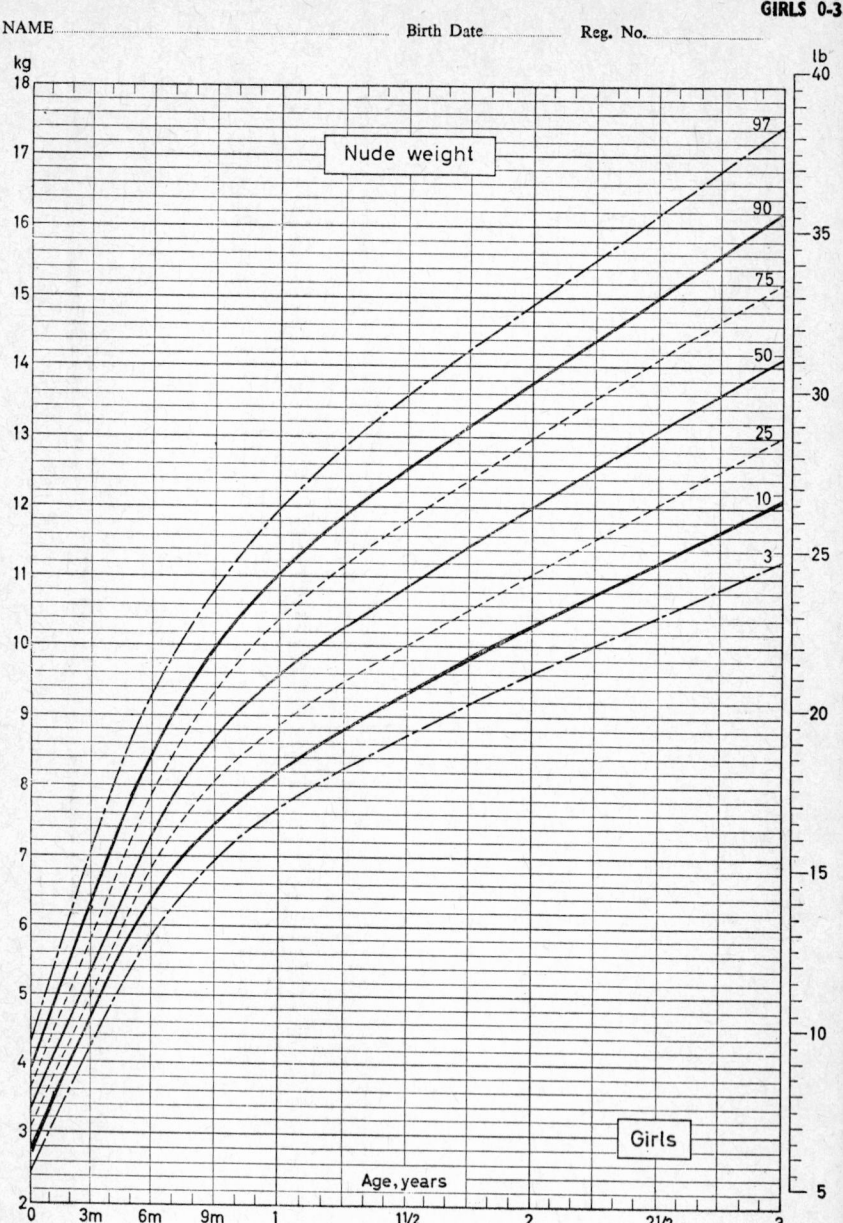

FIG. 14.   Girls 0—3 years. Nude weight.

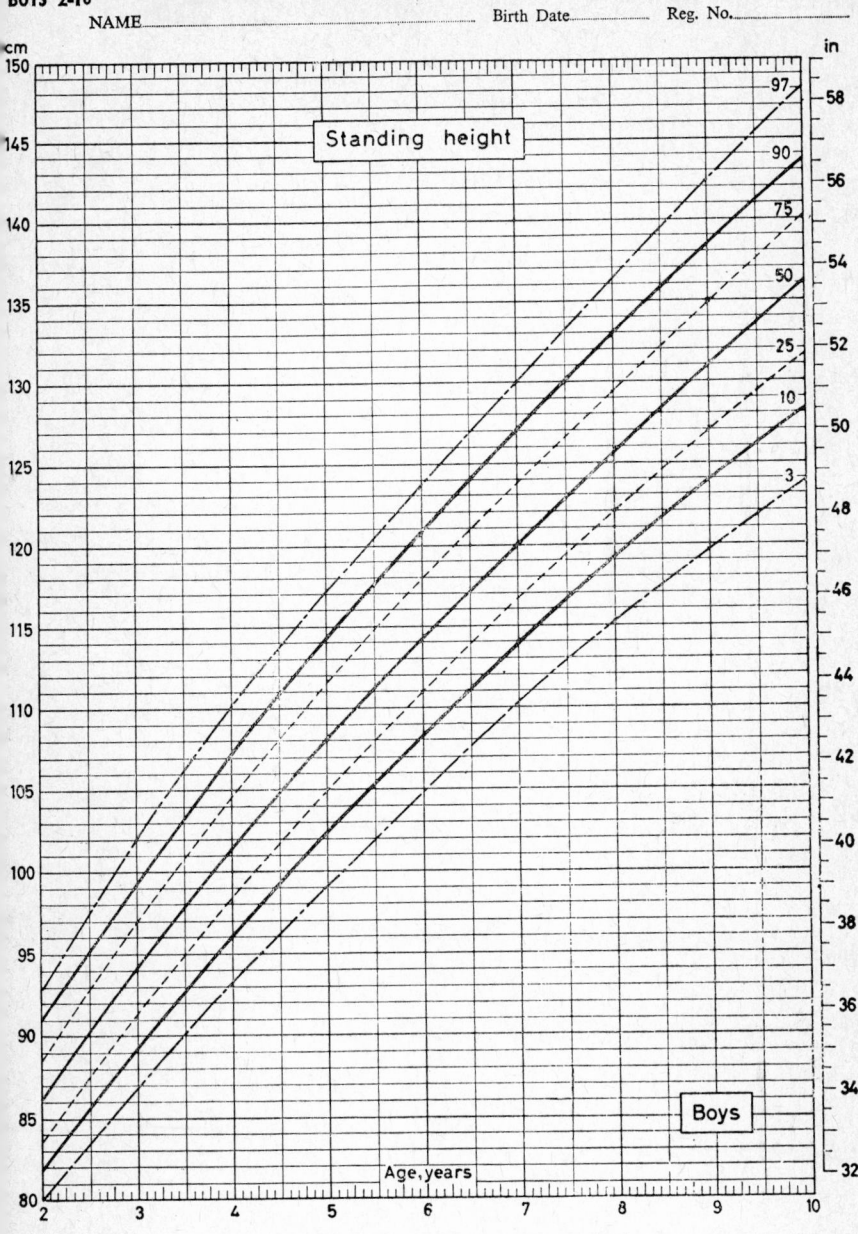

FIG. 15. Boys 2—10 years. Standing height.

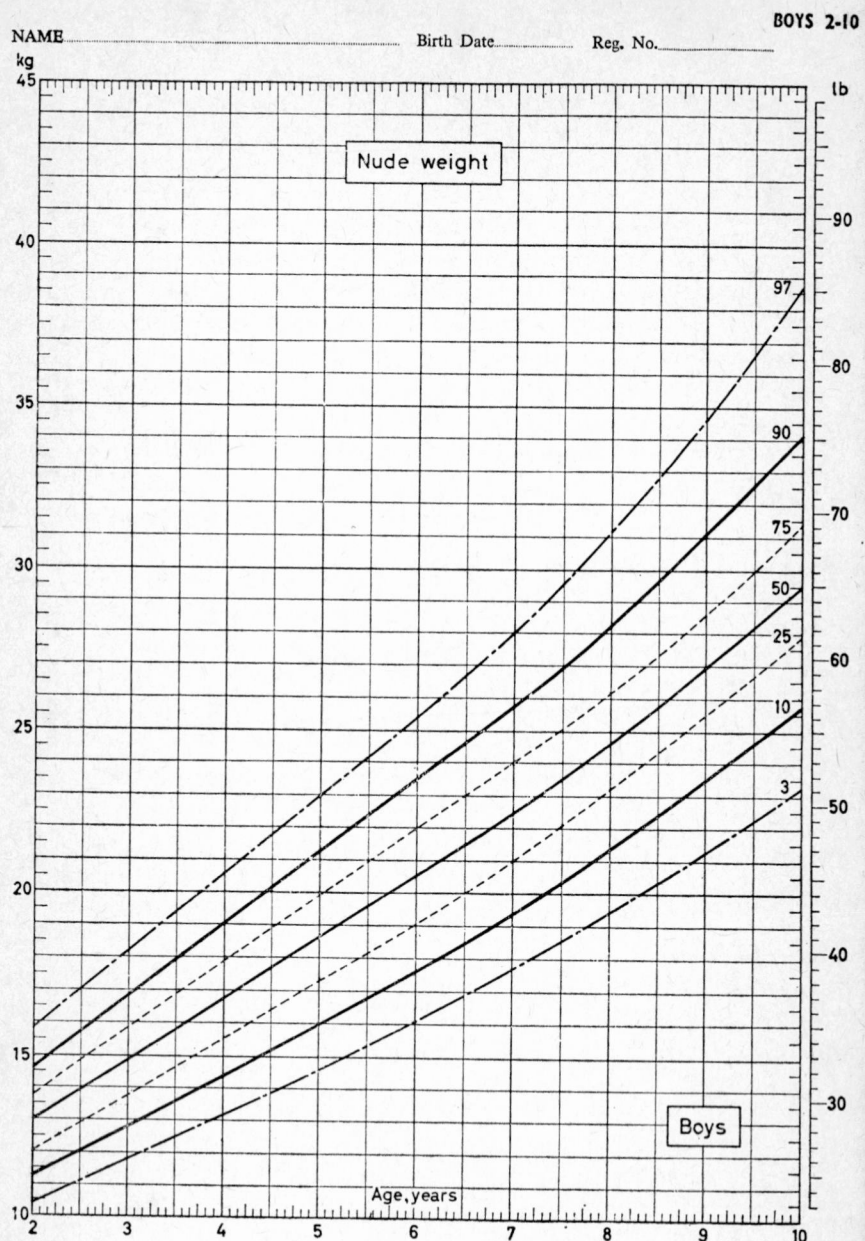

FIG. 16.   Boys 2–10 years. Nude weight.

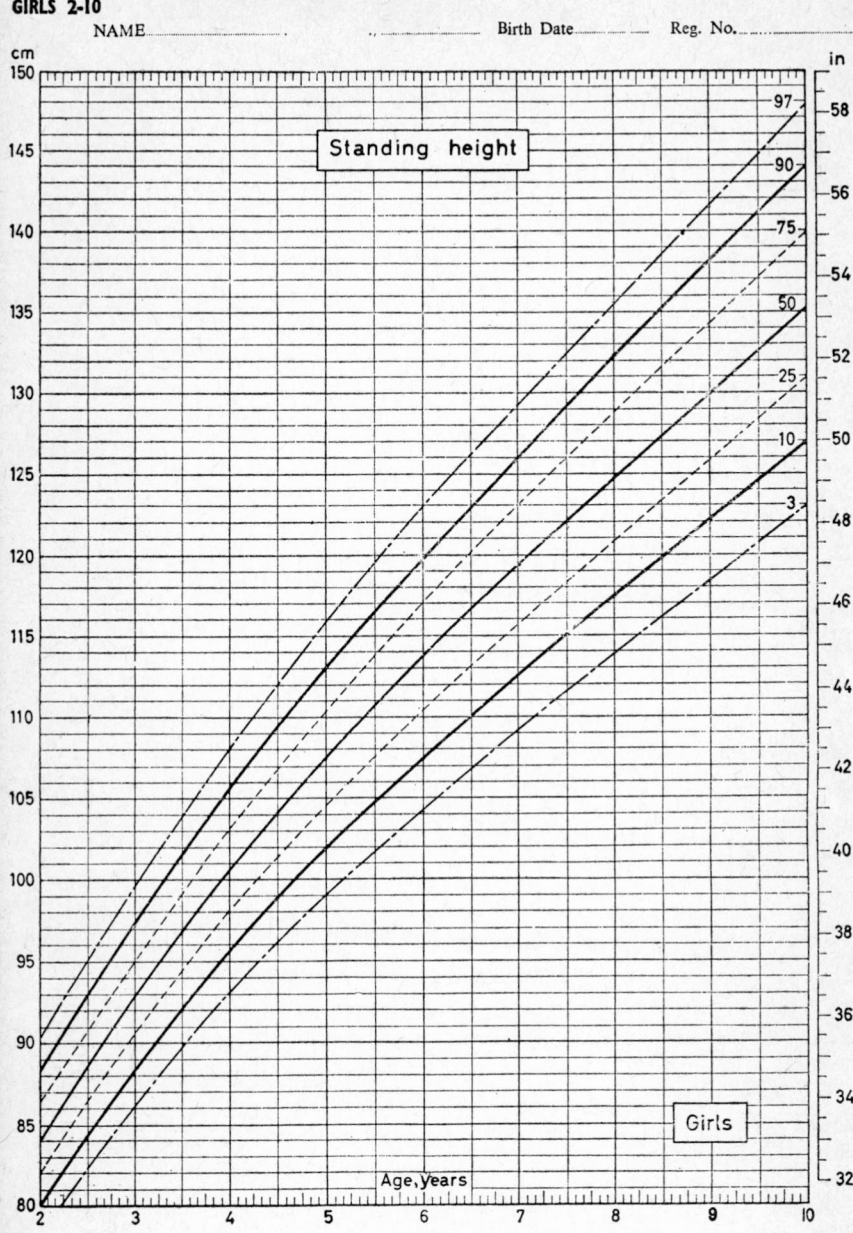

FIG. 17. Girls 2–10 years. Standing height.

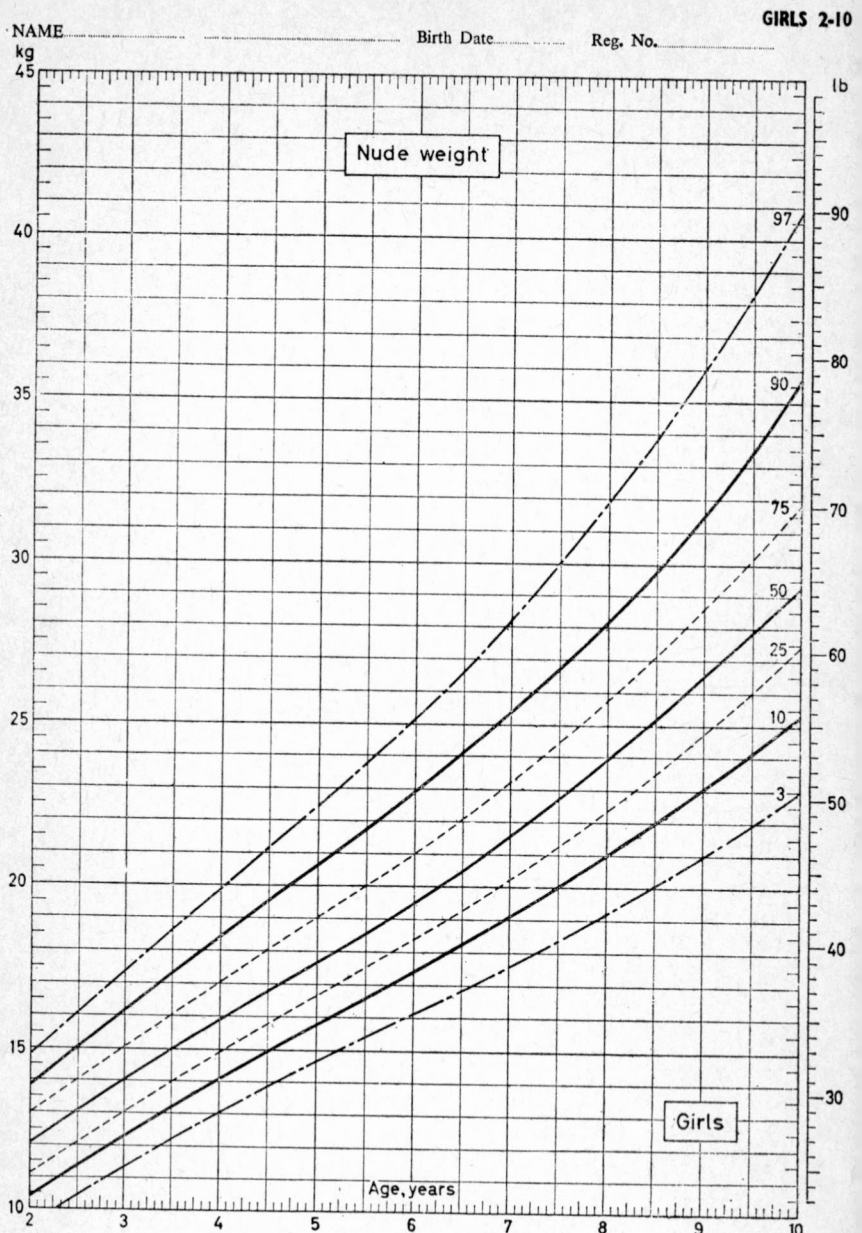

FIG. 18.   Girls 2—10 years. Nude weight.

References

Aicardi, J., and Goutière, S. F. (1971) Les épanchements sous-duraux du nourrisson. *Arch. franç. Pediatr.*, **28**, 233.

Aicardi, J., Baraton, J. and Askeniazi, S. (1973) Paper to European Study Group on Child Neurology, Kungalv.

American Psychiatric Association (1952) *Diagnostic and Statistical Manual for Mental Disorders*. Washington, D.C.

Anthony, J. and Benedek, T. (1970) In *Parenthood*, ed. Steele, B. F. Boston: Little, Brown.

Barnmishandel (1969) Socialstyrelsens redovisar, No. 9, Sweden.

Barrett, J. H. W. (1971) In *A Handbook of Prenatal Paediatrics*, ed. Batstone, G. F. *et al*. Aylesbury: Medical Technical Publishing Co.

Bennie, E. H. and Sclare, A. B. (1969) The battered child syndrome. *Amer. J. Psychiat.*, **125**, 975.

Bernard, V. W. (1971) In *Young Children of mentally ill Parents*, Pavenstedt, E. and Bernard, V. W. New York: Behavioral Publications.

Bertanalffy, L. von (1968) *General System Theory*. London: Penguin.

Bierman, G. (1969) *Kindeszuchtigung und Kindesmisshandlung*. Munchen and Basle: Reinhardt.

Birrell, R. G. and Birrell, J. H. W. (1968) The maltreatment syndrome in children: a hospital survey. *Med. J. Austral.*, **2**, 1023.

Caffey, J. (1972) World Medicine, 28 July 1972.

California Pilot Survey. *See* Gil, D. G. (1968).

Castle, R. L. and Kerr, M. (1972) A study of suspected child abuse, N.S.P.C.C.

City of Birmingham (1972) *Abstracts of Statistics (1970–71)*. Central Statistics Office, City of Birmingham.

Cobb, W. A. (1963) In *Electroencephalography*, ed. Hill, D. and Parr, G. London: Macdonald.

Cooper, C. (1972) Personal communication.

Court, J. (1970) Psycho-social factors in child battering. *J. Med. Women's Fed.*, **52**, 99.

Court, J. and Kerr, A. (1971) The battered child syndrome—a preventable disease. *Nursing Times*, **67**, 695.

Department of Health and Social Security (1970) The battered baby. Memorandum prepared by the Standing Medical Advisory Committee for the Central Health Service Council, 31 July 1970.

Ebbin, A. J., Gollub, M. H. *et al*. (1969) Battered child syndrome at Los Angeles County General Hospital. *Amer. J. Dis. Child.*, **118**, 660.

Elmer, E. (1965) Child abuse, a symptom of family crisis. In *Crises of Family Disorganization*. Univ. of Pittsburgh Press.

Elmer, E. (1967) Children in Jeopardy. In *A Study of Abused Minors and their Families*. Univ. of Pittsburgh Press.

Elmer, E. and Gregg, G. S. (1967) Developmental characteristics of abused children. *Pediatrics*, **40**, 596.

Eysenck, H. J. and Eysenck, S. B. G. (1964) *Manual of the Eysenck Personality Inventory*. Univ. of London Press.

Franklin, A. W. (1971) Personal view. *Brit. med. J.*, **4**, 167.

Galston, R. (1973) Preventing the abuse of little children. American Psychological Association, Annual Meeting, 10 May 1973.

Gibbens, T. C. N. and Walker, A. (1956) *Cruel Parents*. Institute for the Study and Treatment of Delinquency, London.

Gil, D. G. (1968). *See* Helfer and Kempe (1968).

Gil, D. G. (1969) Physical abuse of children: findings and implications of a nationwide survey. *Pediatrics*, **44**, 857.

Goldberg, D. P. (1972) *Detection of Psychiatric Illness by Questionnaire*. Oxford University Press.

Gregg, G. S. and Elmer, E. (1969) Infant injuries: accident or abuse. *Pediatrics*, **44**, 434.

Harding, G. (1973) Personal communication.

Helfer, R. E. and Kempe, C. H. (1968) *The Battered Child*. Univ. of Chicago Press.

Hill, D. (1943) Cerebral dysrhythmia: its significance in aggressive behaviour. *Proc. roy. Soc. Med.*, **37**, 317, **5**, 47.

Hill, D. and Watterson, D. (1942). Electro-encephalographic studies of psychopathic personalities. *J. Neurol. Psychiat.*, **5**, 47.

Joseph, Sir K. (1973) Spring Study Seminar on the Cycle of Deprivation, Association of Directors of Social Services, Brighton.

Kempe, C. H. (1969) *Hospital Practice*, **44**, 4.

Kempe, C. H. (1971) Paediatric implications of the battered baby syndrome. *Arch. Dis. Childh.*, **46**, 28.

Kempe, C. H., Silverman, F. N. *et al.* (1962) The battered-child syndrome. *J. Am. med. Ass.*, **181**, 17.

Kempe, C. H. and Helfer, R. E. (1972) *Helping the Battered Child and his Family*. Philadelphia: Lippincott.

Köttgen, U. (1967) Kindesmisshandlung. *Mschr. Kinderheilk.*, **115**, 186.

Lancet (1971) Annotation on violent parents. *Lancet*, **2**, 1017.

Lukianowicz, N. (1971) *Psychiatria Clinica*, **4**, 257.

Martin, H. (1972) The child and his development, *see* Kempe and Helfer.

Martin, H. P. (1974) In *Advances in Pediatrics* (in press).

Morse, C. W., Sahler, O. K. Z. *et al.* (1970) A three year follow-up study of abused and neglected children. *Amer. J. Dis. Child.*, **120**, 439.

Moszer, M. and Bach, C. (1969) Le syndrome des enfants maltraités. *Progrès Medical*, **97**, 303.

Nau, E. (1968) Kindesmisshandlung. *Mschr. Kinderheilk.*, **115**, 192.

Newson, J., and Newson, E. (1965) *Patterns of Infant Care in an urban Community*. London: Penguin.

Oliver, J. E., and Taylor, A. (1971) Five generations of ill-treated children in one family pedigree. *Brit. J. Psychiat.*, **119**, 473.

Oliver, J. E. and Cox, J. (1973) A family kindred with ill-used children: the burden on the community. *Brit. J. Psychiat.*, **123**, 81.

Ounsted, C. (1968) In *The Mentally Abnormal Offender*, ed. de Reuck, A. V. S. and Porter, R. London: J. & A. Churchill.

Ounsted, C. (1972) Proceedings of the Eighth International Study Group on Child Neurology and Development. (Unpublished.)

Pavenstedt, E. (1971) The meaning of motherhood in a deprived community. In *Crises of Family Disorganization*, ed. Pavenstedt E. and Bernard, V. W. New York: Behavioral Publications.

Registrar General (1972) Statistical Review of England and Wales for 1970, Part 2, London: H.M.S.O.

Richards, M. P. M. and Bernal, J. F. (1972) An observational study of mother–infant interaction. In *Ethological Studies of Child Behaviour*, ed. Blurton Jones, N. Camb. Univ. Press.

Robson, K. S. (1967) The role of eye to eye contact in maternal-infant attachment. *J. Child Psychol. Psychiat.*, **8**, 13.

Scott, P. D. (1973) Fatal battered baby cases. *Medicine, Science and the Law*, **13**, 197.

Skinner, A. E. and Castle, R. L. (1969) 78 Battered Children: a retrospective survey. N.S.P.C.C., London.

Smith, S. M. and Hanson R. (1972) Failure to thrive and anorexia nervosa. *Postgraduate med. J.*, **48**, 382.

Smith, S. M., Honigsberger, L. and Smith, C. (1973) *Brit. med. J.*, **3**, 20. See present work, chapter 6.

Stafford-Clark, D. and Taylor, F. H. (1949) Clinical and electro-encephalographic studies of prisoners charged with murder. *J. Neurol. Neurosurg. Psychiat.*, **12**, 325.

Steele, B. F. and Pollock, C. B. (1968) *See* Helfer, R. E. and Kempe, C. H. (1968).

Till, K. (1968) Subdural haematoma and effusion in infancy. *Brit. med. J.*, **3**, 40.

Trube-Becker, E. (1971) Obduktion beim plötzlich gestorbenen Kind. *Medizinische Klinik*, 66, 58.

Walton, H. J. and Presly, A. S. (1973) Use of a category system in the diagnosis of abnormal personality. *Brit. J. Psychiat.*, 122, 259.

Wechsler, D. (1955) *Manual for the Wechsler Adult Intelligence Scale*, New York: The Psychological Corporation.

Weston, J. T. (1968) *See* Helfer and Kempe (1968).

Williams, D. (1941) The significance of an abnormal electro-encephalogram. *J. Neurol. Neurosurg. Psychiat.*, 4, 257.

Wolfe, R. H. (1959) Observations on newborn infants. *Psychosomatic Med.*, 21, 110.

Woolley, P. V. and Evans, W. A. (1955) Significance of skeletal lesions in infants resembling those of traumatic origin. *J. Am. med. Ass.*, 158, 539.

World Health Organization (1968) *International Classification of Diseases*. Geneva: W.H.O.

Young, L. (1964) *Wednesday's Children: A Study of Child Neglect and Abuse*. New York: McGraw-Hill.

Index

Note: As this book is devoted to aspects of 'battered babies' and 'non-accidental injuries' under the title 'child abuse', these headings have been avoided as far as possible in the index.

Printed by R. & R. Clark, Limited, Edinburgh